THE
CROFTERS' WAR

I.M.M. MacPhail

The
Crofters' War

I M M MACPHAIL

acair

The publisher acknowledges subsidy from the Scottish Arts
Council towards the publication of this volume.

Published in Scotland in 1989 by Acair Ltd, Unit 8a, 7 James Street,
Stornoway, Isle of Lewis.

Designed by Acair Ltd. and Heather Delday
Printed by Highland Printers, Henderson Road, Inverness.

ISBN 0 86152 860 3

ACKNOWLEDGEMENTS

I have been fortunate in the valuable assistance I have received over the years in the course of my research and I have pleasure in acknowledging my gratitude to the staffs of the Scottish Record Office, the National Library of Scotland, the British Library, Glasgow University Library, the Mitchell Library Glasgow, Inverness Public Library and Dumbarton Public Library; the late Duke of Argyll, Viscount Harcourt, Lord MacDonald, Sir Donald Cameron of Lochiel for access to estate papers and correspondence; the late Mr James Philp of Messrs MacDonald and Fraser, Portree, for the perusal of the firm's records relating to the period of Alexander MacDonald's factorship of estates in Skye; Messrs Skene, Edwards and Garson, Edinburgh, for access to the papers of the Marquis of Lothian and Lady Gordon Cathcart, The Clan Donald Lands Trust for permission to reproduce a statement of the rental of Lord MacDonald; the owners and editors of the following newspapers for access to back files — *Inverness Courier*, *Highland News* (including the *Northern Chronicle*), *Oban Times*, *Ross-shire Journal*, *Stornoway Gazette*; the Gaelic Society of Inverness for the back files of the *Highlander*, and Mr W.H. Easson, former Town Clerk of Invergordon, for the back files of the *Invergordon Times*; and the following persons for guidance and encouragement — Mr Hugh Barron, Professor A.A.M. Duncan, Dr James Shaw Grant, the late Mr Rory MacKay, the late Mr George MacLeod, Dr J.G. Kellas, the Rev. William Matheson, the late Dr T.M. Murchison.

I wish also to pay tribute to the members of my family for their assistance and forbearance, in particular my sister, Mrs Catherine MacKenzie, my son, J.R.M. MacPhail, my brother, the late Dr Angus Norman MacPhail, and my uncle, the late Murdo MacLeod, the Borriston spokesman at the Napier Commission hearing in 1883, in whose house I spent many happy days in my youth and from whom I first learned about the crofters' struggle for their rights; and finally, I must express my gratitude to Miss Esther Hepburn for her cheerful assistance in dealing with a variety of problems in the making of this book.

For reproduction of illustrations from contemporary sources I am indebted to the Mitchell Library, Glasgow, the Highland Regional Library Service, the Scottish National Portrait Gallery, the National Portrait Gallery, the Scottish Record Office, Dr Charles Ferguson, and for the maps Mr Arthur F. Jones.

FOREWORD

The Crofters' War is a comparatively modern name for the social unrest and political agitation which prevailed in the Highlands and Islands of Scotland a century ago. After the landlords' clearance of the small tenants to make room for sheep farms and deer forests, the crofters and cottars remained for some time cowed and submissive, the threat of eviction ever-present in their minds. A change, however, was on the way in the 1870s, when there occurred two spontaneous and unrelated displays of defiance of the landlords — one at Bernera on the Atlantic coast of Lewis and the other on the estate of Kilmuir in Skye. The succeeding decade of the 1880s saw widespread, organized defiance of landlords, confrontations of crofters and officers of the law, military expeditions to what were officially described as "disturbed districts".

In support of crofters threatened with eviction in Skye, organizations for reform of the land laws were formed in Glasgow, London, Edinburgh and Sutherland, later combining in a Highland Land League with branches in crofting townships. As a result of the mounting pressure of public opinion, Gladstone's Government, already in trouble over the demand for Irish Home Rule, decided in 1883 to appoint a Royal Commission to inquire into the condition of the crofters and cottars in the Highlands and Islands. The publicity given by the press to the hearings of the Commission, called the Napier Commission after its chairman, Lord Napier, roused nationwide sympathy for the crofters, and with the extension of the parliamentary franchise in 1885, entitling crofters (and working men generally) to vote, the crofter question became the dominant issue in the general elections of 1885 and 1886 in the Highlands and Islands, a new political party emerging in support of the crofters. Scottish affairs seldom received priority at Westminster, but in 1886 a grudging approval was given to the Crofters' Holdings (Scotland) Act, by which crofters obtained security of tenure and a Crofters Commission was appointed to fix fair rents. Even after the passing of this Crofters Act, the Government found it necessary to send military expeditions to the north-west, and it was not until the last year of the decade, when the beneficial work of the Crofters Commission bore fruit and punitive sentences deterred would-be lawbreakers, that at last peace prevailed.

My interest in the subject goes back a long way. Both my parents were natives of Lewis, which was always referred to in our family as "home". I started serious study of the subject in 1965, when I was granted sabbatical leave to attend Glasgow University as a research student. I had the good fortune at that time to locate the papers of Alexander MacDonald, lawyer, Portree, hitherto unavailable, and thus obtained access to a unique source for the study of landlord-tenant relations, as he was factor for almost all the estates in Skye in the 1880s. In my retirement, I have had ample opportunity to widen and deepen my knowledge of the subject, using a variety of sources — estate papers, official records, politicians' correspondence, contemporary newspapers, as well as recent publications, including some in the Gaelic language, connected with the centenary of the Crofters Act. I have read five papers on various aspects of the subject to the Gaelic Society of Inverness, and the papers, fully documented, have been published in the Transactions of the Society from 1974 to 1985. In this volume they appear, modified and expanded, along with five new chapters, notes and appendices, providing a study of the period which, it is hoped, will interest a wide range of readers.

I.M.M. MacPhail.

CONTENTS

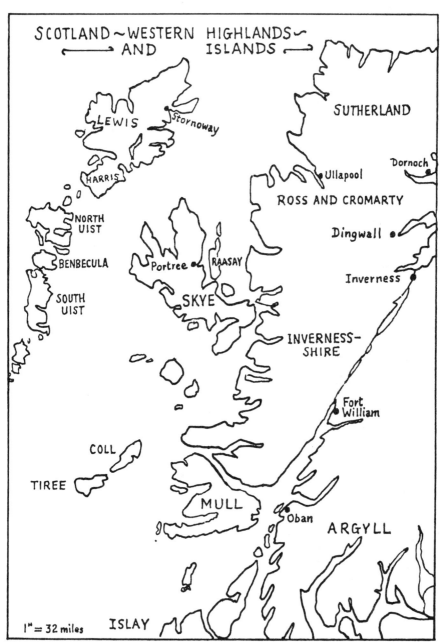

SCOTTISH WESTERN HIGHLANDS AND ISLANDS.

CHAPTER 1

AFTER THE CLEARANCES

The Free Church of Scotland

The 1850s, which saw some of the worst clearances in the history of the Highlands and Islands of Scotland, were succeeded by two decades of comparative quiet in the crofting areas. Memories of the clearances, imprinted deep in the minds of the crofters, left them cowed and submissive; and on some estates the factors, wielding the threat of eviction to exact obedience, ruled as petty tyrants. Sir Frederick Millbank, who was a shooting tenant at Aline in Lewis for fourteen years, spoke of the Lewis chamberlain or factor, Donald Munro, tyrannising over the poor crofters, for example appointing the time for meeting as "after breakfast", without specifying the hour, and then fining them for coming late or keeping their caps on or leaving the door ajar. John Murdoch of the *Highlander* newspaper, on a tour of the Gordon estate of South Uist in 1875, found the crofters in such "a state of slavish fear" that, although they had many grievances, they dared not complain to the factor, Ranald MacDonald, in case he "would drive them from the estate". Murdoch had a similar comment about the crofters of South Harris, whose "manhood had been paralysed by terror, and torpor had supervened". In 1884 at a land reform meeting at Dunvegan in Skye, one of the speakers, Donald MacAskill, openly admitted: "I am ashamed to confess it now that I trembled more before the factor than I did before the Lord of Lords".

Like oppressed races in other lands and at other times, the people of the Highlands and Islands were able to find consolation for their troubles in religion. The Disruption of 1843 had involved a mass exodus in the north and west of Scotland from the Established Church, so that later it was said in the Free Church — "*Thàinig an Eaglais a mach* (The Church came out)", as if nothing was left behind. Indeed, in some of the parish churches in the crofting areas, ministers were preaching to empty pews. According to a survey of church membership, there were in 1890-91 in the parish churches of Lewis only 5 members in Barvas, 4 in Knock, 2 in Lochs, and none in Cross. In Skye the figures were slightly better: 168 in Sleat and 122 in Strath but only 21 in Snizort, 16 in Stenscholl, 12 in Bracadale, 3 in Hallin-in-Waternish; and in Wester Ross, there were only 6 members in Gairloch, 2 in Shieldaig and none in Plockton. Most landlords

1

remained faithful to the Established Church but this only served to widen the cleavage between them and their tenants. The sufferings of the "Destitution Years" of the middle of the century were accompanied by the struggles of many Free Church congregations to obtain church sites from their landlords. Lord MacDonald, then by far the chief landowner in Skye, refused sites to the Snizort, Kilmuir and Portree congregations so that for years services were held in the open air like the conventicles of the Covenanters. Of the Rev. Roderick MacLeod of Snizort, his successor, the Rev. Joseph Lamont, once said: "My predecessor often preached with the hailstones dancing on his forehead, his hearers wiping away the snow before they could sit down". The Strontian congregation overcame the difficulty imposed by the landlord's refusal to grant a site by having a "floating Church", moored in Loch Sunart. These years of travail not only helped to fortify the Free Church members and adherents in their faith but also to harden their attitudes against their landlords.

Religious Revival

In 1859 there began in Britain a religious revival (not the first nor the last of the nineteenth century) which reached its peak in the Highlands and Islands of Scotland and left its mark there for many years to come. Vast assemblies listened with awe and trembling or drew spiritual refreshment from preachers like Dr Kennedy of Dingwall and the Rev. John MacRae (MacRath Mór) of Lochs in Lewis. Nor were the ministers the only agents in the Revival of 1859-60 and in the years of heightened religious awareness which followed. Since the eighteenth century there had existed in the north and north-west of Scotland a religious aristocracy, that of the elders or "Men" (so called to distinguish them from the ministers). Their characteristics have been delineated by Dr John MacInnes — a retentive memory, a preference for allegorical interpretation of the Scriptures, fervour in prayer, austerity of behaviour, strictness in their guardianship of the Sabbath, a consciousness of belonging to an extensive and influential brotherhood and of a singular intimacy of fellowship with God. "A Lewis elder is the holiest man alive". So wrote in 1883 a native of the island, where every form of amusement was regarded as the work of the Devil and piping and singing of profane songs almost vanished. On the gravestone of Roderick MacLeod of Bayble, Rory Bàn, are the words — "Terrible in rebuking sin". For the "Men", the natural leaders of their communities, religion came first and secular matters a poor second.

The revival of 1859-60 was followed in the Free Church by the protracted debate over the proposed union with the United Presbyte-

2

rian Church. Dr James Begg, the diehard who led the opposition to the Union, made a propaganda tour of the Highlands in 1866 and won over Dr Kennedy of Dingwall, whose eloquence and forcefulness were employed against the Union and automatically ensured the support of the thousands who revered him. The Revival and the Union Debate helped to equip many of the crofters spiritually, morally and intellectually for the political struggle of the 1880s, the Crofters' War. When Land Law Reform and Franchise meetings were opened invariably with prayer, it was unlikely that they would end in violence, which was notably absent from the crofters' agitation of the 1880s. Some of the "Men" like Rory Bàn MacLeod became earnest protagonists of Land Law Reform, and many of the witnesses before the Napier Commission were Free Church elders whose eloquence carried conviction with their hearers. But in the 1860s and the 1870s the absorption of the "Men" in religion and in ecclesiastical affairs precluded their participation in such secular matters as crofting grievances. As we shall see, the leadership in the agitation of the Crofters' War was at the outset almost entirely in the hands of the exiled Highlanders in the large towns and cities.[1]

Victorian Heyday

The 1860s and 1870s have been described as "the heyday of British capitalism". Britain was then the leading world power, indeed the only real world power: its textile, iron and steel, engineering and shipbuilding industries were all booming and its overseas trade expanding every year. It was also the "Golden Age" of British farming, just before competition from the United States, Canada, Australia and New Zealand brought ruin to the farmers. Both in industry and farming the burden of taxation was slight, and successive Chancellors of the Exchequer sought to abolish income tax. The Highlands and Islands, although remote from industry and the area of intensive farming, benefited to a certain extent by the "spin-off" from the buoyant economy of the Victorian heyday. This was the period of "Balmoralism", when wealthy English and Scottish magnates vied with one another in acquiring sporting estates and erecting neo-Scottish-baronial dwellings in which to spend a few months each year. Deer-stalking, grouse-shooting, salmon-fishing provided employment for only a few and almost inevitably clashed with the interests of the indigenous inhabitants. Nevertheless, it would be wrong to consider all owners of sporting estates as extirpators of the native population. Duncan Darroch of Gourock, who bought Torridon in 1872 and believed that the only hope for the Highlands was to restrict sheep-farming and start the rearing of cattle and deer, was

3

very proud of the good relations existing between himself and the crofters. When the Napier Commission went on its rounds in 1883, Torridon was one of the few estates where there were no complaints and no arrears of rent.

Railways and Steamers

The advent of railways and steamboat services owed much to wealthy proprietors like the Duke of Sutherland and Sir James Matheson. The capital of the Highland Railway included £355,000 from the Duke of Sutherland, £75,000 from the Earl of Seafield, £73,000 from Sir Alexander Matheson. The 1860s saw a rapid increase in railway construction. The Inverness-Nairn line had been opened in 1854, Inverness-Dingwall in 1862, Dingwall-Bonar Bridge in 1866, Dingwall-Strome in 1870. In the areas served by railways there was undoubtedly a rise in the standard of living, partly as a result of the employment made available in the construction of railways and the roads connected with them (although many of the "navvies" were migratory Irishmen and Lowlanders), and partly from the greater variety of consumer goods made available by railway transport. Sir James Matheson of Lewis subsidised a number of steamers operating between Glasgow and the Hebrides before David Hutcheson and his partner began to develop the coastal trade of west and north-west Scotland. One of the early Hutcheson steamers, the *Glencoe*, which ran for seventy-five years down to 1931, was originally owned by Sir James Matheson, who had named it *Mary Jane* after his wife. The extension of the railway from Dingwall to Strome Ferry in 1870 made a regular steamer service to the Isles commercially viable; and by 1880 David MacBrayne put on a daily service to Portree in the summer months. The *Oban Times* hailed it as a triumph for MacBrayne, describing him as "the admirable managing partner of the far-famed fleet of the famous estimable David Hutcheson and Co." The railway and steamer links with Skye gave an increasing impetus to the annual migration of Skyemen to the mainland to work on farms or on roads and railways — a custom which had its disadvantages in that the croft tended to be neglected and some of the less useful habits of the south such as tea-drinking and wearing watch-chains (according to Miss Emily MacLeod of MacLeod), became popular in the Isle of Skye.[2]

Fisheries

Railways, steamers, telegraphic communications (the first cable to Lewis was laid in 1872 but Barra, Tiree and other islands were to wait much longer for the telegraph), combined to promote commercial activity and definitely benefited the fishing of the north and west. Fishing provided for many a crofter and cottar a profitable, if somewhat precarious, livelihood. Before the advent of trawlers in the 1880s, shoals of herring frequented the sea-lochs: it was estimated that as many as one thousand fishing boats were operating at one time in Loch Hourn. In pre-trawler days, a rich harvest of cod and ling was to be had off the Atlantic coasts of the Hebrides; but the trade there was controlled by the fish-curers, who provided the boats, the fishermen paying up the purchase price over the period of years. The truck system was widely used by the curers, and, if seasons were poor, the fishermen were sometimes unable to get out of debt. The Caithness and east-coast fishing could prove more lucrative. In 1877, a good year, it was estimated that a Lewis fisherman with a one-sixth share in a cod or ling boat might draw from it £12, and if he went to the herring-fishing, he could earn £10 at Wick or £15 at Peterhead. Added to these, he could receive £6 as a member of the Royal Naval Reserve and £4 for a stirk, which gave him a total of £25 or £30, a tidy sum in those days of an almost self-sufficient economy. But this was in a good season, and his money income in a poor season might only be a few pounds, not to mention that the arduous cod-and-ling fishing was conducted on an exposed and dangerous coast, nearly 300 Lewis fishermen losing their lives at sea between 1848 and 1883.

In Skye, the fishing industry existed on a smaller scale. Formerly as many as 800 boats went out of Portree for the herring-fishing but thereafter the number declined until the great herring seasons of the early 1880s, which unfortunately brought the trawlers into inshore waters. Their depredation of the spawning beds could ruin the local fishing for years, and despite the setting-up of a Royal Commission on trawling in 1883 and official measures to prevent inshore trawling, the situation worsened as time went on. From 1875 onwards Skye fishermen were going regularly to the Irish fishings. There seems to be little doubt that the summer migration of the crofter-fishermen, whether to the east coast or to Ireland, provided opportunities for exchange of ideas and opinions; and it certainly was the case in the 1880s that crofter agitation became more noticeable after the men returned from the fishing.

Crofters' Grievances

The 1870s, as it can be argued, were years of a rising standard of living among the crofter-fishermen of the north and west, and a number of impartial observers bear testimony to this. Indeed, it was partly because standards began to decline in the 1880s that the Crofters' War developed. But the same impartial observers were not blind to the numerous grievances of the crofters. Witnesses who appeared before the Napier Commission in 1883 were full of complaints. In Skye, the factor's method of dealing with arrears of rent was by sending a summons of removal to the tenant, where a summons to the Small Debt Court would have sufficed, the factor reckoning that the mere threat of eviction from the croft would bring the tenant to heel. When a tenant was removed for non-payment of rent, the factor insisted on the payment of the arrears by the incoming tenant. The purchase of the goodwill of the croft was how the factor explained it, but others, including the Home Secretary, Sir William Harcourt, considered it unjustifiable.[3] The collection of sea-ware on certain shores was either forbidden or had to be paid for; in the Broadford district of Skye, the right of the tacksman to the sea-ware was written into their leases, a relic of the days of the kelp industry.

Relations between crofters and tacksmen or farmers were seldom good: complaints were made of the loss of the best grazings to neighbouring farmers without a corresponding reduction in rent and of the encroachment by farmers on the common grazing, which, where there was no adequate dyke or fence, was thus reduced. Complaints also arose out of the impounding of crofters' stock which strayed. Tenants with shooting rights could be more troublesome than farmers. Deer were sometimes pursued by sportsmen into the cornfields at the Braes in Skye. According to John Nicolson of Sconser, "It would give the apostle Paul himself enough to tell of it. The women would be quietly herding and would have to fly home because of the bullets". Where deer fences had been erected, as at Sconser near Sligachan in Skye, they were inadequate as protections for the crops. In the interests of shooting tenants, dogs were forbidden at Sconser, Glendale and Raasay.

Overpopulation, so common in the crofting areas, gave rise to many grievances. The sub-division of crofts in some areas had led to serious congestion, with the inevitable impoverishment of the land, the stock and the people. In Skye, at Drumfearn in Sleat, there was only one crofter with a whole croft, and at Lusta in Waternish because of sub-division there were 38 families where formerly there had been only 14. In Lewis, where the population had increased between 1851 and 1881 by 29 per cent (as compared with a decrease of 21 per cent in Skye in the same period), sub-division was rife in almost every village. Cottars differed from crofters in possessing only a house with a small piece of "potato ground". It was estimated in 1886 that of the 3,786 families living in crofting townships in Skye, 1,174 were cottar families. At Elgol, where there were 45 crofter families and 17 cottar families, none of the latter were paying any rent. Of the 582 families in the twelve townships in the *quoad sacra* parish of Knock in Lewis, 183 were those of cottars, many of whom made a livelihood as fishermen but still contributed to the impoverishment, by overuse, of the land available. Cottars were often to be found on the farms of the tacksmen and were sometimes treated like the *sgalag* (the menial farm-servant) of old. At Talisker in Skye, cottars had to give up to 28 days' labour a year, being paid only one shilling a day and their food, those who refused to work being evicted. In Barra, which according to a report in 1886 was "overrun with cottars", Dr MacGillivray of Eoligarry demanded 60 days' labour for every acre of "potato ground". In addition to sub-division of crofts, crofters sometimes encouraged, to their own detriment, "squatting" by relatives on the common grazing.[4] For the evils of sub-division and squatting and the consequent overuse of the land, the crofters were to blame, but the principal responsibility was that of the proprietor or his factor. On well-run estates such as those of Sir Kenneth MacKenzie of Gairloch and Cameron of Lochiel, both members of the Napier Commission of 1883, sub-division was strictly prohibited. As for squatters, the crofters realised only too well the harm done to the grazings; at Balallan in the parish of Lochs in Lewis, they petitioned the chamberlain for the removal of 32 squatters.

The new parish school boards, set up with the introduction of compulsory education in 1872, took some years to overcome the difficulties imposed by geographical considerations — large parishes like Glenelg with only small, scattered communities. In the Catholic islands of South Uist, Barra and Eriskay, where, previous to 1872, the only schools had been provided by Protestant organisations, there were special difficulties, because of religious differences.[5] These educational problems may seem to have little connection with crofting; but the school boards tended to be dominated by the factors and tacksmen, and the crofters were all the more critical as school rates had to be paid for attendance at badly-situated schools, involving long journeys over rough and boggy ground for the children. In Islay, it was not the school board but the proprietor, Ramsay of Kildalton, who proved difficult: he refused the school board a suitable site at Port Ellen despite the fact that an Inspector of Schools had condemned the old school after the deaths of several pupils. There were thus plenty of grievances among the crofters during the period of the Victorian heyday.

The Gaelic Movement

The grievances were ventilated in 1883 by crofters who appeared before the Napier Commission; but in the early 1870s there was little or no sign of revolt in the crofting areas. During the 1870s, however, there was a tremendous upsurge of Gaelic sentiment and a growing

7

awareness of their Gaelic heritage among the exiled Highlanders and Islesmen in the large cities — Glasgow, Edinburgh, Greenock, Aberdeen, Dundee, Inverness. This Gaelic movement manifested itself in various forms — in Gaelic poetry, in Highland societies, in Highland newspapers and journals, in the campaigns for a Gaelic Chair in Edinburgh University and for Gaelic in the state schools. Although primarily orientated towards preserving Gaelic tradition and culture, almost all of these manifestations contributed indirectly towards bringing the condition of the crofter before a wider public and eventually towards the rectification of their grievances.

The subject of the poetry of the clearances has attracted considerable attention in recent years. According to Dr Sorley MacLean, himself a poet, there existed in most of the poetry in the Highlands and Islands prior to the Crofters' War of the 1880s, an uncritical idealisation of the pre-clearance period, a strongly nationalist spirit and a detestation of the Sassenach landlord and sheep-farmer. With this judgement no one would disagree who reads the poems (nearly three hundred of them) in Archibald Sinclair's *An t-Oranaiche* (The Songster), published in the late 1870s. The finest poems prior to the Crofters' War were mainly love songs or those of the exiled or emigrant Gael, full of nostalgia, such as *"An gleann 's an robh mi òg* (The glen where I was young)"*, composed by Neil MacLeod of Glendale and Edinburgh and *"Och nan och tha mi fo mhulad* (O, sadness overwhelms me)"* composed by Mary MacIver of Valtos in Lewis. Although these poems are not at all anti-landlord, it is not difficult to appreciate that they would appeal to those who were critical of landlords and factors and the crofting system as it existed in the 1870s.

It is easier to describe the content of a poem of any period than to assess the extent of its appeal and influence. Many of the best-known poems appeared in periodicals and newspapers like the *Highlander*, the *Oban Times* and the Gaelic journal, *An Gaidheal*, which was the first to publish songs with sol-fa notation in 1874, the song honoured in this way being *"Muile nam Mór-bheann* (Mull of the high mountains)"*. In a letter to the Napier Commission in 1883 there is an interesting reference to what was described as the most popular song in Lewis and Skye at the time, *"Moladh a'Bhàta* (In praise of the boat)"*, composed by John MacLeod of Carloway in Lewis, who was actually refused baptism for his children unless he abandoned his song-making. It does not seem to have been printed until 1916 (in *Bàrdachd Leòdhais*) but songs could achieve a wide circulation by oral transmission through the annual migration of the crofter-fishermen to the herring fishing.

8

Highland Societies

There was certainly an increasingly appreciative audience in the cities of the south, what with their soirées (as *ceilidhs* were then called), and their Annual Gatherings. The Rev. Donald MacCallum, himself a minor poet of the Crofters' War period, wrote of the Lewis bard, Murdo MacLeod (*Murchadh a' Cheisteir*), who composed *"Eilean an Fhraoich* (Isle of heather)" a few years after he arrived in Glasgow in 1861, that he was a regular attender at meetings of High-landers in Glasgow, often singing his own compositions. The first time he sang his *"Fàsachadh na Duthcha* (The desolation of the homeland)", a bitter attack on the iniquitous practices of evicting factors, was at the Annual Gathering of the natives of Ross-shire, who however greeted him with silence, shocked at such criticism of landlords and their servants. But his popularity grew, and the Rev. Donald MacCallum (who mistakenly referred to him as a native of Skye) main-tained that "in imparting courage to the sufferers and in strengthening the hands of their deliverers in the time of the crofters' agitation, no one did more than Murdo Mac-Leod".

The 1860s and 1870s saw the formation of numerous Highland societies in the large

REV DONALD MACCALLUM.

towns, most of them established with the purpose of enabling the natives of a district to meet socially but also with the object of dispensing charity to impoverished fellow-countrymen. In the 1870s there were in Glasgow regular meetings of the Sutherlandshire Asso-ciation, founded in 1860, the Skye Association (1865), the Tiree Association (1870), the Lewis and Harris Association (1887), the Mull and Iona Association, the Ross-shire Association, the Islay Society,

9

the Lochaber Society, the Appin Society, the Coll Society, and, last but not least, the Ardnamurchan, Morvern and Sunart Association, whose secretary, John MacDonald, was a perfervid champion of the crofters' cause.[6]

The Gaelic Society of Inverness was formed in 1871, the first of its kind in Scotland. Its rapid success encouraged Gaels in other towns to follow the example of Inverness, and soon Glasgow, Greenock, Aberdeen and Dundee had their Gaelic societies. These societies and many of the Highland societies mentioned became involved during the 1870s in the promotion of Gaelic teaching in the schools and in the campaign to set up a chair of Gaelic in Edinburgh University, a campaign in which a notable part was played by that polyglot admirer of the Gael, the indefatigable Professor John Stuart Blackie, professor of Greek at Edinburgh University. The position of Gaelic in the new state schools was most unsatisfactory as the newly-set-up Scotch Education Department was slow to act, and the Gaelic societies returned again and again to the subject in their discussions and resolutions. Most of the societies tended to treat with deference the proprietors of their native soil, who were sometimes invited to act as chairmen at the Annual Gatherings. One proprietor, Lachlan Mac-Donald of Skeabost, came out strongly in December 1877 in defence of the crofters at the "Annual Gathering of the natives of Skye resident in Glasgow". The first petition to Parliament for a commission of inquiry into the condition of the crofters was presented by the Gaelic Society of Inverness in the same month, December 1877, following a paper on the Strathglass clearances by one of the founder-members, Colin Chisholm. The Federation of Celtic Societies, which was formed in the following year, 1878, soon became involved in crofters' affairs. Many of the members of the Gaelic Society of Inverness, notably John Murdoch of the *Highlander* newspaper, Alexander MacKenzie, Charles Fraser Mackintosh, M.P., and of other societies, such as John Gunn MacKay of Glasgow (later of Portree), John MacDonald of Glasgow and Morvern, Angus Sutherland of the Glasgow Sutherlandshire Association, John Whyte, later librarian in Inverness, and his brother Henry Whyte ("Fionn") were to become prominent in the land law reform movement of the next decade.

Newspapers and Journals

Like the Highland societies, newspapers and journals interested in crofters' problems multiplied during the 1880s, while old-established newspapers devoted more and more space to the Highlands and Islands. This was possible because of the improved opportunities for education even before the Education Act of 1872.[7] In addition to the

Invergordon Times, dating from 1856, and the *Ross-shire Journal*, dating from 1875, there was the *Oban Times*, which however did not begin to champion the crofters' cause until 1882, when Duncan Cameron became editor, but was still very much a Highland newspaper before that. James Cameron, himself a reporter in the 1880s, wrote many years later: "Printed paper in the shape of newspapers proved the most deadly tool against the Highland landowners". The Radical Glasgow newspaper, the *North British Daily Mail*, the property of Dr (later Sir Charles) Cameron, M.P., was sympathetic to the crofters, and its weekly edition circulated in the Highlands and Islands, while the daily edition had a large circulation in Glasgow and west Scotland, where so many exiled Gaels lived. The old-established *Inverness Courier*, like the Edinburgh *Scotsman*, was a Whig paper, a staunch supporter of landlords and farmers; but it did not eschew the publication of news and articles about the crofters and, like other newspapers of those days, reported *verbatim* speeches on the important issues of the day. The *Courier's* rival, the *Inverness Advertiser*, was anti-Whig, representing a left or radical wing of the Liberal Party. It was in the '*Tizer*' (as it was familiarly known) that the antiquarian notes of Charles Fraser Mackintosh first appeared and it was with the newspaper's backing that he became Liberal M.P. for Inverness Burghs in 1874.

The other Inverness newspaper of the 1870s was the *Highlander*, which had a brief existence of just over eight years. Founded in 1873, it was the first newspaper to cater primarily for the interests of the people of the Highlands and Islands. Its founder and editor, the Radical John Murdoch, an exciseman who had been forced by ill-health to resign his post at Inverness, was an outstanding figure in the land reform movement. Born at Ardclach in Nairnshire but reared in Islay, he had served in many parts of the kingdom, including Ireland, and had contributed to several newspapers and journals on a variety of subjects — paedobaptism, agricultural chemistry, temperance, the Irish question, Gaelic culture, land law reform. Production of his weekly newspaper was bedevilled by financial problems and latterly by the conduct of his manager, Hugh Fraser. Much of Murdoch's time had to be spent in collecting subscriptions, advertisements and payment of accounts. More than once, when the paper was ready for the printers on a Thursday, he would set off for Glasgow or Edinburgh or Fort William to collect enough money to pay the printers on the Saturday. His manuscript autobiography, preserved in the Mitchell Library, Glasgow, throws a rather lurid light on the intrigues of Inverness councillors and their cliques in the 1870s.

In addition to the newspapers, there were journals dealing with the Highlands but mainly concerned with literary matters. Foremost

11

among these was *An Gaidheal*, founded in 1871 by Angus Nicolson, a native of Lewis resident in Toronto, who shortly afterwards was appointed Canadian Emigration Agent for the north of Scotland, as a result of which publication of the journal was transferred from Canada to Glasgow and later to Edinburgh. It was a monthly devoted to Gaelic literature; but its appearance tended to be erratic and it ceased publication after 1877.[8] It performed a notable service in providing a forum for Gaelic scholars but in its earlier issues avoiding controversial issues such as crofters' grievances. A poem in praise of Sir James Matheson of Lewis appeared in its first issue and was criticised by a correspondent, who deprecated the fulsome flattery bestowed on Highland lairds, "*daoine's miosa a tha ri fhaighinn* (men as bad as can be found)"; but the editor, admitting that this remark might be true of some Highland lairds, claimed to share the sentiments expressed in the poem. Twice, in 1874 and 1875, the editor expounded his views on the conditions of the Highlands, with a shrewd analysis of the situation and some trenchant criticism of factors and, to a lesser extent, proprietors; but his only solution was one which came naturally enough from an emigration agent but was unacceptable to the people themselves — large-scale emigration, assisted by the Government.

The other important Highland journal of the period, written however mostly in English, was the *Celtic Magazine*, edited by Alexander MacKenzie of Inverness from 1875 to 1886, when Alexander MacBain became editor, MacKenzie having started a weekly newspaper, the *Scottish Highlander*, in 1885. According to John Murdoch, who was not alone in regarding MacKenzie as an opportunist, the latter intrigued to become secretary of the Gaelic Society of Inverness, thereby obtaining for the *Celtic Magazine*, on the title page of which his name appeared along with his designation as secretary of the Society, a cachet it would not otherwise have achieved. It was in the *Celtic Magazine* that MacKenzie first published his clan histories, his genealogical researches enabling him to trace the descent of Gladstone through the statesman's grandfather, Provost Robertson of Dingwall, to Kenneth MacKenzie, 10th Lord of Kintail, from whom he himself was also descended.[9] MacKenzie, usually referred to as the "Clach", was an active propagandist for the crofters in the 1880s both in speech-making and in writing.

The Bernera Dispute

It was on the west coast of Lewis, far away from Celtic societies, newspapers and journals and their influence, that the first resistance by crofters to the domination of their landlords and factors was taken in the post-clearance period. It was the action of a community of crofters on the island of Bernera in Loch Roag, goaded beyond endurance by the petty, stupid management of the factor or chamberlain of Lewis, Donald Munro. Reference has already been made to his bullying treatment of the crofters on rent days. One witness before the Napier Commission of 1883, Malcolm MacLean of Swainbost, was of the "firm conviction" that Munro's policy "from the first day of his factorship to the last was to extirpate the people of Lewis so far as he could". This may be termed wild exaggeration but it does illustrate the attitude of Munro to the Lewis people and their attitude to him. A native of Tain in Easter Ross, he had come to Stornoway as a solicitor in 1842, had been appointed chamberlain in 1853, and by 1874 had accumulated a multiplicity of offices — chairman of the four parochial boards in Lewis, the four school boards, joint Procurator-Fiscal of Lewis along with his cousin, William Ross, Chief Magistrate, director of the Stornoway Gas Company and Water Company, vice-chairman of the Harbour Trust, deputy-chairman of the Road Trust, Commanding Officer of the local Volunteers — a veritable "Pooh-Bah". Little wonder that Professor Blackie referred to his "polyonymous omnipotence"!

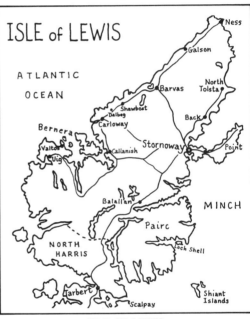

ISLE OF LEWIS.

The trouble with the Bernera crofters arose over summer grazings, which were on the mainland of Lewis and not on the island itself. From early times they had had their shielings on the moor of Beinn a' Chualein, stretching from the Uig road as far as Loch Langavat, one of the lochs which feed the Grimersta river, reckoned by many the finest salmon river in Europe.[10] When the sporting estates of Morsgail and Scaliscro were formed in 1872, the grazings were taken from the Bernera crofters and they were offered instead the moorland nearer the sea which had formerly belonged to the farm of Earshader. These grazings were not considered as good as the old ones but, at a meeting with the *maor* or ground officer, the crofters agreed to accept the factor's proposal and also to build a dyke between

13

themselves and the deer forest of Scaliscro. The ground officer had brought with him a paper which he read to them and according to which the new grazings would be theirs so long as they held their crofts in Bernera. This paper, which most of them could sign only by making their marks, was not produced at the subsequent trial and its very existence was denied by Donald Munro, the chamberlain, but there is no doubt about the promise having been given. The dyke, seven miles long, was built by the Bernera men and then, after a year and a half, the ground officer came again and told them that they were no longer to have the new grazings but instead the grazings of the farm of Hacleit on Bernera, the tenant of which was to receive Earshader on the mainland of Lewis. The Bernera men were naturally very much aggrieved, not merely because of all their labour on the dyke and the promise given to them but because they considered the new grazings offered to be inferior. Donald Munro, the chamberlain, himself went over to Bernera in order to persuade them and, when he failed, he foolishly threatened to bring the Volunteers from Stornoway to prevent them from putting their cattle across to Earshader, although he afterwards maintained that he had intended the remark only as a joke. He finished his harangue by telling them that he would have them all evicted from their crofts in Bernera, even although there was none of them in arrears.

Shortly after his visit, on March 24, 1874, a sheriff officer from Stornoway, Colin MacLennan, a native of Duirinish, Lochalsh, accompanied by the *maor* (ground officer), James MacRae of Miavaig in Uig and a customs officer, Peter Bain, who happened to have business on the west side of Lewis, landed on the island pier and proceeded to serve the 58 summonses of removal.[11] All but three were served, the houses omitted being unoccupied at the time of their visit. They were unmolested in their progress but in the evening between Tobson and Vallasay were set upon by a crowd of boys and girls, who threw "plocs" or divots at them. The sheriff officer, MacLennan, lost his temper and shouted at them: "If I had a gun with me, there would have been some of the women in Bernera tonight lamenting their sons." On the following morning, after serving the three remaining summonses, the sheriff officer and his companions were met halfway between Breacleit and the march of Kirkibost farm by a crowd of about fourteen men, one of whom, Angus MacDonald of Tobson, asked MacLennan if he was the man who had threatened to shoot them. On MacLennan trying to break away from the crowd, his waterproof coat was torn. The sheriff officer and his companions eventually managed to leave the island and return to Stornoway, where a complaint was lodged against the parties who, it was alleged, had assaulted them.

14

The Bernera Riot

A fortnight later, on April 8, Police Superintendent Cameron was on his way from Stornoway to Bernera to arrest three of the men alleged to have assaulted the sheriff officer when trouble of the most serious kind broke out in Stornoway. One of the three accused, Angus MacDonald of Tobson, happened to be in Stornoway that day and was identified by the sheriff and arrested by two policemen. MacDonald and his companion, also from Bernera, put up a violent resistance, and although the distance to the Police Office from Kenneth Street, where they were arrested, was only one hundred yards, it took four hours to get them there. This was due mainly to the obstruction of the police by sympathisers with the Bernera men in Stornoway; and so serious did the situation become that the Sheriff was sent for to read the Riot Act. The next morning, however, Sheriff Spittal, once he had been informed by the Police Superintendent of the comparatively mild offence for which MacDonald had been arrested, decided to release the prisoner on bail. He was also given a new suit of clothes to replace his own garments torn off his back in the struggle. Fortunately his release was effected before the arrival of 130 Bernera men, armed with all sorts of implements and headed by a piper, prepared to liberate the prisoner. Halfway to Stornoway, in the middle of the moor, they met MacDonald (who ever after bore the distinctive title of *Aonghas a' Phrìosan* [Prison Angus]) but they decided to proceed to Stornoway to lay their case before the proprietor, Sir James Matheson. He agreed to hear a small deputation, with Angus MacArthur of Bosta (later of Kirkibost) acting as interpreter, and he was told the story of the summer grazings. Sir James declared he knew nothing of the threat to evict the 58 families on Bernera. (Later, Donald Munro said that he did not think it was a matter to put before the proprietor.) At any rate, the men received a sympathetic hearing from the baronet and light refreshments — bread, beef, coffee and milk — from his wife.

The three men charged with assaulting the sheriff officer, Angus MacDonald of Tobson, Norman MacAulay of Tobson and John MacLeod of Breacleit, all fishermen, appeared for trial in Stornoway Sheriff Court, their defence counsel, Charles Innes of Inverness, having little difficulty in procuring their acquittal. In his cross-examination and his speech for the defence, he was extremely critical of Donald Munro's handling of the affair and of his management of the Lewis estate generally. "Had he been in either Connaught or Munster," Innes declared, "he would long ago have licked the dust he had for years made the poor people of Lewis to swallow". In a second trial on the following day, a Stornoway baker, John Smith, was

15

charged with obstructing the police in their attempt to arrest Mac-Donald; Charles Innes was again defence counsel and the case against his client was found "not proven". Still another trial connected with the Bernera affair was held on the same day: the sheriff officer, MacLennan, was charged with assaulting MacDonald during the attempt to arrest the Bernera man and was found guilty, being fined 21s.

The repercussions of the Bernera case were far-reaching. In Lewis itself, the summonses of removal were allowed to lapse and the Bernera crofters retained their grazing. The people of Lewis had had a demonstration that the chamberlain was not omnipotent, and in November of the same year the crofters of Swainbost in the parish of Ness, who had a dispute over the rent of a grazing, demanded to see the proprietor. Munro, the chamberlain, had promised to rectify the matter but, after waiting for some time, the Swainbost men set off for Stornoway. The chamberlain, hearing of their march, left Stornoway hurriedly in his brougham to meet them halfway and agree to their demands. He also distributed in the Ness district the balance, £600, of the Ness Fund, which had been raised in 1863, when 31 men were drowned off the Butt of Lewis, and which for years had been used by Munro to pay the rents due by some of the widows who had succeeded to their husbands' crofts. Surviving widows, orphans and other dependants received belated payments at the hands of the chamberlain. Munro had been deprived before the trials in the summer of 1874 of his post of joint procurator-fiscal (which he should never have been allowed to combine with that of factor), and then of most of his other posts, one after another. The final blow came in 1875 with his dismissal from the post of chamberlain. The new chamberlain, William MacKay, who had been a clerk in Munro's office, was a reasonable, tactful, well-respected person, but neither he nor the proprietor, already a very old man, introduced any radical changes in the administration, so that ten years later Lewis was to become a hotbed of agitation for land law reform.

The Bernera case received wide publicity in the Scottish press, and an anonymous pamphlet containing a *verbatim* report of the two Stornoway court cases appeared in Edinburgh soon afterwards. Who paid for the publication of the pamphlet? And who hired Charles Innes from Inverness to appear at the Stornoway trial? Innes, who later became Tory agent for Inverness-shire and who could not be called a friend of the crofters, may have undertaken the duty of defence counsel in order to bring into disrepute the administration of Lewis, whose proprietor, Sir James Matheson, had been Liberal M.P. for Ross-shire from 1847 to 1868, when he was succeeded by his nephew, Alexander (later Sir Alexander) Matheson; but the latter,

16

who was highly regarded as a landlord, was able to retain his seat in Parliament until he resigned in 1884. It was seven years before the crofters, this time in Skye, were to make open resistance in 1881 to their factor and proprietor; but the floodgates of criticism had been opened by the Bernera affair and newspapers continued throughout the rest of the decade to ventilate crofters' grievances and create an informed and sympathetic public opinion in the cities of the south.

One man who could have financed the publication of the Edinburgh pamphlet about the Bernera case and the hiring of the Inverness lawyer was Daniel MacKinlay, a native of Lewis who had become a wealthy merchant in Calcutta and had taken a lease of the shootings at Gress in Lewis in 1874, not long after the Bernera riot. MacKinlay himself in 1878 produced a pamphlet containing scathing criticism of the whole Matheson regime from 1844, when Matheson purchased the island from the heiress of the Seaforths. In it he denounced the removal of whole townships to create sporting estates and the transfer of the people to already-overcrowded townships, the neglect of fisheries, the failure to improve housing conditions and crofting conditions generally. In this respect Sir James was unfavourably compared with his nephew, Alexander Matheson, also a wealthy magnate, who had made his fortune in the East but had transformed his estates of Ardross and Strathcarron. Sir James was said to have spent half a million pounds on Lewis with little return, but MacKinlay, in a detailed analysis of the expenditure, proved that the paternalism or despotism of the Matheson regime had been far from a benevolent one and of little benefit to the crofters. It is as well to add, however, that one should discount some of the stories of Lewismen living in misery in their squalid hovels. The best-known song about Lewis in the nineteenth century, "*Eilean an Fhraoich* (Isle of Heather)", composed in the 1860s by Murdo MacLeod, an exile in Glasgow, made the island seem to be almost heaven on earth; and the descriptions of Lewis life which appeared in the *Glasgow Herald* in the 1870s from the pen of W. Anderson Smith reveal a happy, contented, hard-working people.[12]

Improving Landlords

It was often said in the nineteenth century that the solution for the problem of the crofters, who according to the law before 1886 were mere tenants-at-will, was to give them leases. This solution had been tried successfully on some estates, notably that of Sir Kenneth MacKenzie of Gairloch. But many landlords were not in favour: the Duke of Argyll maintained that leases for small crofts would prevent consolidation of crofts, which he claimed to have been successful in

Tiree. Crofters themselves generally distrusted the idea of a lease, as they feared eviction at the termination of the lease. Nevertheless, leases were attempted by some "improving" landlords, one of whom, Evan Sutherland Walker of Skibo Castle, by his tactless and overbearing methods, evoked a barrage of criticism from his tenants and the press, a series of articles on the "Skibo Management" appearing in John Murdoch's *Highlander* in 1876. There were certain peculiarities in the tenures of the Skibo estate (later the property of the millionaire

Andrew Carnegie). Some crofters already had feus, some had leases for ten years, some leases for nineteen years, and there was actually a lease giving a joint tenancy to a number of tenants on the lands of Tulloch, granted by George Dempster as far back as 1798. Sutherland Walker was prepared to ride roughshod over his tenants' rights such as they were; and it is probable that the criticism of the *Highlander* only served to strengthen his resolve. Ten years later he was to cause even more trouble by his attempted evictions and his refusal to implement the decisions of the Crofters Commission.

The *Highlander* in the same period also exposed conditions on the estate of South Uist, John Murdoch taking the matter up by writing to the proprietor, Gordon of Cluny,

JOHN MURDOCH, EDITOR, THE HIGHLANDER.

with proposals, some of which were adopted in a half-hearted manner unlikely to bring success. It was in connection with a Skye estate that the *Highlander* became involved in a *cause célèbre* in Inverness Sheriff Court. The one estate in Skye on which rents had been raised considerably was that of Kilmuir, formerly Lord MacDonald's and bought from his trustees in 1855 by Captain William Fraser, 11th laird of Giusachan, but invariably designated "of Culbokie" and later "of Kilmuir". He had sold Giusachan to Lord Tweedmouth the year he bought Kilmuir for £85,000, and the very next year he raised the rents by 30 per cent. Now, whatever else may be said in criticism of the Skye landlords (and their sins, it may be added, were mainly sins of omission rather than of commission), they were not rack-renters. Fraser was an exception. He was, according to himself, an "improving laird", who took an interest in his estate, reckoned to possess the most fertile land in Skye, and saw no reason why he should not make it profitable by extracting as high rents as he could from the tacksmen or farmers, the sportsmen who took leases of the shootings and fishings, and the crofters. Following a valuation in 1876, Fraser intimated to his tenants an increase in rents, which would then be double what they were in 1855.

The Uig Flood

On Sunday, October 13, 1877, a gale of exceptional severity, accompanied by torrential rain, swept the north-west of Scotland. The north end of Skye suffered worst of all. "The two rivers, the Conan and the Hinnisdale", wrote D. Nairne in his *Memorable Floods in the Highlands*,

"thundered down in terrible volume to Uig Bay, carrying away bridges, obliterating crops, sweeping flocks of sheep into the sea, and entirely changing in several places the face of the country."

Uig Lodge, the residence of Captain Fraser, was completely wrecked and the only occupant, David Ferguson, the estate manager, drowned. Uig graveyard was devastated and bodies were washed out to sea or into the Lodge gardens.

Immediately afterwards, a report on the disaster by the *Highlander* correspondent, Finlayson, appeared in that paper. It included strong criticism of Captain Fraser's treatment of the Kilmuir crofters, whose condition, he stated, was "anything but enviable". "Their lives", the report continued,

"were bitter enough before but now their burdens are unbearable. This is the time for Captain Fraser to show his charity if he has any. The Lord has given him means, which he can turn to good or evil account, just as he pleases, but he must now bear in mind that there is One who is fearful in judgement and that an account must be rendered."

The correspondent went on: "The belief is common throughout the parish that the disaster is a judgement upon Captain Fraser's property."

Murdoch, editor of the *Highlander*, was away on one of his fundraising missions when the article was received for the press but he accepted responsibility for the article, which he regarded as straight

19

reporting of the feelings of the Kilmuir people. He was however soon faced with an action for £1,000 damages, an action which, if success-ful, would mean the end of the *Highlander*. William Burns, of the legal firm, Rule and Burns, who acted for Captain Fraser, told Murdoch's agent in forthright terms: "You escaped in the Skibo case, but we have got you now and will lock the door on you." Murdoch, however, got off comparatively lightly, Sheriff Blair assessing the damages at £50, but with £34:5s. of legal expenses to be added. Murdoch was unable, even with the contributions of various well-wishers, to raise more than £69:5s. wherewith to pay the damages and costs and meet the printers' wages next day. He was sitting in silence with a few friends in the *Highlander* office on the last day allowed for payment, when word was brought to him from the Tory agent, Charles Innes, that John MacKay of Hereford, a staunch supporter of Murdoch, had wired to say he would stand good for £50. The paper was saved and survived for a few more years. Contrary to what has often been written, the case did not harm the paper, which gained added publicity. Captain Fraser, on the contrary, was from that time onwards always under attack from crofters' sympathisers; and it was on his estate that the dispute with the Valtos tenants sparked off the troubles in Skye in 1881. The *Highlander's* financial difficulties were perennial but, according to Murdoch, it was "treachery in the office" and the conduct of the manager, Hugh Fraser, which brought about the collapse of the paper a few years later.

Leckmelm Evictions

Absentee landlords frequently came under fire for their neglect of their estates. But the proprietors who, like those of Skibo and Kilmuir, began to make "improvements" aroused sometimes greater criticism. At the end of the decade, in 1879, the estate of Leckmelm on Lochbroom was purchased for £19,000 from Col. Davidson of Tulloch by an Aberdeen paper manufacturer, A.C. Pirie, who de-cided to convert it into something akin to a Lowland estate, all the crofters to surrender their stock, at valuation price, and become employees on the estate or be evicted. This rationalisation of the rural economy of Wester Ross might well have produced a prosperous estate with contented estate-workers, at least sure of their wages. But, although most of the crofters accepted the terms in time, it was symptomatic of the new atmosphere in the Highlands in the late 1870s that almost immediately a public outcry was raised.

The leader in the agitation was the Free Church minister of Lochbroom, the Rev. John Macmillan, who in June, 1880, sent letters to all the newspapers in the north about Pirie's proposed action. A question on the subject was asked in Parliament by Charles Fraser Mackintosh, M.P. for Inverness Burghs, and Sir William Harcourt, the Home Secretary, in reply said that, although he heard with deep regret of the wholesale eviction and considered the letter of Mr Pirie's factor, C.R. Manners, to the Leckmelm tenants "a most offensive production", yet the proprietor was within his rights so far as the law of Scotland was concerned. By the end of the year, a large public meeting in Inverness, at which the Rev. John Macmillan made a fiery speech, concluded with protests against the Leckmelm evictions and a resolution in favour of land reform. The national press, apart from the *Scotsman*, was full of condemnation of Pirie's action. The *Inverness Courier*, which generally echoed the sentiments of the *Scotsman*, gave ample space to Pirie's critics and to Pirie himself; and the *Courier's* Lochalsh correspondent, who happened to be a native of Leckmelm, permitted himself several critical remarks in his weekly notes. The changed climate of opinion on the crofting question was discernible among exiled Highlanders in Glasgow. At the Skye Gathering in Glasgow in the following month, one of the leading landlords in the Highlands, Cameron of Lochiel, discussing the topical subject of crofting improvements, remarked that it would be worthwhile if Highland proprietors would endeavour to place themselves in the position of their crofters, an oblique reference to the new proprietor of Leckmelm.[13]

A Decade of Change

The 1870s saw the beginning of public criticism of landlords in the Highlands and Islands of Scotland with the launching of the *Highlander*. The Bernera dispute in 1874 and the subsequent dismissal of the Lewis chamberlain, Donald Munro, resulted in a knowledge of crofting conditions in Lewis spreading to the rest of the country. Criticism of the estate management of Sir James Matheson of the Lews and of Captain Fraser, Kilmuir in Skye, brought them adverse publicity in a climate of change.

The pace of change was hastened by the opportunities provided by the Highland societies which proliferated in the cities (as well as in smaller towns like Greenock and Dumbarton) for the expatriate Gaels to discuss affairs back in the homeland. In an early issue of the *Highlander*, John Murdoch urged those who attended "convivial reunions" to devote their time to more practical work for the lasting good of the people. By the end of the decade the Federation of Celtic Societies was criticised as being too political and there was scarcely a musical programme at a soirée of a Highland society which did not include songs about the clearances or the halcyon days of youth. The

21

steady improvement in transport and communications encouraged a greater mobility of the population with a resulting increase in exchange of ideas. The Highlands attracted tourists such as Sir William Harcourt, whose yachting cruises each summer made him sympathetic to the crofters, and critical of sportsmen like Winans, the "American Nimrod", who leased seven deer forests and antagonised the native population. This was the period when the popular press was born. Improved educational facilities provided a larger readership and made it possible for reporters to comment daily on events and give full accounts of speeches. The continuing conflict in the Free Church over disestablishment and union with the United Presbyterian Church created among the leaders of the church an interest in the affairs of the crofters, who were among the most devoted supporters of the church. Finally, it was in the 1870s that the Irish problems of land tenure and home rule began to dominate British politics, and set an example for Scotland to follow.

Notes

1. For accounts of the religious revivals in the Highlands and Islands of Scotland see Dr John MacInnes, *The Evangelical Movement in the Islands of Scotland* (1951); Rev. Alex. MacRae, *Revivals in the Highlands and Islands in the Nineteenth Century* (1905); Rev. Norman C. MacFarlane, *The "Men" of the Lews* (1924); Roderick MacCowan, *The Men of Skye* (1902).

2. According to John Taylor, the navvy-poet from the Black Isle, the navvies from Skye and the west coast were more clannish even than the Irish, with whom they frequently had rows, sometimes clearing them off the line when the Irishmen were fewer in number (quoted in James Handley, *The Navvy in Scotland* (1970), 342).

3. In the *Napier Commission Report*, Appendix A, there is included a table drawn up by Dugald MacLachlan, banker and lawyer, Portree, showing the number of decrees of removal from 1840 to 1883, and a letter from Alexander MacDonald, banker, lawyer and factor, Portree, commenting on the figures. The total number of decrees was 1,740, with an average of four defenders involved in each summons, making a total of 6,960 heads of families. The average number of decrees per year in the period 1870-79 was 15.4%, compared with 35.4% for 1860-69 and 54.4% for 1850-59. The expense of the decrees, 19 shillings, was borne by the crofters who received the summonses.

4. In the parish of Barvas, Lewis, about a third of the total number of families had been squatters and cottars paying rents to the crofters for 15 to 20 years until 1883, when the chamberlain, William MacKay, entered their names in the new rent ledger (*Napier Commission Evidence, 1104*).

5. The connection of the Roman Catholic Bishop of Argyll and the Isles, the Right Rev. Angus MacDonald, with the Hebrides dated only from 1878, and he was impressed by the contrast between the unsatisfactory educational provision in the predominantly Catholic islands of South Uist and Barra and the situation in industrial districts in Central Scotland, where the school boards were overwhelmingly Protestant in composition. Recruitment of teachers for the newly-opened schools in the southern Hebrides gave rise to acrimonious dispute. The Catholic applicants almost invariably had no Gaelic and had been trained in English training colleges, whereas the applicants favoured by the Inspector of Schools and the factor, a member of the school board, were Scottish and better qualified according to inspector and factor, although bishop and parish priest suspected that the choice was based on sectarian grounds. (*Napier Commission Report*, Appendix A).

6. The Lewis and Harris Association, which celebrated its centenary in 1987, was preceded by a Lewis Association, founded in 1876 and registered as a Friendly Society. Two of the founders in 1887, D.J. and A.R. MacKenzie, were sons of a former tacksman of Dalbeg.

7. The percentage of men who signed the marriage register by a mark only, i.e. illiterates, decreased in Inverness-shire in the years 1862-81 from 30.9 to 17.5 and that of women from 49.5 to 27.3 (*Napier Commission Report*).

8. In 1874-75, there were, out of a total of 189 subscriptions to *An Gaidheal*, 132 from Scotland (6 from Lewis, 3 from Skye); 31 from Canada; 16 from England; 5 from Australia; 4 from Ireland; 1 from Wales.

9. The "Clach's" father was third cousin to Sir Kenneth MacKenzie of Gairloch by a descent on the wrong side of the blanket from Sir Alexander MacKenzie, 9th of Gairloch.

10. The record catch for one rod in one day is said to have been made in 1888 by a Mr Naylor, who caught 54 salmon on the Grimersta River. (*Eilean an Fhraoich Annual*, 1975).

11. The number of summonses is usually given as 56, following the anonymous printed account of the trial of the Bernera men in Stornoway Sheriff Court, but in the lengthy and detailed report of Superintendent Cameron, the number was 58. Cameron's report is contained in a letter, dated April 13, 1874, sent to the Chief Constable of Inverness-shire, D. Munro, and is preserved in the papers of Sir Kenneth MacKenzie of Gairloch, then Lord Lieutenant of the county. Oral tradition in Bernera has added some detail to the official report and the anonymous pamphlet — two accounts in Gaelic, that given in the introduction to the poems of John Smith of Earshadar in *Bardachd Leodhais* (1916) and the chapter "*Aramach am Bearnaraigh*" by Donald MacAulay in *Oighreachd agus Gabhaltas* (1980), and two accounts in English by writers with Bernera connections, that of Dr Donald MacDonald of Gisla in *Tales and Traditions of the Lews* (1967) and that of Anne M. Whitaker in *Eilean an Fhraoich Annual* (1974).

12. A number of these articles were reprinted in W. Anderson Smith's *Lewsiana* (1874). In a second edition in 1886, Smith gave expression to his strongly-felt criticism of the management of Lewis, about which he had made no comment in the original articles.

13. The chapter on the Leckmelm evictions in Alexander MacKenzie's *Highland Clearances* first appeared in pamphlet form and was the earliest of MacKenzie's many accounts of the Crofters' War. Pirie remained adamant in his policy. When, at the Napier Commission hearing in 1883, he was asked by Charles Fraser MacKintosh, "Physical conditions may be improved, but what of dignity and status?" Pirie replied, "It is a matter of sentiment and I can quite understand the feeling of sentiment. I do not see it in the light of sentiment when it is a question of subsistence".

CHAPTER 2

THE SKYE TROUBLES

Skye Estates

The Isle of Skye differed from Lewis in the number of proprietors.[1] By far the most important in the 1880s, Lord Macdonald, had an estate which extended from Sleat to north of Portree. The rental in 1881 amounted to nearly £13,000, a total made up mainly of crofters' rents, farm rents and shooting lets. The estates of MacLeod of MacLeod, once extensive, had been considerably reduced in size through the extravagance of previous chiefs and the misfortunes of the destitution years in the 1840s. MacLeod himself had been compelled by the burden of debt on the estate to follow a career in the civil service, rising to the rank of Principal Secretary in the Department of Science and Art. His rental still amounted in the 1880s to nearly £9,000, but more than half of this went each year to debt interest and repayment.[2] The other chief proprietor in Skye in this period was Captain (later Major) William Fraser of Kilmuir, who was an improving landlord and whose rental amounted to about £7,500, more than half of it from tacksmen. It was on the Kilmuir estate that crofters complained most bitterly about increased rents, whereas on the other Skye estates there had been comparatively little change in crofters' rents for many years. Besides these three large estates,

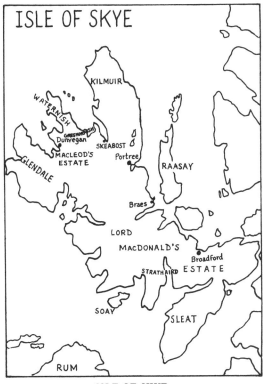

ISLE OF SKYE.

25

there were a number of small estates:— Greshornish, the former proprietor of which, Kenneth MacLeod of Gesto, had bought the estate after making a fortune as an indigo planter in India, and had also endowed the first hospital in Skye at Edinbane; Bernisdale, owned by another wealthy proprietor and philanthropist, Lachlan MacDonald of Skeabost; Treaslane, the property of Alexander Mac-Donald, the Portree lawyer, banker and factor, who was held in high regard by his own tenants; Waternish, whose proprietor, Captain Allan MacDonald, also had the reputation of a good landlord; Lynedale, owned by another Alexander MacDonald; Strathaird, the MacKinnon homeland, whose laird in the 1880s was Alexander MacAllister. Over in the west of Skye were the two Glendale estates, the larger owned by the Rev. Hugh MacPherson, heir of Sir John MacLeod, who had purchased the estate from MacLeod of MacLeod thirty years before, and the smaller owned by Dr Nicol Martin of Husabost. Lastly, the Isle of Raasay, which had been subjected to many changes of ownership in the nineteenth century, was in the 1880s a sporting estate in the possession of Edward Herbert Wood.

Alexander MacDonald — lawyer, banker, factor

The factor for most of the estates in Skye in the 1880s, Alexander MacDonald, *Alasdair Ruadh* (Red Alick) was the son of Harry MacDonald, founder of the legal firm known later as MacDonald and Fraser, Portree, and grandson of Dr Alexander MacLeod, *An Dotair Bàn* (the fair-haired Doctor), who had earned universal respect as a doctor and as factor for Lord MacDonald. Three of the factor's brothers spent some years in India, two of them as planters and the third as a surgeon in the army, while a fourth practised as a lawyer in Edinburgh. In one respect Alex. MacDonald resembled Donald Munro, chamberlain or factor for Lewis: both held a multiplicity of offices in addition to that of factor, MacDonald for Lord MacDonald, MacLeod of MacLeod, Fraser of Kilmuir, MacDonald of Skeabost, MacAllister of Strathaird. He was a member of most of the parochial boards and parish school boards of Skye and chairman or clerk of some. He had a busy practice as a lawyer and was also agent for the Portree branch of the National Bank of Scotland. There were some offices not so demanding — Collector of taxes and distributor of stamps, Collector for the Road Trustees, Clerk of the Peace, Secretary of the Skye Gathering Committee and Captain, Skye Volunteers. MacDonald was himself the proprietor of a small estate, Treaslane, with 23 crofts, small in comparison with Kilmuir with its 380 crofts, and Lord MacDonald's estate with its 863 crofts. Conscientious and diligent in his dealings with landlords and tenants, intelligent and capable of working hard (often until 2 o'clock in the morning) he had a prodigious output of letters, which were hand-written by clerks or by himself.[3] At the time of the trouble over rents in Kilmuir, the proprietor, Captain Fraser, who faced criticism on all sides, kept in touch with MacDonald in weekly letters and was on several occasions saved from worse trouble by the factor's advice. As a lawyer, MacDonald felt bound by the legal system prevailing, harsh though it was and as he knew it to be. The small tenants would have preferred as factor someone less diligent and particular about obligations being fulfilled. It is significant that at the mass meeting of crofters and cottars at the Quirang in October, 1884, a resolution, accepted unanimously, called for the dismissal of MacDonald and his replacement by someone "with a practical knowledge of agriculture" — in other words, not a lawyer. Unfortunately, the strains and stresses of overwork told on his health, and although only in his forties "the uncrowned king of Skye" resigned most of his factorships in 1886.

Kilmuir Estate

The estate of Kilmuir in the north end of Skye had some of the best farm land in the island as well as extremely rugged scenery such as Quirang. There were 380 crofts on the Kilmuir estate in 55 crofter townships, many with only a small number of tenants, the most populous being Bornaskitaig with 46 crofts, while 4 townships in Glenhinnisdal totalled only 15 crofter tenants altogether. Valtos, the township which first showed organised resistance to the proprietor and the factor, contained 6 crofts, all but one subdivided, i.e. with 11 crofter tenants. The estate had been purchased in 1855 from the trustees of Lord MacDonald, then in dire straits financially, by Captain Fraser, who generally spent half a year at his mansion house in Uig until it was destroyed in the flood disaster of 1877. When, in 1874, after the Bernera dispute in Lewis, the subject of crofting was discussed in the press, the Glasgow-based *North British Daily Mail* drew attention to the condition of the people of Skye, blaming "feudalism and tenant-at-willism, with the heavy rents that keep the people from ever getting out of difficulties", an allusion to the crofters of Kilmuir, the most highly-rented estate in Skye. It was the action for libel brought by Captain Fraser against John Murdoch of the *Highlander* in which, as has been stated, he was awarded only £50 damages of the £1,000 he had claimed, that left his reputation worse than before.

Captain William Fraser

The publicity given to the Kilmuir estate management following the Uig floods in October, 1877, hurt the pride of the proprietor, Captain William Fraser, who earlier in the year, writing to his factor, Alex. MacDonald, had said, "I do not want to do anything but what is reasonable, for they are a fine race of people". After the attack on him in the *Highlander* newspaper, he suggested to the factor that he could mention to the tenants on the east side of the estate that he had felt hurt by hearing of grumbling instead of the reverse. Four years later, after trouble arose over the Valtos rents, he made an offer to any tenant who was dissatisfied of a sum equal to three years' rent to leave his croft, adding,

"if all is carried out in good spirit up to the point of leaving. You can point out to them that I should like to be on good terms with my tenants, the Valtos ones not excepted, i.e., if they remain it must be on a pleasant footing".

These statements are in contrast to the denunciation by one of his Valtos tenants, Norman Stewart, who described Fraser as — "the evictor of 21 townships, the rack-renter, the process-server, the persecutor of 'the brave old crofter'". Fraser's reputation did not improve with the years, and a quarter of a century later he was described by Cameron, one of the early writers on the Crofters' War, as "a greedy and grasping Highland laird", guilty of "shameless rack-renting" and —

"the most conspicuous example of a ferocious and peremptory land merchant, hungering for a large return upon his capital".

Sheriff Speirs of Portree partly confirmed the last charge in his remark to Sheriff Ivory about Fraser as a "speculator in property". Fraser was one of the "hard men" who had brought "discredit on their class by conduct which nothing could justify", according to Sir William Harcourt, Home Secretary, in a letter to Queen Victoria.

What kind of man and what kind of landlord was he? A member of the landed family of the Frasers of Culbokie in the Black Isle (the most notable of whom was the Canadian explorer, Simon Fraser), he served in the Army for a time, rising to the rank of captain, and later became first, major then colonel, of the Inverness-shire Artillery Volunteers. A Liberal in politics, he was at one time chairman of the Inverness-shire Liberal Association and won the gratitude of the Free Church in Skye by granting sites for building churches in Kilmuir and Snizort. An improving landlord, he cleared 14 townships (21 townships, according to Norman Stewart) or deprived them of the better part of their grazing or arable to provide ground for farms or for his own mansion house and woodland. Some of the large farms on the Kilmuir estate like John Stewart's Duntulm farm were well-run and profitable to the farmer until the 1880s, when prices of stock slumped. As farmers and tacksmen (like innkeepers and fishery-lessees), were tenants with leases terminable or renewable after a definite period of, say, 9, or 19 years, it was possible for the proprietor, Captain Fraser, after negotiation with the tenant, to impose increases, so that the total of tacksmen's rents rose from £1,300 in 1856, the year after his purchase of the estate, to £4,365 in 1880, an increase of over 300 per cent, compared with a rise in crofters' rents over the same period from £2,220 to £2,873, an increase of just under 30 per cent. Fraser argued, on the basis of these figures, that the crofters' rents were far below the market rate; but the comparison was defective. For one thing, as a result of removals, there were in 1880 120 fewer crofters and in most townships the grazings had been curtailed; for another, the tacksman's grazing had in many cases been enlarged. Increases in rents were justified by Fraser and his factor, MacDonald, on the grounds that the improvements in roads, subsidies to the Post Office, investment in the Dingwall and Skye Railway, had added to the amenities of life in Kilmuir. According to the *Scotsman* in April, 1882, Fraser, who had purchased the estate in 1855 for £85,000, had recently been offered £170,000 for it but had refused, saying he wanted £30,000 more. Financially, he would have done well to accept but as the crofters' agitation continued and even worsened, a sale was out of the question. It was not until 1888, after the Crofters Commission had reduced crofters' rents from a total of £2,761 to a total of £1,716, that he sold the estate to G. Abinger Baird of Stitchell near Kelso, news of which deal was celebrated by the Kilmuir tenants at Bornaskitaig with a "gigantic bonfire".

Kilmuir Re-valuation

A re-valuation of Kilmuir estate, which started off the Skye troubles, was carried out in 1876 by William Malcolm, "an experienced and competent person and practical farmer" (as Captain Fraser called him), who farmed at Crook near Nairn, where Fraser resided for most of the year. As an east-coast farmer, Malcolm was later criticised because of his unfamiliarity with west-coast conditions. Malcolm was favourably impressed by the potential value of the estate: he considered the soil "very good, in some places exceptionally rich", describing the crops of oats, clover, hay and turnips on land improved and cultivated by the proprietor as splendid in contrast to the crofters' crops on soil exhausted by repeated cultivation. The survey was carried out, critics alleged, in good weather and in late summer when the crops were at their best. Malcolm's survey resulted in the swinge-ing rent increases for both tacksmen and crofters already mentioned. The new rents, double the original, were to be made payable as from Martinmas, November 15 1877, and in anticipation of complaints from the crofters Fraser wrote to MacDonald, the factor,

"Wishing to be as indulgent as I can to my tenantry at large, I have had the valuations looked over with a view to the circumstances of the people and the result is this reduced valuation . . . I cannot continue letting at the present extremely low rental."

One would think that these words came from a humane but realistic landlord, reluctantly driven to take a painful decision, but, in his next letter to the factor, he appears more like a callous, hypocritical, Victorian factory owner, expatiating on the virtues of hard work.

"I think it would be a mistake to allow the rents to continue at their present low rate, which indirectly seems to encourage a want of industry. The present state of croft agriculture throughout Kilmuir is very far back but with an increase of the rents it will become necessary to those who wish to continue to improve their lands a little."

Then, as if recognising his failure to encourage the crofters to improve their method of cultivating their lands, he added that he was prepared to help with grass seed, draining (although he would charge interest on any money laid out), and offer prizes for cattle at the show to be held at Uig that year. These letters were written in February, 1877, when the inevitable criticism of the rent increases was expressed in moderate terms and was confined to tenants. The *Scotsman's* special correspondent was one of the few who took the landlord's side but he annoyed Fraser as he failed to mention that the rents paid by the crofters were much less than what could be paid if the ground was let to a single tenant on a long lease or tack; and Fraser frequently in his letters referred to that form of tenure as a solution to the trouble with crofters' rents. The factor, MacDonald, collected the rents with difficulty, some of the tenants at first offering partial payment, that is, by refusing to pay the increase. Reluctantly they paid it under the threat of eviction and Fraser's decision not to supply seed corn to any tenant in arrears of rent.

Three years passed and trouble boiled up again when some of the tenants of the east side of the estate withheld their rents or the portion represented by the increase imposed in 1877. Opposition to the increased rents was led by Norman Stewart, a Valtos crofter and fisherman, who shared a croft of 7-8 acres arable with "a kind of pasture" and 6 cows, 1 horse and 20 sheep,[4] while he could earn £10 to £16 as a salmon fisher during the short summer season. Stewart had been sent to prison for a week for taking heather and rushes for the thatch of his house, a sentence which must have left more than a trace of bitterness. He became active in the agitation for reform and was christened "Parnell" after the Irish nationalist leader. Stewart in 1877 refused at first to pay the increase, in his case as joint tenant a rent of £7.10s. instead of the old rent of £4.15s. Later, in 1880, Stewart was able to make the most of an apparent error in the valuation, the valuator having been given by the ground officer the wrong figure for the souming of the township, 8 cattle per croft instead of 6 per croft. Souming was the number of cattle, horses and sheep which experience had shown a township would carry all the year round (as Alex. MacDonald defined it), and was primarily intended to prevent over-stocking of the grazing. More important, the souming was used as a basis for calculating the rents — cattle at £2 per head for a year's grazing, horses at £3 per head, sheep at 2s. per head — in most townships of Kilmuir estate. The estate management at first accepted that an error had been made but later both Fraser and MacDonald denied that the ground officer and Stewart were right. The ground officer, a minor estate official, may have been uncertain or in error as there seems to have been a considerable amount of over-stocking on the estate. But Fraser himself admitted privately in a letter to the factor on March 31, 1881, that the souming was carefully looked into in 1876 and that it was found that Valtos was "under-summed". The Captain, however, also maintained (in an earlier letter) that the first he heard about a souming error was in 1880.

Landlord and Tenants

When agitation revived in 1880 and some tenants at Martinmas refused to pay the increased rent, Captain Fraser at first confined himself to threats of eviction and attempts to discover the identity of the agitators. In March, 1881, in an attempt to improve his public image, he arranged to send out "a little remembrance" to the poorer people on the estate — 80 one-pound packets of tea and 80 two-pound packets of sugar — at Uig, Staffin, Kilmuir and at Culnacnock (a township two miles from Valtos), preference being given to any deserving person not on the poors' roll. A fortnight later, following an obvious case of incendiarism on the farm of Monkstadt on the west side of the estate, he sent a telegram to the factor, Alex. MacDonald, to warn six tenants in Valtos and six tenants of Elishader, a neighbouring township, where rents were also unpaid, the warnings being the first stage in removals or evictions. In a letter the next day, he urged MacDonald to pick out the troublesome tenants, preferably well-off ones and not to "overlook Stewart at Valtos". The factor advised him

31

to restrict the warnings to Valtos and Fraser agreed, stating however that he intended to be "firm, quite firm" with the ringleaders but that the rest of the tenants could remain, provided he received a signed statement that they were satisfied and intended to continue as his "good tenants". He threatened to remove any tenant who was an agitator or in communication with agitators, but any well-disposed tenants who would prefer smaller holdings would be accommodated if possible, and he added that the same concession would apply to tenants in Elishader. Then, in this letter of March 26, almost as an afterthought, he introduced the subject of a reduction of rents.

"By the way, considering the somewhat depressed state of the times it occurred to me it might not be amiss by way of a little recognition on my part with reference to those who have been anxious to pay the rent punctually and are otherwise well-disposed to make such tenants a little allowance (not much but as much as I can afford) but before doing so I would like your private opinion on the subject. Would you think that the following little gift would be appreciated? I would make all these tenants who paid their last half-year's rent punctually 5 per cent off the Martinmas rents but not off arrears of Whit rents then due. Further, as to all who have since paid or may yet pay up to the end of April, I would charge no interest on their Martinmas rents, a similar deduction to be made to those who pay their rents punctually — I except from this arrangement the Valtos tenants who, if they remain, must pay interest and legal expenses with reference to them."

The question of souming remained unsettled. MacDonald was able to report a good response in the payment of arrears but advised Fraser to increase the rebate from 5 to 10 per cent, which was nearer the rent increase of 1877. Fraser accepted the advice and expressed his willingness to extend the rebate (or abatement as he called it) to Valtos tenants who paid punctually and who expressed their regrets at what had occurred and their appreciation of his acts towards them. He went further and instructed the factor to draw up a list of those tenants who wanted a reduction on account of flood damage or had sustained recent losses or were very poor but really deserving, and he would then consider what could be done for them. In his new philanthropic mood, he declared his readiness to discuss the whole question of souming and adjust the rent accordingly. His concessions were not immediately implemented and when they were announced were regarded as constituting a victory for the crofters and a defeat for the landlord.

Although a settlement of the Valtos dispute was imminent, criticism of the Fraser regime was becoming more widespread and more outspoken than ever. Evictions provided a constant theme for letters to the editors of various newspapers and for reports of Highland societies' meetings, and Irish politics began to influence crofting affairs. The Irish Land League had been founded by Michael Davitt in May, 1879, with Charles Stewart Parnell as president. In 1880 over 10,000 people were evicted in Ireland and it was to combat evictions that Parnell introduced the policy of "boycotting", which led to the prosecution of himself and members of the Irish Land League executive on charges of sedition and conspiracy in December, 1880. When the jury failed to reach a verdict and the charges were dropped, Gladstone, the Liberal Prime Minister, turned to a policy of conciliation and brought in the Irish Land Bill, which was to serve as an example for Scottish crofters to follow. Captain Fraser was aware of the possible effects of the nation-wide agitation in connection with the bill and on April 16, 1881, he wrote to MacDonald, asking him to arrange a meeting with the Valtos tenants at once "in consequence of the state of Ireland". Two days later, Easter Monday, at a meeting in Glasgow addressed by Parnell, a motion was passed unanimously to the effect that in view of the threatened evictions on Kilmuir estate, support was pledged for the Highland crofters "whatever form the struggle might ultimately assume". A meeting of the council of the Federation of Celtic Societies was held in the Christian Institute, Glasgow, on May 6 and a similar motion was carried, expressing sympathy with the Valtos tenants and promising support in resisting "this gross outrage on humanity and public decency". Soon afterwards, on May 17, 1881, at a meetng in Fleming's Hotel, Bridge Street, Glasgow, the Skye Vigilance Committee was formed to "watch the future dealings of Captain Fraser". From then onwards, crofters' complaints were taken up by this group of Glasgow Highlanders, whose connection with the Irish Land League was denounced and exaggerated by the newspapers of the establishment such as the *Scotsman* and the *Inverness Courier*.

Valtos Settlement

The meeting with the Valtos tenants which Captain Fraser asked the factor to arrange took place on April 21, three days after Parnell's meeting in Glasgow. Although Fraser complimented MacDonald on having conducted the meeting with "great good judgement", the compromise agreement did not last long. In a statement headed "Obligation by Valtos Tenants", both sides accepted the reduced souming as the correct souming, Captain Fraser "having yielded to our representations"; and the tenants agreed to pay their rents for the year from Whitsunday, 1880 to Whitsunday, 1881, less a rebate of £1.2.6 for each whole lot or croft. This "Obligation" included the names of the tenants, all but one, John Lamont, signing with a cross, and the bargain was sealed with a dram of whisky. The dispute between landlord and tenants was not at an end: some of the tenants suspected that the rebate of £1.2.6 off the rent of each whole lot meant that, as five of the six lots or crofts were shared, the rebate for the majority would be halved. When the factor confirmed their suspicions and reminded them of the agreement (signed and sealed with whisky), they reverted to their original demand for the rent to be reduced by the amount of the increase of four years before. Captain Fraser's first reaction to the breakdown of negotiations with the Valtos tenants was one of disappointment and a determination to avoid any further leniency "as it would be mistaken for weakness". Among the possible measures he considered was legal action for recovery of the whole rent and arrears, while he also asked the factor for his views on procuring a policeman and a ground officer for the east side of the estate. A ground officer, if a "canny fellow" were chosen, would, Fraser suggested, be useful in giving information about ring-leaders and parties who were inciting the tenants. The difficulty of serving notices of removal without involving the sheriff officers in violent reprisals and the need for backing by a small force of police Fraser discussed in letters to MacDonald and with his lawyers in Inverness, Messrs Rule and Burns, but he was reluctant to use force, although he was advised that he was within his legal rights in taking such action in cases of tenants badly in arrears.

At the beginning of June he took the first steps towards satisfying the Valtos tenants' demands by proposing a rebate of 25 per cent to tenants having paid or paying punctually at Whitsunday collections, this rebate to apply to all crofters on the estate except Valtos. The reasons he gave to the ground officers for transmission to the tenants were —

"the difficulty of tenants getting loans, a harder winter than usual, and last but not least, the Irish agitation and unprincipled people endeavouring to draw tenants from paying that which they owe".

The rebate of 25 per cent amounted to £742 for the whole estate compared with £766, the amount of the increase in the rental imposed in 1877, so that the stand made by the small number of tenants had brought about a reversal of estate policy which was of benefit to all the tenants. The Valtos tenants agreed to pay their rents with the 25 per cent reduction allowed to all Kilmuir tenants and an extra sum to be the equivalent of the increase in respect of the wrong souming.

The Kilmuir Petition

Captain Fraser's troubles over rents did not end after the agreements with the Valtos tenants. Already, the factor, MacDonald, was writing

34

warning letters to the crofters at Digg and Glenhinnisdal. Fraser had prided himself on having "a fine race of people" as tenants, with whom he would like to be on good terms, but although he continued with rebates after 1881, he regarded them as temporary concessions or he applied conditions such as expressions of gratitude. At the time of the Martinmas rent collection of 1882 he suggested to MacDonald that if the tenants of Digg, Brogaig, Glaspheinn and Glenhinnisdal paid their rents, gave up their agitation and expressed their thankfulness, he would reduce the rents by 12½ per cent. He added to the factor's difficulties at the rent collection by insisting on excepting "discontented persons" from the benefit of a rebate on rents unless they wrote "suitable notes of appreciation". He included a short list of "malcontents" — Norman Stewart, Valtos, Donald Ross, Culnacnock, Archibald MacDonald, Garrafad, and Murdo MacLeod, Digg. This was at Martinmas, 1883, the year of the Royal Commission under Lord Napier, the year when Captain Fraser, almost continually in pain from rheumatism, faced open criticism from the witnesses at the Commission's hearings and the press. It was also the year of the Kilmuir petition fiasco.

James Urquhart, inn-keeper at Uig, and Alexander MacLeod, farmer, Skudiburgh, two tacksmen on the Kilmuir estate, who had attended the Napier Commission's hearing at Portree in May 1883 but were not called, protested in a letter to the Commission about the one-sided evidence presented by crofter witnesses. They referred to the expressions of appreciation of Fraser's kindness in a memorial, requesting the erection of a pier at Uig (from where there is today a regular service to the Western Isles). The petition, 24 feet long, was signed in April, 1883, by almost all the adult males on the estate, many of whom later admitted that they were unaware of the praise of the proprietor and had thought it was a simple request for a pier. One person behind this ingenious scheme was the local policeman, John MacKenzie, who because of his involvement in local affairs was given notice of his removal by the Chief Constable of Inverness-shire, Alex. MacHardy. Before his removal he was offered and accepted the post of local manager, a move which did not improve relations between landlord and tenants. The opening paragraph of the petition read as follows:—

"We, the undersigned tenants and others on the Kilmuir estate, Skye, desire to convey to our esteemed proprietor, Major Fraser, our best thanks for the kindly interest he has always taken in everything calculated to promote our welfare" . . .

During the summer of 1883, after the method of obtaining signatures had been exposed, Fraser admitted that the petition's presentation

35

had been bungled and for a time considered a suggestion for another, shorter statement but eventually decided to let sleeping dogs lie. Just before the Martinmas rent collection, however, he declared in a letter to the factor that the time was ripe for a show of firmness, that the law had to be respected and that Glenhinnisdal should be taken as the battleground. By this time most of Skye was involved in crofting troubles and Fraser had his hands full with another grazing dispute at Garrafad on the east side of the Kilmuir estate.

Agitation in the Braes

As the trouble with the tenants of Valtos on the Kilmuir estate subsided (temporarily, as it turned out), Alex. MacDonald became involved in a more serious dispute with the tenants of three townships of the Braes of Portree on Lord MacDonald's estate — Gedintailear, Balmeanach and Peinchorran, situated six to eight miles south of Portree. There were many differences in the new situation for Mac-Donald, who had become factor for Lord MacDonald as recently as 1880. In contrast to Captain Fraser, proprietor of Kilmuir, Lord MacDonald displayed little interest in the management of his estate. Partly in consequence, there was no history of rack-renting, and little if any animosity shown by the Braes tenants towards Lord Mac-Donald, who relied on his factor and his Edinburgh agents, J.C. Brodie and Sons, to deal with the running of the estate. Not yet thirty years of age, and despite the encumbrance of a debt of over £100,000 on the estate, he maintained a lifestyle comparable to that of the wealthy English magnates, owners of sporting estates in the High-lands and Islands. When in summer time he travelled north from London to Armadale Castle in the south end of Skye, it was by special train to Strome, the railway terminus at that period, and from there by his steam yacht, the *Lady of the Isles*, to Skye, the homeland of his ancestors.

The Valtos trouble affected far fewer people than the problems of the three Braes townships, which contained 29 crofts held by 48 crofter tenants, while the Valtos township contained only 6 crofts, divided among 11 crofter tenants. There were also some other Braes townships, not directly involved at first in what became known as the Ben Lee dispute. For all the Braes townships there were two schools for the 150 pupils. The headmaster of one of them, Kenneth Mac-Lean, a native of Coigach in Wester Ross, had a son, Norman, who became a minister of the Church of Scotland. In his autobiographical *The Former Days* he painted a vivid picture of the crofters' struggle as seen through the eyes of a young boy. John Murdoch, who visited the Braes, as also many other Highland villages, to publicise his newspaper, the *Highlander*, made a lasting impression on the schoolmaster's son. After the visit of Murdoch, who was the first man MacLean ever saw wearing the kilt, about a dozen copies of the *Highlander* arrived by post until it closed down at the end of 1881. It was from the *Highlander*, in which there appeared from time to time excerpts from Donald MacLeod's *Gloomy Memories*, that the young MacLean learned about the clearances and the grievances of the people of the crofting communities. The politically-conscious among the crofters also found in the *Highlander* ammunition to reinforce their arguments about their own particular grievance, the grazing on Ben Lee.

1881 was a year full of troubles for the crofters and fishermen. Apart from the success of the small-scale haddock fishing, it was a poor season for the Skye fishermen. A terrible storm on November 21, when 250 Skye fishing boats were completely destroyed and over 150 severely damaged, increased the agitation for reduction of rents. It led to the raising of relief funds in Glasgow and other cities, incidentally focussing more attention on the Highlands and Islands. Nor were the crofters and fishermen alone in seeking rebates of rent. The Aberdeenshire farmers in late August demanded immediate remedies for the depressed state of agriculture, and at a meeting of Ross-shire farmers in December, one speaker, Mr Adams of Hamberston near Dingwall, asserted that "five disastrous seasons in ten is surely no common occurrence". Landlords were compelled to grant rebates to farmers as well as to crofters: on Kilmuir estate, John Stewart, tacksman of Duntulm and one of the most notable breeders of Highland cattle, threatened to give up his lease if there was no reduction in his rent, and Nicolson, tacksman of Staffin Inn, became bankrupt. On Lord MacDonald's estate, Dr MacKinnon, minister of Strath parish and tacksman of the farms of Suishnish and Boreraig, asked to be relieved of his lease; John MacKay of the Home Farm, Portree, and tacksman of Ben Lee, was "financially embarrassed" and unwilling to renew his lease, and the tenant of Glenvarigill lapsed into bankruptcy.

As has been stated, the most important factor influencing the course of events in the Highlands and Islands in 1881 was the emergence of the Irish question — first, agrarian reform, followed by the demand for self-government. These two movements and the accompanying violence produced in Britain a cleavage of opinion which has survived to the present day. The passage through Parliament of the Irish Land Bill, which was later used as a basis for the crofters' claims for land law reform, was regarded with alarm by landlords like Fraser of Kilmuir, who feared that it could only increase the agitation already present among the crofters. On the other hand, the proprietor of Greshornish in Skye, John Robertson, who had spent some years in Ireland, welcomed the bill as a reform long overdue. John Murdoch, who had also lived in Ireland, openly supported the Land Bill so that the last few issues of his newspaper were reckoned by some more Irish than Highland. From 1875, the year which marked the beginning of a period of prosperity for the fishery on the west coast of Ireland, many Skyemen hired themselves as crews in the Campbeltown and Carradale fishing boats for the summer in Ireland instead of the north and north-east coasts of Scotland. There they became imbued with Irish ideas such as "No Rent" campaigns. Alex. MacDonald had little doubt over the rôle played by the Irish and those influenced by the Irish. When questioned at the Napier Commission hearing in 1883 about the Valtos dispute having sparked off the Skye troubles, he admitted the mistake over the Valtos souming but claimed that Fraser had "at once agreed to reduce the rents", a rather disingenuous admission considering his many changes of policy. He added, "There was no combination until after the Irish affair". This may have been an indirect reference to the setting-up of the Skye Vigilance Committee in 1881 after the Easter meeting of the Irish National Land League in Glasgow. The Braes dispute first came to MacDonald's notice following the return of the young men from the Irish fishing in 1881. In a letter to Lord MacDonald's Edinburgh agents, he wrote:

> "Shortly before the term of Martinmas a body of young men, the sons of tenants, most of whom had been fishing at Kinsale in Ireland and had imbibed Irish notions, came to my office and presented a petition which they had almost the whole tenants to sign, to the effect that they demanded Ben Lee in addition to their present holdings without paying any additional rent."

This was the first step in the course of events culminating in a confrontation between Braes people and a body of Glasgow police, which gained nation-wide publicity.

The Ben Lee Dispute

The crofters' argument was based on the fact that Ben Lee, near the Braes, once a common pasture, had been taken from them without deduction of rent and let to a farmer, Angus MacDonald, in 1865, by Lord MacDonald's factor at that time, MacKinnon of Corry (*Fear a' Choire*, as he was known in Skye). The tacksman farmer in 1881, John MacKay of the Home Farm, Portree, held Ben Lee, estimated to be able to carry 1200 to 1400 sheep, on a lease due to expire at Whitsun 1882, and although he had a right of renewal, he had difficulty in paying the rent of £120 per annum, a fact which was known to the tenants of the Braes townships. Donald MacDonald of Tormore (usually known simply as "Tormore"), who had been factor for Lord MacDonald until 1880, when Alex. MacDonald took over the factorship, was said by the Braes tenants to have promised them the grazing of Ben Lee at the expiry of MacKay's lease. Alex. MacDonald, in his correspondence with Lord MacDonald's Edinburgh agents, J.C. Brodie and Sons, had a different account of the origin of the Braes people's claim. At one time there had been an important cattle market at Sligachan, the busiest market in Skye, and during the period of the market, cattle from all over Skye were allowed to graze on Ben Lee. Since the grant of the first lease in 1865, the three Braes townships nearest to Ben Lee had at times grazed their cattle on Ben Lee and had come to regard it as having been their exclusive possession. Alex. MacDonald admitted to having some sympathy for the Braes people but could not condone their refusal to pay rents or the intimidation of tenants reluctant to sign an agreement over non-payment of rents. On December 8, the day for rent collection, none of the Braes tenants turned up at first, but after MacDonald had sent a notice to the Braes a band of young men marched into Portree to the factor's office, where MacDonald's reasonable advice received a poor hearing. Their march back to the Braes was accompanied by Colin the piper, a kenspeckle figure in Portree. A few days later, two widows from the Braes complained to the factor that they had been threatened by an angry crowd because they had refused to sign an agreement not to pay rent. MacDonald reported the matter at once to the Procurator Fiscal in Portree as a serious case of intimidation, but after some delay and consultation with the Crown Office in Edinburgh, MacDonald

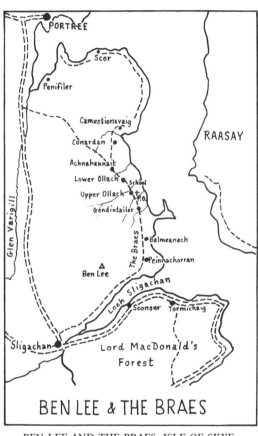

BEN LEE AND THE BRAES, ISLE OF SKYE.

learned that their decision was not to proceed with a charge for lack of evidence. Eight tenants, who had been summoned to Portree to be precognosced arrived with a retinue of about 50 supporters for their preliminary examination and only after a good deal of peaceful persuasion were the precognitions completed. Sheriff Speirs of Portree was in no doubt, after seeing the precognitions, that intimidation had taken place but concluded that there was insufficient evidence to convict. MacDonald had still to deal with the tenants' refusal to pay their rent and their demand for the restoration (as they viewed it), of the grazing on Ben Lee. Speirs was himself sympathetic to the Braes people: in a letter to Sheriff Ivory, he admitted, "I would do anything rather than have a row with poor, ignorant fellows".

Not all the tenants of the three townships were prepared to run the risk of eviction for non-payment of rent. Lachlan MacLean of Peinchorran, who had held his croft for less than two years, at first complained to Alex. MacDonald of threats from his fellow-tenants and ultimately had his rent paid privately into the National Bank of Scotland, of which MacDonald was agent. At the end of March, MacDonald received a letter from Peter and Angus Nicolson of Peinchorran asking for the names of tenants who had paid their rents and in his reply, declining to reveal their identities, he warned them not to force him to serve summonses of removal, adding —

"Any man of sense can see that three small townships cannot long resist the law although they may give trouble for a time."

He seemed to have forgotten the protracted dispute with the tenants of a smaller township and the opposition which the Valtos dispute aroused among sympathisers with the crofters throughout the kingdom. When another request for approval by the Crown Office of the charge of intimidation was turned down, MacDonald decided to press for eviction on grounds of non-payment of rent of those whom he regarded as "the ring-leaders of the organisation" — Donald Nicolson, Samuel Nicolson, John Nicolson, John MacLean and James Matheson from Balmeanach; Widow C. Nicolson and William Nicolson from Gedintailear; Widow F. MacKinnon, widow of Neil Buchanan, John Stewart, and Donald MacQueen from Peinchorran.

Deforcement

On Friday, April 7, 1882, MacDonald instructed Angus Martin, his chief clerk and a sheriff officer, to proceed to the Braes and serve summonses of removal. He was accompanied by Norman Beaton, the ground officer, whose duty it was to point out the persons named in the warrants, and Ewen Robertson, a Portree labourer, who acted as concurrent or witness to the sheriff officer's service of the summonses. As they approached the first township, Gedintailear, two boys appeared in the distance and then ran off, to reappear with flags in their hands. They were followed by two young men, also with flags, as if to warn their neighbours. Within a short time a crowd had gathered, and before they reached Gedintailear, they were surrounded by a hostile mob. Martin was asked what his business was and when he produced a bundle of summonses they were snatched from him by Donald Nicolson of Balmeanach, one of those named as ring-leaders by Alex. MacDonald. When the papers were scattered on the ground and set on fire with a burning peat, Martin watched the burning in apparently unconcerned fashion, an attitude which was later interpreted as indicative of his intention of seeking to be deforced, that is, prevented from performing the service of the summonses. He did not suffer physical violence but was castigated by the tongues of some of the women, who accused him of having made slighting remarks in Portree about the women of Gedintailear. It was a different story so far as Ewen Robertson was concerned. Whereas Martin and Beaton were regarded as performing official duties in execution of the law (which was being put in defiance by the crofters), Robertson was considered to be involved only for the sake of money and was assaulted with stones and clods by young people, who chased him back down the road to Portree. For the time being, the proposed eviction of the "ring-leaders" was dropped and instead charges of deforcement and assault were brought against Alexander Finlayson, Donald Nicolson, James Nicolson, Malcolm Finlayson (son of Alexander Finlayson), and Peter MacDonald, all of Balmeanach. The first two, Alexander Finlayson and Donald Nicolson, were mentioned as "ring-leaders" in the factor's list of tenants to be evicted. Kenneth MacLean, the schoolmaster, in response to a letter of enquiry from Alexander MacDonald, had given a list of the leaders of what he called the "rebellion", which, according to him, had started in Balmeanach. John MacLean in that township was the first or at least one of the first to raise the question of Ben Lee, and among his best supporters were four Nicolsons — Donald, John, James and Samuel, all of Balmeanach. Among the more prominent supporters of the movement in Peinchorran were Donald MacRae, John Stewart and Neil Buchanan. Gedintailear produced only two "rebels" — Alexander MacLennan and the son of Widow Nicolson. The arrest of those accused of the deforcement on April 7 was undertaken on April 19, 1882, in what came to be known as the "Battle of the Braes", when a band of Glasgow policemen fought hand-to-hand with men, women and children of the Braes.

The Battle of the Braes

There had been an immediate reaction by the authorities to the failure of the sheriff officer to serve summonses at the Braes on April 7. The Portree Sheriff, Peter Speirs, wrote on the same day as the alleged deforcement to Sheriff Ivory in Inverness:—

> "If not calmed down we must have 100 soldiers quartered at Portree till there is quiet in the island . . . I cannot allow the police to go there."

A week later, he repeated to Ivory his advice about the need for 100 soldiers, adding that the Braes men have "watchers all over the hills". Chief Constable Murray, soon to retire, did not consider the situation so serious as to require such a drastic measure and thought 20 policemen would be an adequate force to provide protection for sheriff officers in the execution of their duties. Sheriff Ivory, after consultation with Lord Lovat, Lord Lieutenant of Inverness-shire, decided to call upon an outside police force for assistance and to by-pass the Police Committee of the county, in order to avoid unwelcome publicity. Off to Glasgow went Ivory and there he met with the Lord Provost, the Sheriff and the Chief Constable, who promised to send 40 policemen to assist in the projected service of summonses on the Braes men. The meeting was held in private to ensure secrecy for the dispatch of the small force, which it was arranged would travel by steamer from Glasgow to Portree, arriving there late on Tuesday, April 18, and carry out a dawn raid on the Braes villages. At Oban, Sheriff Ivory joined the *Clansman*, the Mac-Brayne's vessel chosen for this unprecedented mission, and at Strome a small detachment of 10 men from the Inverness-shire constabulary came aboard. Secrecy however was impossible to maintain. The Glasgow *Citizen* reporter, MacLeod Ramsay, actually travelled to Portree on the *Clansman* along with the police and was able to give an eye-witness account of events as also was Alexander Gow of the *Dundee Advertiser* and *People's Journal*, who had arrived in Skye a few days earlier. On the evening of the *Clansman's* departure from Glasgow, meetings were held by the Skye Vigilance Committee and the Glasgow Inverness-shire Association in support of the crofters, and telegrams of warning were sent by sympathisers. The Braes people were thus awaiting with some confidence a confrontation with the authorities but not, as it happened, at such an early hour as planned by the sheriff and Captain Donald, the officer in charge of the Glasgow policemen.

The small expeditionary force, from the time it entered Skye waters, encountered unforeseen difficulties. The *Clansman* steamed into Portree Bay about 1.30 a.m. at low tide and ran aground some distance from the quay. Some delay occurred in ferrying the sheriff and other officials ashore. More delay ensued in conscripting the sheriff officer, Angus Martin, and his assistant, both of whom, when roused and informed of their duties, were terror-stricken. Considerable persuasion was required and eventually they were put under the charge of a policeman. Waiting on the quay were the local sheriff, Peter Speirs, and Procurator Fiscal MacLennan, who expressed surprise at the smallness of the force and advised postponement of the mission and requisitioning of military assistance. Sheriff Ivory, Anderson, the Inverness Procurator Fiscal, and Captain Donald, the Glasgow police officer, were however in favour of an immediate start and once the Glasgow and Inverness-shire policemen were landed at the quay the expedition got under way.

The weather could hardly have been worse for the Glasgow policemen, torrential rain pouring down most of the six miles to the nearest village, Gedintailear. The muddy roads made the going heavy and latterly impossible for the two waggonettes, the sheriffs and other officials having to walk the last two miles. A grey dawn was breaking when they arrived about 6 a.m. to find not a soul stirring. The Braes people had anticipated the arrival of a powerful force and expected to muster as many as 300 men but were literally caught napping. By the time the next village, Balmeanach, was reached, figures were appearing on all sides, men, women and children half-dressed, the women with their hair dishevelled, the men and boys whistling and shouting to rouse the heavy sleepers. The five men, Alexander Finlayson, Malcolm Finlayson, Donald Nicolson, James Nicolson, Peter Mac-Donald, who were to be summonsed, all lived at Balmeanach and their arrests were effected within half an hour. The task of escorting the prisoners back to Portree, rendered more difficult by the determination of the Braes people to rescue their fellow crofters and kinsmen, called for courage on the part of the Glasgow police. The local inhabitants carried sticks and had gathered piles of stones in order to block the march of the police back at Portree, and in retaliation the police used their truncheons. At a part of the road where it passed through a defile called *An Cumhang* (a narrow strait), a ding-dong struggle developed. Women dealt and received blows, and seven women and girls (five of them Nicolsons) were seriously injured by blows from the police truncheons. Above the uproar could be heard shouts — *"Cait' am bheil fir Pheighein a' Chorrain?"* (Where are the Peinchorran men?) but the men of Peinchorran were still in bed, more than a mile away from the conflict. Despite a hail of stones and clods, Captain Donald and his men were able to force their way back and bring their prisoners to Portree.[5]

The first judgement of those who supported the establishment was one of congratulations and praise for Sheriff Ivory's expedition to the Braes as an effective vindication of the law. Sheriff Webster, writing from Lochmaddy in North Uist, complimented Sheriff Ivory on "a most successful coup". "Nothing", he wrote, "could have turned out better. This must have a great moral effect on all the West of Scotland". The Lord Advocate, J.B. Balfour, congratulated Ivory on discharging "a most difficult, delicate and perilous duty with admirable judgement, energy, temper and courage on the part of all concerned". The Inverness-shire Police Committee, which had been by-passed by Ivory, gave him their approval for "his promptitude and energy displayed in vindicating the law". The *Scotsman*, not unexpectedly, praised the authorities for acting "with vigour and discretion in dealing with the crofters in Skye who have set the law at defiance", and recommended "sharp punishment of the assailants of the police as the truest mercy". The majority of the press, which gave wide coverage to the events of April 19, tended, however, to examine more critically the underlying causes of the disturbances in Skye, "stirring up trouble", according to Alexander MacDonald. Immediately after news of the Braes violence reached the south and the east, the *Scotsman*, *Glasgow Herald*, the Glasgow-based *North British Daily Mail*, the *Inverness Courier* and *Northern Chronicle* sent their representatives to the island; and by the end of the week more arrived from the *Glasgow News*, the London *Standard*, the Dublin *Freeman's Journal*, and also in addition, the editor of the *Inverness Courier* in person.

The question of the prosecution of those involved in the "Battle of the Braes", as the newspapers soon dubbed the affair, troubled the minds of those in authority. Violence, it was argued, should not go unpunished, but there was a trial of Braes crofters already fixed for May 11 and both Sheriff Ivory and the factor, MacDonald, saw disadvantages in another trial. Ivory suggested to the Lord Advocate on April 26 that it would not be advisable to have another Braes trial and thus keep open the sore for weeks. MacDonald, writing to Lord MacDonald's Edinburgh agents in favour of a negotiated settlement, remarked very wisely, "Every day lost in using repressive measures is adding strength to the agitation." That was his opinion on April 11, when he was hoping that "the authorities would send a proper force so as to keep order." He was faced with the choice of two courses of action — yielding to what he considered the unreasonable demands of the crofters, who would claim it as a victory and demand more concessions, influencing others to follow their example, or insisting on a rigorous implementation of the law, which in Skye at that time involved too frequently the threat of a summons of removal. It was little wonder that the strain began to bear heavily upon him. Writing to an Inverness solicitor in mid-May he apologised for delay in dealing with a request for information. "I have since Christmas been so annoyed and put about by the agitation among the crofters that I have had too little time to attend to my own business."

Trial of the Braes Men

The trial of the Braes men arrested by the Glasgow police was held on May 11, 1882, in Inverness Sheriff Court before Sheriff Blair, sitting without a jury. This represented a departure from established practice in Scotland, where summary trials were held by sheriffs without a jury in subsidiary courts such as Portree while more serious offences were heard by sheriffs with a jury in the principal court of the sheriffdom. Protests against what seemed a subterfuge to avoid the pressure of local opinion in Skye in a summary trial or in Inverness with a jury trial were made by the defence counsel and by Scottish M.P.s. There was ample justification for the suspicions of the crofters' friends: Sheriff Ivory, writing on April 22 to the Lord Advocate about the possible trial of persons engaged in "mobbing and rioting" at the Braes on April 19, recommended a hearing in Edinburgh, "considering the risk of acquittal in consequence of the sympathy of an Inverness jury". Kenneth MacDonald, Town Clerk of Inverness, who defended the accused, challenged the ruling of the Lord Advocate, J.B. Balfour, in what Balfour termed an insolent letter. Balfour defended his decision in the House of Commons in answer to questions from Fraser Mackintosh and J. Dick Peddie, who were signatories along with five others to a lengthy letter in the London *Times*. Kenneth MacDonald's defence at the trial was skilfully conducted: he managed to have the charge of deforcement withdrawn, and obtained for the accused, who were all found guilty, moderate sentences ranging from £2.10s. or one month's imprisonment for Alexander Finlayson and Donald Nicolson to 20s. or 14 days' imprisonment for the others. Kenneth MacDonald in his cross-examination elicited the fact that Martin had been frequently the worse of drink and absented himself from the office when the factor was in Glasgow on business connected with the Skye Boat Disaster Fund. The trial did not show Alexander MacDonald in a favourable light either: Kenneth MacDonald grilled him over the numerous posts held by the factor, who for the first time was called by the Inverness lawyer "the uncrowned king of Skye".[6]

The trial had proved a moral success for the crofters. Just as after the Valtos affair, sympathy for them soon manifested itself in the cities. A mass meeting had been held in Glasgow before the Inverness trial on May 11, and in the following week the London Inverness-shire Association sponsored a meeting of protest about crofters' grievances. Before Parliament rose for the summer recess, in a debate on crofting conditions on August 4, Donald MacFarlane, M.P. for County Carlow, in Ireland, and others, failed to convince the Lord Advocate, J.B. Balfour, that an inquiry was necessary or desirable. Whitsun rent collection had come and gone without any rents, far less arrears, being paid by the Braes tenants. To add insult to injury, they drove their sheep or allowed them to wander on to Ben Lee. Edward MacHugh, a paid emissary of the Irish National Land League, had arrived at the end of April and was soon engaged, according to Sheriff Speirs of Portree, in "preaching his vile doctrines all over Skye". He was aided and abetted in his mission by the veteran champion of the crofters and enemy of "landlordism", John Murdoch, and the sight of MacHugh and Murdoch walking arm-in-arm through the streets of Portree was sufficient to confirm the worst fears that Irish agrarian disorders — dynamiting outrages, boycotting, murder — were soon to be copied in Skye. MacHugh, who was not an advocate of violence, probably had little influence on the Presbyterian crofters of Skye when it became known that he was a Roman Catholic.

Edinburgh Agents

When Lord MacDonald arrived back from Istanbul at the end of May, 1882, he was presented with a report on the disorders on his estate from his Edinburgh agents, J.C. Brodie and Sons, a firm of high standing in the Capital. John Clerk Brodie, the senior partner, had been Crown Agent in the 1850s and later Keeper of the Register of Sasines and Deputy Keeper of the Signet. In his seventies at the time of the Braes troubles, he signed some letters to important clients but left most of the firm's business to his son, Thomas Dawson Brodie, who had held the post of Deputy Keeper of the Privy Seal and was to become a baronet in 1892. When Alex. MacDonald was appointed factor for Lord MacDonald's estate at Martinmas, 1879, he was directed by Thomas D. Brodie to address all communications regarding Lord MacDonald's affairs to him personally and not to his firm. He made it clear to MacDonald that no decision should be taken in regard to the Braes dispute without prior consultation. The situation was complicated because of the attitude of John MacKay, the farmer, who was financially embarrassed and wished to renounce his lease on the ground that because of the crofters' actions he was unable to conduct his affairs to reasonable advantage. As a first step towards a settlement, Brodie adopted a proposal by Alex. MacDonald that a new survey and valuation of the Braes townships and Ben Lee should be undertaken by a competent surveyor. The appointment of John

Forsyth, factor for Sir Charles Ross of Balnagown, was again criticised as that of an east-coast farmer who conducted his survey in fine summer weather, the same criticism as had been levelled against William Malcolm's re-valuation of Kilmuir. But Forsyth seems to have been extremely well received by the Braes people, according to John C. Brodie, writing to Lord Lovat four months later. Brodie had a high opinion of Forsyth, whom he described as "shrewd, judicious, firm and experienced". There would have been little difficulty in effecting an amicable arrangement in July, Brodie wrote, had not the factor, Alex. MacDonald, insisted that any settlement should be made through him. Forsyth's report was as objective as could be expected. The rent, £128, paid by the farmer, John MacKay, for Ben Lee was considered a fair rent "provided he has undisturbed use of the grazing". If let to the Braes crofters, he recommended a rent of £90 "or even considerably less". The survey supported the claim of the tenants of Gedintailear, Balmeanach and Peinchorran to the grazing on Ben Lee but along with the tenants of the Lower Braes townships. Forsyth found most of the crofters' rents on the low side and made slight increases, e.g. John Stewart's rent of £5.9/- he raised to £5.16.6 for his croft in Peinchorran, but he recommended for special consideration three poor tenants, two of whom were widows. If it proved impossible to let Ben Lee to the crofters, Forsyth concluded, the only course left to Lord MacDonald would be for him to "vindicate his rights", which meant taking legal action against the crofters.

The summer of 1882 passed quietly in the Braes villages, and the Braes sheep and cattle remained on Ben Lee. John MacKay, tenant of Ben Lee, ignored the letters of Alexander MacDonald, who argued that it was MacKay's duty to protect his grazings and who tried unsuccessfully to persuade MacKay to join with Lord MacDonald in legal action against the Braes trespassers. At the end of August, the Edinburgh agents, J.C. Brodie and Sons, obtained from the Court of Session an interdict against the Braes tenants with the purpose of bringing anyone in breach of the interdict before the Court of Session in Edinburgh, where he could be charged with contempt of court and if found guilty could be sentenced to imprisonment or fined a substantial sum. For serving a Court of Session summons, a messenger-at-arms was required. He was a glorified sheriff officer, distinguished by his blazon and ceremonial wand of peace. His functions were similar to those of a sheriff officer, but deforcement of a messenger-at-arms was considered a serious crime and therefore regarded as not so likely to be attempted. As it happened, the sheriff officers in Skye were most unwilling to be involved in disputes relating to crofters, which had already produced such violent scenes. An attempt on September 2 to serve the summonses was unsuccessful:

Alexander MacDonald, the messenger-at-arms from Inverness, managed to serve most of the summonses in the first village, Gedintailear, but once the alarm was raised, a crowd of men, women and children gathered, "howling in a frightful manner", and determined to prevent MacDonald, his assistant, Charles Clunas from Inverness, and Norman Beaton, the local ground officer, from going any further. Both Clunas and Beaton were struck by stones and clods, and MacDonald formally declared himself deforced, "breaking" his wand in token of his deforcement. The humiliating reverse of those entrusted with vindicating the law was naturally enough regarded as a moral victory for the defiant Braes crofters. Once more the local officials — the sheriffs, the sheriff clerks, and the procurators-fiscal in Portree and Inverness — were advocating military assistance in the enforcement of the law: billeting a hundred soldiers in the affected districts (for by this time trouble was brewing in Glendale), and the stationing of a gunboat near Portree seemed to offer a way out of the predicament in which the authorities found themselves. The Government officials resisted such demands, which might affect adversely future recruitment to the armed forces, and suggested the use of extra police from other authorities.

Autumn in the Highlands and Islands in the nineteenth century as now was the season for grouse-shooting and deer-stalking for the proprietors, native Scots and English incomers, and shooting tenants of many races. For many, particularly the ladies, the highlight of the season was the sports meeting or Highland Games, then more often called Gatherings, and the ball held on the evening of the Gathering. These were important social occasions and were attended by all the notables of the distrct, indigenous or temporarily resident. At the Argyllshire Gathering at Oban in mid-September the main topic of conversation was the Skye crofters' agitation, and many proprietors, worried about the possibility of similar troubles on their own estates, expressed the opinion that Lord MacDonald should reach a settlement with his crofter tenants. Soon afterwards, at the Northern Meeting in Inverness, which Lord MacDonald attended, he came under pressure from his fellow proprietors to find some solution which was acceptable to the Braes tenants. The Skye Gathering, the principal social event of the year in Skye, was held in the last week of September and since 1878 had formed part of a three-day programme, the two other days being given over to balls. These balls were held under the aegis of the Skye Gathering Society and were very exclusive affairs. Numbers were restricted to 60, the gentlemen were dressed in Highland garb, the ladies wore tartan sashes, and the reels and strathspeys were danced with vigour until the dawn. Despite these distractions, Lord MacDonald had more serious matters on his mind.

On September 25 he set off with his factor, MacDonald, to the Braes for a meeting with the crofter tenants. The crofters proved surprisingly reasonable, admitting at the outset that they were prepared to pay a rent for Ben Lee. They were in a strong bargaining position: they had the use of Ben Lee grazing without payment of rent, they had successfully resisted attempts to enforce the law, and they had the weight of public opinion behind them. Hitherto, the more vociferous people in the Braes (mainly young men who were not themselves tenants and also some women), had asserted a claim to Ben Lee without additional rent. Lord MacDonald's first and only offer of £100 for Ben Lee he considered as an abatement of £28.10/- on the rent paid by the farmer, MacKay, but it was above the rent recommended by Forsyth, the valuator — £90 "or even considerably less". The crofters countered with an offer of £45 for the three townships, or £1 per croft. Lord MacDonald was not prepared to haggle and withdrew his offer.

Police or Soldiers?

The Skye authorities, worried by the failure of Lord MacDonald's meeting with the Braes crofters and the emergence of a similar challenge to the law at Glendale on the other side of Skye, appealed to the Government for military assistance. The Home Secretary, Sir William Harcourt, in a letter to Sheriff Ivory, deprecated the use of a military force except when there was "a certainty of violent and riotous resistance by large bodies of men to the execution of the law". At the same time Ivory was told by the Lord Advocate, J.B. Balfour, that Lord MacDonald should settle soon with the Braes men "at some pecuniary sacrifice: otherwise the Land Question will be raised in a form of which no man can predict the end". A fortnight later, Balfour insisted in a letter to Ivory that there was no need to expect forcible resistance to "a well-conducted service with a more intelligent and resolute messenger-at-arms, as the Braes men had shown themselves 'quiet and respectful' during the talks with Lord MacDonald". The Inverness Procurator Fiscal, James Anderson, however, told Ivory that "the Lord Advocate and Home Secretary would look very foolish if this leads to loss of life". The Edinburgh agents thought differently. Thomas Brodie, writing to Lord MacDonald on October 11, feared that the use of troops might lead to loss of life, which Lord MacDonald would very much regret, and suggested that it would be prudent to accept a rent considerably below the offer made on September 25. He added that

"in the present excited state of feeling, an amicable settlement may be best effected by the intervention of someone who has not hitherto been mixed up in this dispute like Mr MacDonald".

At attempt to serve notices of interdict was made on October 24 with a small force of 11 policemen accompanied by a band of newspaper reporters. The Gedintailear tenants had been served with summonses on September 2 but a large body of Braes men, women and children prevented the officers of the law from reaching Balmeanach and after a discussion of more than an hour the police and officials withdrew. On the previous day a telegram had been sent by Alexander MacKenzie of Inverness, advising the tenants to accept the writs peaceably and to trust to the support of public opinion. Part of the advice was taken but the refusal to accept the notices left the legal situation unchanged. More public sympathy was shown for the Braes crofters in the newspaper reports and editorials, even the *Inverness Courier* correspondent criticising the authorities rather than the crofters. One reader of the *Courier* report, Malcolm MacKenzie of Guernsey, a wealthy expatriate Scot, was so impressed by the account of the crofters' stand in defiance of the law that he telegraphed Alexander MacKenzie to offer to Lord MacDonald £1,000 in payment of two years' arrears of rent on condition that all proceedings against the crofters should be dropped. The offer was not accepted, the Edinburgh agents pointing out that the case pending was one of trespass. Unwilling to have their further course of action restricted, they regarded the offer as an unwelcome piece of propaganda.

A way out of the impasse by accepting arbitration Lord MacDonald was unwilling to consider despite the arguments of his fellow landlords, Lord Lovat, Lord Lieutenant of the county, and Donald Cameron of Lochiel, M.P. At a meeting on November 11 with Lord Lovat and the Lord Advocate, Lord MacDonald at first actually agreed to accept arbitration but changed his mind. Thomas Brodie confirmed him in his original opinion, by pointing out that he could not be held to be committed to any decision in a conference at which he had not his agent present to advise him. The Lord Advocate reflected the views of the Home Secretary, who two years later, in a letter to the Marquis of Lorne, wrote:

"With the help of Lovat and Lochiel I persuaded (almost coerced) Lord MacDonald into an arrangement which has given peace to his estate".

Lochiel, after a meeting with Harcourt on November 3, described the Home Secretary as "ranting and storming like a maniac", who would listen to "neither reason nor argument". Harcourt, who had a reputation for being short-tempered, was insistent on the use of police rather than troops, declaring that he would not sanction a military expedition unless the county provided 150 police. The County Police

Committee, discouraged by the stubborn attitude of the Home Secretary and the failure of the appeal to other authorities for assistance, finally accepted the proposal of the Lord Advocate to increase the police force by 50 constables, making a total of 94 for the whole of Inverness-shire. The county Commissioners of Supply, the predecessors of the County Councils, reluctantly confirmed the decision of the Police Committee, a drastic step for them in contrast to the response to Captain Fraser's request for an extra policeman on Kilmuir estate.

Braes Settlement

Before another attempt to serve summonses was made, a settlement was achieved in the Braes dispute. Lord MacDonald, still standing on his dignity, maintained that it was for the crofters to make an offer and for him to accept or refuse. For the choice of an intermediary acceptable to both sides Alexander MacKenzie of Inverness suggested Dugald MacLachlan, Sheriff Clerk Depute at Portree, as one who could persuade the crofters to reach an agreement. MacLachlan, a native of Mull, had been resident in Portree since 1866, when he was appointed Sheriff-Clerk Depute. He was also agent for the Portree branch of the Caledonian Bank, a leading elder and Sabbath School superintendent in Portree Free Church, the church attended by the crofters. MacKenzie's suggestion met with the approval of the Lord Lieutenant, the Sheriff Principal, the Procurator Fiscal of the county, and the Edinburgh law agents of Lord MacDonald. MacLachlan persuaded some of the moderate crofters to accept a compromise but because of his official position in the Sheriff Court he left the final stage of negotiations to the factor, Alex. MacDonald. He met the crofters on November 27 and after more than seven hours of argument with the factor and among themselves the crofters offered to pay a rent of £74.15/- for Ben Lee, a figure which Lord MacDonald approved the following day. Because of the delay involved in settling with the farmer, MacKay, it was some time before the transaction was completed. Within a year the factor was pressing the tenants of the three Braes townships for payment of rent arrears, which was one of the conditions attached to the let of Ben Lee. Two years later, when the Braes tenants had joined a "No rent" campaign, MacDonald complained to Harcourt that Ben Lee had become a desolation through the crofters' inability to place enough stock (sheep and cattle) on the hill. This was a familiar argument used by landlords and factors in criticism of crofters' demands for more land; but the results of under-grazing (such as the spread of bracken), would hardly manifest themselves to a serious extent in such a brief interval. There is some evidence that the Braes crofters had second thoughts about the settlement of November 27 and felt that they had been persuaded to accept too high a rent for Ben Lee. The Braes witnesses at the Royal Commission hearing in May, 1883, were agreed about their rents being too high (although they fell far short of rents on Kilmuir estate), and when in 1887 the Crofters Commission fixed fair rents for the Braes, the total rental for the three townships was reduced by almost half and almost all the arrears cancelled, while the question of Ben Lee was decided in favour of the crofters. The Braes tenants must have felt justified in the stand they had made although difficult times still lay ahead for proprietors like Lord MacDonald.

The Glendale Estates

On the western side of Skye, far away from the Braes of Portree, lies the MacLeod country, *Duthaich MhicLeoid*. The centuries-old Dunvegan Castle is still occupied by the MacLeod chief but much of the MacLeod patrimony had been in the possession of others before the middle of the nineteenth century, sold off to ease the burden of debt incurred by the MacLeod chiefs' extravagance. Two small estates, both called Glendale, were to be the scenes of at least as much defiance of the law as was shown in the Braes townships. Glendale was, strictly speaking, the valley of the Hamara river which flowed north-west to Loch Pooltiel, where a pier had been built in order to promote fishery there, but for lack of fishing-boats it was seldom used. Most of the villages in Glendale were situated in the valley — Fasach, Holmisdal, Lephin, Hamaraverin — on the estate of Sir John MacPherson MacLeod but to the west of the valley and nearer the pier were the townships of Upper and Lower Milovaig, where opposition to the estate management first developed. Sir John M. MacLeod bought the Glendale estate from the trustees of MacLeod of MacLeod in 1852, adding it to his property of Colbost and Skinidin, which he had inherited. Sir John had a distinguished career in India but visited Glendale only once in the thirty years of ownership. After his death in 1881, the estate passed to his nephew, the Rev. Hugh MacPherson,

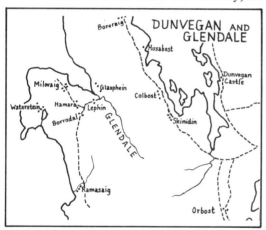

DUNVEGAN AND GLENDALE, ISLE OF SKYE.

The reaction of the crofters was to prepare themselves for a confrontation with the factor and summon a meeting to ventilate their grievances:

"We, the tenants on the estate of Glendale do hereby warn each other to meet at Glendale Church on the 7th day of February, on or about one p.m., of 1882, for the purpose of stating our respective grievances publicly in order to communicate them to our superiors, when the ground officer is requested to attend."

At the meeting there was a general discussion about the clearances effected by the factor, the most recent at Ramasaig, where 15 years before there had been 22 crofters but in 1882 only 2, the rest having been removed to other townships to the detriment of the inhabitants of these townships and involving hardships for those removed. This meeting, which Alexander MacKenzie of Inverness called the start of a revolutionary movement, was unprecedented and marked a new stage in the revolt of the crofters against "landlordism". MacKenzie had special praise for the men of Glendale, most of whom appeared to be "hard-working, industrious, thoroughly intelligent, some of them reading newsapers regularly and holding definite political views".

The most significant result of the meeting was the co-ordination of the protests from the tenants of the various townships on the estate, who were invited to submit petitions to the trustees about their grievances. The response was encouraging to the activists. The crofters of Skinidin complained about the ban imposed on the collection of sea-ware on the shores of Loch Dunvegan. Tenants of the neighbouring township of Colbost were highly rented but the soil was exhausted by constant tillage. The crofters of Hamaraverin asked for the redress of the grievances laid upon them by a "despotic factor", grievances unknown to the late "good and famous proprietor", and requested the trustees to reinstate the tenants turned out from Ramasaig, Lorgill and Hamara by the "ill-ruling factor". In Holmisdale and Lephin, there was much overcrowding and the tenants criticised the factor for "causing the downfall of his fellow-beings in order to turn their small portions of the soil into sheep-walks". On the neighbouring estate of Glendale petitions were also sent to the proprietor, Dr Martin, and given due publicity in the press. Particularly obnoxious to the crofters was the exaction of 10 days' labour as part of the tenants' rent, a practice which had formerly been common on the farms of tacksmen and still persisted in parts of the Hebrides.

The various township petitions were submitted at the rent collection on March 23 but before that date two notices were displayed at Glendale post office. The anonymous, mischievous author of the first seemed to have some knowledge of Irish threatening letters.

"Any one of the tenants at Skinidin who will pay the rent, not only that his House and Property will be destroyed, but his life will be taken away or any one who will begin backsliding. Not to be removed."

The other notice was couched in moderate terms but was more serious as representing the views of the leaders of the three townships nearest to Waterstein.

"Notice is hereby given by the Milovaig and Borodale Alliance that Dr Martin must clear Waterstein of his stock at Whitsunday punctually, if not, they will be driven off with full force."

At the rent collection, Peter MacKinnon, the Glendale postmaster, read out a letter he had received from Dr Martin's newphew, Nicol Martin, who maintained that MacKinnon had allowed notices to be posted inciting the "ignorant people to violence". Nicol Martin's brother, Donald Archibald, also offended the assembled tenants, after he saw the notice at Glendale post office, by threatening that he would "settle the whole of the Glendale people" and that half of them should emigrate to America. The crowd became incensed at the disparaging remarks of the Martin brothers and started miscalling them, both Nicol Martin and Tormore looking very much frightened. According to Sheriff Speirs, Tormore had become so alarmed for his safety that he armed himself with a revolver for his journey to Glendale, and would have carried another had not Alexander Mac-Donald, the Portree lawyer, who was Captain of the Skye Volunteers, refused his request. It seemed, from a later conversation with John Murdoch, of the now-defunct *Highlander* newspaper, that Tormore had been impressed by rumours of Irish pamphlets circulating in Skye. The three townships of Upper Milovaig, Lower Milovaig and Borrodal, formed an alliance and sent a petition to Tormore, who in front of a large crowd at Colbost, informed the tenants of the three townships that he had taken the lease of Waterstein himself but would give it up for the sake of the Alliance. The crofters offered to pay the same rent as Dr Martin and petitioned the trustees to let them have the Waterstein grazing instead of Tormore. In May the trustees at last visited the estate but the visit was a disappointing one so far as the crofters were concerned. Tormore not only retained the lease but had his shepherds drive his stock away out of sight of the crofters' grazings and told them that he would bid them goodbye and never see them again.

The trustees found themselves involved in a dispute between factor and tenants. They answered the tenants' complaints about not receiving the lease by stating that there had been advertisements of the lease for eight months, to which the crofters replied that they had never seen the advertisement and that until they were given the lease of

Waterstein they would withhold their rents. The trustees obviously preferred dealing with one tenant rather than with three townships and at first tried to hold Tormore to his contract but he claimed that because of trespass by crofters' cattle and sheep the trustees had failed to provide full access to the grazing for Tormore's stock. Not only did he withdraw from his contract but he compelled the trustees, in terms of the lease, to take over his stock at valuation. Tormore had other farms and other interests and, faced with a possible protracted confrontation with the crofters, he resigned his factorship. A year later, at the Royal Commission hearing at Dunvegan, he maintained that his relations with the crofters during the period of his factorship had been of the most friendly nature until the Waterstein dispute, which he attributed to the influence of evil-minded agitators. As for his resignation of the factorship, he said:

"I could not be humbugged with it. I did not care to be trying to govern people who would not be governed."

After a brief interval, the trustees asked John Robertson, proprietor of the small estate of Greshornish in north-west Skye, to assist them in the management of their farms, and in October appointed him factor. He had a difficult task ahead of him and, if anything, made his task even more difficult. John Murdoch referred to him as "poor Robertson . . . silly enough to put his foot in the mud so much muddled by his more astute predecessor." John MacPherson, the Glendale leader, criticised Robertson for his ignorance of Gaelic and said that the people would even prefer Tormore or any factor who knew Gaelic and was of good character.

Interdicts

The trustees sought to clear the grazing at Waterstein and Ramasaig of crofters' livestock in June, 1882, by obtaining notices of interdict against Alexander MacLennan and others, tenants at Upper and Lower Milovaig and Borrodal, a neighbouring township, but the interdicts were not enforced. Immediately after his first visit to Glendale, Robertson proposed that a portion of Waterstein be given to the Milovaig crofters but the trustees and their Edinburgh agents, Messrs Tods, Murray and Jamieson, decided that the crofters must first remove their stock from the Waterstein grazing. The townships had united in an alliance but Borrodal withdrew and Upper and Lower Milovaig were left to go it alone. At the beginning of July there was a mass exodus from Skye of young and active men to the east coast fishing — over 500 men according to Chief Constable Murray. Sheriff Speirs informed Sheriff Ivory on July 11 that there were hardly a dozen men left in Glendale so that the women and boys would be the delinquents if there was any disturbance or breach of the law. Mention has been made of the militancy of the young Braes men after their return from the Irish fishing. The east coast fishing also helped to create a more critical attitude by the exchange of ideas. A meeting at Fraserburgh in the summer of 1883 passed a resolution pledging those present to join the Highland Land Law Reform Association on their return to the west coast to their home. (A correspondent of the *Scottish Highlander* complained in the summer of 1885 that with the young men away at the fishing the H.L.L.R.A. meetings at Shawbost in Lewis had been suspended until the young men return, "as the old people have not much life and have the fear of the factor and his officials before their eyes".) In August, 1882, Robertson received a complaint from John Morrison of Upper Milovaig that Borrodal sheep were trespassing on the Milovaig hill grazing. Borrodal tenants had a considerable overstock of sheep and were told by Robertson either to sell their overstock or pay the Milovaig tenants one shilling per sheep, and in compensation he offered the Milovaig tenants a portion of the Waterstein grazing. When they saw how small the portion was — 360 yards by 2 miles — the Milovaig tenants declined to accept. In his few months in Glendale Robertson had succeeded in satisfying no one except the Borrodal people, and more trouble lay ahead of him.

The young Glendale men came back from the east coast at the beginning of September to find that Robertson had engaged two shepherds, both elderly men, to keep the Milovaig cattle and sheep off the Waterstein grazing. The young men were not long in taking action. On the morning of September 13 a band of Milovaig men marched up to Waterstein and threatened the shepherds, bawling and blowing horns, warning them that if they did not give up their jobs or if they drove the Milovaig cattle away their heads would be broken. The ringleaders were mainly from Lower Milovaig — Archibald Gillies, Alexander MacLean, John MacPherson and Malcolm Matheson, and John Morrison and Neil MacPherson from Upper Milovaig. Colin MacAskill, the grandson of one of the shepherds, who was present on the morning of the 13th, refused to give evidence at a precognition and, in honour of his loyalty to the crofters' cause, he was presented with a sum of money collected from the tenants. A case of intimidation, in addition to the threatening of the shepherds, came to light in October 16, when Ewen MacKenzie of Upper Milovaig reported to the police that he had received threats from Murdoch Matheson and John Bruce because he had stopped going to the tenants' meetings. A week later, the local policeman, Alexander MacVicar, informed Sheriff Speirs in Portree that the Milovaig cattle were all over the Waterstein grazing and that the shepherds were in bodily fear but were not interfering with the crofters' cattle. He added that not a penny of rent would be paid in Glendale or Husabost and that there were in the two estates 400 able-bodied, fine-looking, well-built men who would stick at nothing.

It was not long before the Milovaig crofters made a show of strength. The two shepherds, Donald MacDonald of Hamara and Donald Nicolson of Lephin, on November 8 cleared the Waterstein grazing of crofters' cattle. The following day a band of about fifty men and youths made their way up to Waterstein and although MacDonald attempted to evade them, they soon made up with him. "Surround the bugger at once", they shouted. One of the crofters, Malcolm Matheson, seized MacDonald by the throat and when he tried to run away he was knocked down and kicked. He was chased, along with Nicolson, the other shepherd, down through Glendale, a distance of four miles. Nicolson was warned by John MacPherson, Alan MacKinnon and Archibald Gillies that it was not safe for him to continue in the job and that no one would be allowed to drive the tenants' cattle off Waterstein before they obtained a settlement. The action of the Milovaig tenants gave encouragement to the tenants of Skinidin, who sent a letter to the factor, Robertson, expressing their determination not to pay their rents until they received satisfaction in regard to the islands in Loch Dunvegan opposite their township, where they formerly gathered sea-ware.

All through the autumn the county authorities had been engaged in negotiations with the Government over assistance by a military force for the law officers, and with the prospect of a settlement of the Braes dispute their attention was turned to Glendale. But it was not until after the New Year that a decision was taken to vindicate the law in Glendale. The remoteness from Portree and the presence of sentries on the neighbouring hills meant that a surprise raid was difficult, if not impossible, and when an attempt to serve notices of interdict was made on January 17, 1883, a messenger-at-arms from Glasgow, MacTavish, his two concurrents, and 14 policemen under the charge of Sergeant MacKenzie from Kingussie, were stopped and severely mauled in Glendale by a crowd mainly of youths, estimated in thousands. A few days later, a rumour swept the district that the steamer, *Dunara Castle*, with 50 policemen on board was lying storm-bound in Bracadale Bay. The following day, January 20, the steamer entered Loch Dunvegan and by the time it reached Dunvegan pier a huge crowd, consisting mainly of youths and boys, armed with sticks, had gathered. Discretion proved the better part of valour and the officers of the law retreated, the Glendale and Dunvegan police constables taking refuge in Dunvegan Castle.

Arrest of Crofters

It is difficult to assess to what extent the older men in the crofting townships approved of the use of violence against the police and sheriff officers, even when it seemed to be to their benefit. Their advisers, such as Alexander MacKenzie and John Murdoch, advocated respect for the law and the avoidance of violence. The crofters' spiritual leaders were faced with a dilemma: their sympathy for the aims of the crofters in their opposition to unjust laws was not in conflict with their Christian beliefs and practice. But a stage had been reached in defiance of the law which called for action on the part of the church. A meeting of ministers and crofters at Hamara Lodge in Glendale was arranged for January 30, when the Free Church ministers of four parishes of Skye were present — Rev. John MacPhail of Kilmuir, Rev. Finlay Graham of Sleat, Rev. Joseph Lamont of Snizort and Rev. John MacRae of Duirinish. The meeting opened with prayer, and to the ministers' queries about recent events the crofters answered by denying assaulting the police and sheriff officers but admitting that some men and boys had acted foolishly. The ministers urged the crofters to respect the law and not to use violence. The men agreed and promised to obey the orders of the Court of Session. The authorities, acting on information from the ministers, arranged for a gunboat, the *Jackal*, to sail round to Loch Pooltiel. The *Jackal*, with a civil servant, Malcolm MacNeill, on board, anchored off Lower Milovaig, and a meeting was held in Glendale Free Church, where MacNeill addressed the crofters. MacNeill, who was a Gaelic speaker and who was to be the secretary of the Royal Commission under Lord Napier, persuaded the crofters named in the warrant on charges of breach of interdict and contempt of court to surrender and stand their trial in the Court of Session. The crofters — John MacPherson (46), John Morrison (60), Donald MacLeod (45) and Malcolm Matheson (37) had been selected as recognised ring-leaders and all but one intimated their willingness to surrender to the authorities with the proviso that they should not be compelled to travel by the *Jackal* but allowed to make their own way south, which they did by the *Dunara Castle*. The fourth man, Malcolm Matheson, was absent in Stornoway for the annual training of the Royal Naval Reserve and surrendered separately. The trial took place in the Court of Session on March 15, 1883, and each was found guilty of breach of interdict and contempt of court and received a sentence of two months' imprisonment. They were well looked after by members of the Edinburgh Highland Association during their spell in Calton Jail and emerged on May 15 to a heroes' welcome. An even more rousing reception greeted the Glendale Martyrs (as the popular press already

60

called them), when they arrived at Portree by steamer, to see three bonfires ablaze and flags flying. Since the beginning of May the Royal Commission set up by the Government (see Chapter 3) had been touring Skye and on May 19 reached Glendale, where the first day's hearing in the Free Church was taken up with the evidence of John MacPherson.

Lachlan MacDonald of Skeabost

Conflict between landlords and tenants was not so bitter in the smaller estates in Skye as on the properties of Lord MacDonald, Captain Fraser and the Rev. Hugh MacPherson. Life seemed to flow smoothly on the estates in the north-west corner of Skye — on Waternish, Treaslane and Skeabost. Lachlan MacDonald, proprietor of Skeabost (also spelt Skaebost), the richest man in Skye, whose fortune came from his time in India as an indigo-planter, could well afford to be a philanthropist, but he was genuinely interested in the welfare of the crofters.[8] He and his wife were wildly opposed to the use of the military in Skye in the opinion of Sheriff Speirs of Portree, who described them as fanatics so far as the crofters were concerned. In his address to the Skye Association Annual Gathering in Glasgow in 1877, MacDonald maintained that, with the decline in wool and sheep prices, a crofting township could be as profitable as a sheep farm. He shocked the Inverness conference of proprietors by declaring that he could not condemn the people who deforced sheriff officers, as sending sheriff officers into crofting townships brought back memories of the clearances. No less than the provisions of the Irish Land Act would be acceptable to the crofters and he was later, like most other champions of the crofters, to be very critical of the Crofters Act of 1886. He was generous in his benefactions, cancelling all the arrears of his tenants at the Crofters Commission setting of fair rents, coupled with granting permission to fix their own rents. Many other small gestures of liberality, such as a rent-free house for Mary MacPherson, the poetess and singer of the crofters' movement, and £5 to John Murdoch, editor and owner of the *Highlander*, revealed his sympathy with the crofters' generally. His relations with the crofters of Bernisdale, where most of the crofts were situated, were of a friendly nature. In 1884, when a branch of the Highland Land Law Reform Association was set up, he was kept informed of the proceedings. Another local organisation, the Temperance Association, was responsible for a most unusual development in landlord-tenant relations. The minute of a resolution passed unanimously at a largely-attended meeting, contained the following clauses, copies of which were sent to the proprietor and factor:—

"1st. That this Society disapprove of whisky at funerals, and resolve to give it no countenance.

2nd. That, if proprietors and factors are not to make further concessions, they be asked to cease offering whisky on rent days — the money so spent in kindness would be put to better purpose in giving tea to the many poor people in the district."

When the Royal Commission toured the Isle of Skye in May, 1883, the second hearing after the Braes was in Skeabost Free Church. One of the witnesses, William MacLure, Glen Bernisdale, gave a distorted and confused statement which was refuted by Lachlan MacDonald himself. In addition, five tenants submitted a letter at a later hearing at Portree supporting the proprietor. They affirmed their support for the proprietor, declaring that they were exceedingly sorry to hear the "incredible evidence" of MacLure. Four years later, the Skeabost tenants presented their landlord with an illuminated address, a unique occasion in Skye and indeed for the crofting area.[7]

Notes

1. There is no lack of source material for the story of the Skye troubles. The Napier Commission hearings in 1883 presented both proprietors and factors on the one side, crofters and their supporters on the other, with an opportunity to state their cases in public and also to respond to any misrepresentations by their opponents. Newspapers in the Highlands and Lowlands of Scotland (and even in England) provided constant coverage of events and were able, with the aid of the recently-installed telegraph, to publish eye-witness accounts of the confrontations between the crofters and the forces of law and order soon after they occurred. The papers of William Ivory, Sheriff of Inverness, which were kept by him with meticulous care and are now preserved in the Scottish Record Office, present the views of the chief executive officer responsible for the maintenance of law and order in Inverness-shire. The private correspondence of landlords and factors may be studied in the papers of the legal firm, MacDonald and Fraser, Portree, which have recently been made available for research and which sometimes reveal opinions at variance with public pronouncements. As Alexander MacDonald was factor for most of the estates in Skye, these records are useful aids to the understanding of the problems facing landlords and tenants in the 1880s.

2. A copy of a financial statement for the estate of Lord MacDonald is reproduced in the Appendix.

3. On January 12, 1882, 46 letters and telegrams were sent from Alexander MacDonald's office in Portree, some of which are reproduced in the Appendix.

4. A table showing the rents and stock of the Valtos tenants is included in the Appendix.

5. Many accounts of the Battle of the Braes have appeared, all of them more or less based on the eye-witness report of Alexander Gow, special correspondent of the *Dundee Advertiser*. Two accounts written in Gaelic by persons with local connections — that of Dr T.M. Murchison in a series of articles in the *Stornoway Gazette* in 1982 and the chapter, *"Blàr a' Chumhaing"*, by John A. MacDonald in *Oighreachd agus Gabhaltas* (1980) — add little to Gow's report.

6. A verbatim report of the trial on May 11, 1882, along with a detailed account of events leading up to the trial and also of the disturbances in Glendale, is contained in Alexander MacKenzie's *History of the Highland Clearances*, first published in February, 1883, and reprinted in a paperback edition in 1979. MacKenzie had increasingly since 1877 used the *Celtic Magazine*, of which he was editor, as a vehicle for propaganda on behalf of the crofters. The 1883 volume was a composite production, including Donald MacLeod's *Gloomy Memories*, the harrowing story of the Sutherland clearances, and long quotations from MacKenzie's own contribution to the *Celtic Magazine* and reports by other newspaper correspondents. MacKenzie's early career as an author (apart from his journalism) had been in a different field. His *History of the Clan MacKenzie* was the first of a series of clan histories, appealing to the Gael's pride of ancestry; and two early works, *The Tales and Legends of the Highlands* and *Prophecies of the Brahan Seer*, attracted the reader with an interest in the supernatural.

7. Lachlan MacDonald in 1886 published a pamphlet with the cumbersome title, *Position of the Bernesdale Crofters from 1843 to 1885 and Progress of the Land League in 1884-85*, which showed that, even with a landlord sympathetic to the crofters, some problems in a crofting township could prove intractable. He expressed surprise at the support accorded to the Land League and suggested as an explanation that his crofting tenants, although well treated by any standard, wished to see "all their sons and daughters married and settled down on the island on those large farms now under sheep".

CHAPTER 3

THE NAPIER COMMISSION

Petition to Parliament

On April the 19th, 1877, Colin Chisholm, late president of the London Gaelic Society and a retired exciseman, read a paper to the Gaelic Society of Inverness on "The Clearances of the Highland Glens", much of it dealing with his native Strathglass. He ended with an appeal to his fellow-members:

> "And now the simple and important question is — Will you do all in your power to alter this state of things? . . . My humble opinion is that you ought to petition Parliament forthwith, praying that they may be pleased to interpose between misapplied capital and the cultivators of the land in the Highlands."

ALEXANDER MACKENZIE, AUTHOR OF THE HIGHLAND CLEARANCES.

The petition, which was duly signed and presented to Parliament by the Gaelic Society of Inverness, was the first of many directing the attention of the powers-that-be to the grievances of the crofters. Later that year, at a public meeting in Inverness in October, the possibility of a Royal Commission on crofting affairs was first publicly mooted.

The person who raised the subject in a question to the main speaker, Charles Fraser Mackintosh, M.P. for Inverness Burghs, was Alexander MacKenzie, familiarly known as the "Clach", his first place of business before he changed to journalism with the *Inverness Advertiser* being a drapery shop called the Clachnacuddin House. MacKenzie had a varied career, and was regarded by some of his contemporaries, as has been stated, as an opportunist. Born in Gairloch, in Wester Ross, he worked as a labourer before going to England to take up the drapery trade. It was in England that he met his wife and began his journalistic career. After eight years in England he returned to Scotland, settling in Inverness. In 1875 he started the *Celtic Magazine*, a monthly journal, in which there appeared in serial form his clan histories. His interest in public affairs increased with his election to Inverness Town Council in 1877 and for many years he held the post of Dean of Guild. He was a staunch supporter of the crofters and an active propagandist for them both before and after the Napier Commission. In October 1877, the same month as the public meeting in Inverness, there appeared in the *Celtic Magazine* an article by him on "The poetry and prose of a Highland Croft". In both Lewis and Skye, as has been shown, the estate management (landlords and factors) was under severe attack, that of Lewis by Daniel MacKinlay in a pamphlet and in letters to the press, and that of the estate of Kilmuir in Skye by John Murdoch in the *Highlander* newspaper. MacKenzie's question to Fraser Mackintosh was to ask if he would move in Parliament for a Royal Commission to inquire into —

> "the scarcity of men and women in the Highlands; the cause of this state of things; and the most effective remedy for ameliorating the condition of Highland crofters generally."

For a month or two the crofting problem was constantly under discussion. At the Annual Gathering of the natives of Skye in Glasgow in December, 1877, Lachlan MacDonald of Skeabost, reckoned to be the best landlord in Skye by his fellow-Skyeman, Sheriff Nicolson, devoted his entire address to the theme of crofting. Some of the newspapers in the south, e.g. the Radical *North British Daily Mail* and the Whig *Scotsman*, took the matter up, the *Scotsman* sending on a tour of the Highlands and Islands a reporter dignified by the title of "Special Commissioner". More petitions to the Government and to the Queen followed. But the Government and the Prime Minister, Disraeli, in particular, were too involved in the Eastern Question to bother about the crofters in Scotland.

Sir William Harcourt, Home Secretary

It was not, however, until 1882, after trouble had flared up in Skye, once again at Valtos, then at the Braes and in Glendale, that Gladstone's Government, which had been absorbed in Irish affairs, began to consider a Royal Commission inevitable. Questions on Skye affairs had been asked frequently in the House of Commons by Fraser

Mackintosh, by Dr Charles Cameron, the Glasgow M.P., who owned the *North British Daily Mail*, and by Donald MacFarlane, M.P. for the Irish constituency of County Carlow and later to be M.P. for Argyll. It was MacFarlane who initiated a debate on crofters' conditions in the Commons on August 4th, 1882, but his request for an inquiry was refused by J.B. Balfour, the Lord Advocate, who in those days, before the creation of the office of Secretary for Scotland in 1885, managed Scottish affairs under the aegis of the Home Secretary. The Lord Advocate was scathing in his criticism of MacFarlane, whose speech he described as containing "a good deal of exploded nonsense about depopulation and a little spurious sentimentality intermixed with wild assertions". In a memorandum Balfour sent to the Prime Minister, Gladstone, in September, commenting on a letter received from the librarian of Inverness Public Library, John Whyte (a brother of Henry Whyte, "Fionn"), on the same topic, he reiterated his opposition and informed Gladstone that he had been assured by the Sheriff of Inverness, William Ivory (who was later to lead two military expeditions against the crofters), that there was no public support for an inquiry.

The decision to appoint a Royal Commission was taken not by the Lord Advocate but by the Home Secretary, Sir William Harcourt, who had overall control of home affairs and who, over many years of yachting holidays in the Hebrides, had come to regard the crofters with great affection. In November 1882 he had refused permission for a military expedition to Skye, despite the urgent representations of Sheriff Ivory and the Inverness-shire Police Committee about the critical situation in Glendale, where the crofters had become increasingly bold in their defiance of the law. The Sheriff and the Lord Lieutenant of Inverness-shire, Lord Lovat, travelled to London to press their views upon the Home Secretary and Lord Advocate, who in reply merely suggested the use of more police. In a letter to Gladstone, however, at the end of November 1882, Harcourt revealed a change of mind about a Royal Commission, in which it is probable he saw an alternative to the dispatch of a military expedition. Hitherto he had regarded an inquiry (quite rightly, as it transpired), as "opening the floodgates of a Highland land question"; but circumstances, he said, were forcing the Government's hand and there was a growing conviction amongst "decent people" that the crofters had much to complain of. The poor harvests of 1882 foreshadowed famine and distress, and the opinion of the Highland M.P.s, especially "the wiser and more prudent sort", was that a court of inquiry was necessary, an opinion which he now shared.

Appointment of Royal Commission

A memorial to the Home Secretary in favour of a Royal Commission was got up at the end of February 1883 by Fraser Mackintosh, who mentioned, *inter alia*, that even the *Scotsman* regarded it as necessary. It carried the signatures of 21 Scottish M.P.s, and even Lord Colin Campbell and Sir Alexander Matheson of Ardross expressed their support. On March 19, 1883, Harcourt announced the appointment of a "Royal Commission of Inquiry into the condition of the Crofters and Cottars in the Highlands and Islands of Scotland". The composition of the Commission was announced at the same time — Lord Napier (chairman), Sir Kenneth MacKenzie of Gairloch, Donald Cameron of Lochiel, M.P., Charles Fraser Mackintosh, M.P., Sheriff Alexander Nicolson and Professor Donald MacKinnon. Harcourt had hoped to include a minister, one who might be regarded as a "friend of the crofters", and he asked Lochiel, if he agreed, to nominate one. But the cleavage between the Church of Scotland and the Free Church and the divisions within the Free Church itself would have made any choice seem invidious, and no minister was appointed. The presence of four landed proprietors and the son of a proprietor (Sheriff Nicolson) was unfavourably commented on by the crofters' friends. Alexander MacKenzie of Inverness feared the worst, especially as the selection was approved by the Whig and Conservative papers like the *Scotsman*, the *Inverness Courier* and the *Northern Chronicle*, while Donald MacDonald, Tormore, the former Glendale factor, considered the personnel of the Commission unexceptionable. MacKenzie was later pleased to admit that his forecast had been wrong, as the Commissioners gave the crofters sympathetic treatment at the hearings.

Lord Napier, the chairman, was a Border laird (his full title was Lord Napier and Ettrick), and the only member of the Commission possessing no connection with the Highlands and Islands. A member of a family which had produced many brilliant soldiers and sailors (not to mention the inventor of logarithms, the father of the first Lord Napier), he had spent much of his life abroad in the diplomatic service. Among the posts he held were a number of ambassadorial rank and his last had been that of Governor of Madras. Since his retiral in 1872 at the age of 53 he had taken an interest in social affairs and had acted as President of the Social Science Association and Chairman of the London School Board. As far back as 1873 he had asked the House of Lords (but without success) for statistics of land in Scotland under cultivation, land used for deer forests, land capable of reclamation. As the wording of such a question would imply, his attitude to crofters' problems could be described as that of a sympathetic observer.

CAMERON OF LOCHIEL

FRASER McINTOSH

SHERIFF NICOLSON

LORD NAPIER
CHAIRMAN.

PROF. McKINNON

SIR KENNETH McKENZIE

MR MALCOLM McNEILL
CLERK.

NAPIER COMMISSION AT GLASGOW 1883.

68

Sir Kenneth MacKenzie, sixth Baronet of Gairloch, succeeded his father in 1843, when he was only nine years of age, and it was his mother who had to cope with the troubles of the "Destitution Years." Sir Kenneth studied under the famous Professor Liebig, the founder of agricultural chemistry, at the university of Giessen in Germany, where he took his doctorate. There, in the years following the abortive Revolution of 1848, he imbibed Liberal ideas. He deservedly enjoyed the reputation of a good landlord: he cleared off arrears on his estate by getting the tenants to make new roads, work on drainage and improvement of the croft land, part payment being made in meal and the rest towards wiping off arrears; leases of 12 years were given to every crofter on the property, and there were no evictions. He was appointed Convener of Ross and Cromarty in 1855 at the age of 23, and Lord Lieutenant in 1881. In 1880 he stood for Parliament as a Liberal in Inverness-shire, but was defeated by the Conservative, Cameron of Lochiel. Alexander MacKenzie of Inverness, a genealogist as well as a propagandist, could claim a relationship with Sir Kenneth, as a third cousin of his (Alexander MacKenzie's) father, whose great-grandmother was born on the wrong side of the blanket to the second baronet of Gairloch.

Donald Cameron of Lochiel was another Highland laird held in high regard by his tenants. Like Lord Napier, he had been in the diplomatic service, holding posts in Denmark, China and Germany. His father had wiped out £1,300 of arrears accumulated during the "Destitution Years" and reduced the rents by 20 per cent. Lochiel, who succeeded his father in 1858 at the age of 33, would not sanction evictions or sub-division, a practice too prevalent in Skye and Lewis and one bound to impoverish the crofters themselves in the end. He had been M.P. for Inverness-shire since 1868, and in 1882, as has been stated, had played an active rôle as mediator in the Braes dispute, joining with Lord Lovat in persuading Lord MacDonald to accept a settlement not only in his own interest but in the interest of proprietors generally. It was his opinion which was the decisive factor in influencing Sir William Harcourt when he refused the request of the county authorities for a military expedition in November 1882. Lochiel's attitude in this matter came in for a good deal of criticism from some of the proprietors and factors. One of his election agents, James Mollison, factor for Baillie of Dochfour, described him (privately) as an "officious goose"; and the Duke of Argyll, perhaps unfairly, considered that Lochiel was "no doubt looking to crofter votes" (i.e., at the next election, as they were not enfranchised until 1885). That Lochiel was not unsympathetic to the crofters was evident from his speech at the Skye Annual Gathering in Glasgow, in 1880, when he remarked that it would be well sometimes if Highland proprietors would place themselves in the position of their crofters. His name was associated with the famous clause 67 of the Scottish Education Act of 1872, whereby 7s 6d was paid out of state funds for every scholar in average attendance less the amount produced by the 3d rate, a provision intended to subsidise poorer parishes. It may seem small enough today but in 1883 the minister of Barvas in Lewis referred to it as "that most splendid grant, commonly known in this part of Scotland as Lochiel's Clause".[1]

The other M.P. member of the Commission was Charles Fraser Mackintosh, M.P. for Inverness Burghs from 1874 to 1885 and after that date for Inverness-shire. His efforts to persuade the Government have been referred to already. He was the son of Alexander Fraser of Dochnaluirg but changed his name to Fraser Mackintosh at the request of an uncle, Eneas Mackintosh. He qualified as a lawyer and had acted as commissioner or factor on the Mackintosh estates. He himself owned lands near Inverness — the estate of Drummond, on which there were in the 1880s still a few crofters, and that of Ballifeary. He was keenly interested in the promotion of Gaelic in the schools and took a leading part in the formation of the Federation of Celtic Societies in 1878. He wrote extensively on Highland history, and his *Antiquarian Notes*, published in 1865, and *Invernessiana*, published in 1875, still have value for the historian a century later. His opposition to Gladstone's Home Rule policy brought an end to his long parliamentary career in 1892, when he stood as Unionist and was defeated by Dr MacGregor, the crofters' candidate.

Sheriff Alexander Nicolson was a native of Skye, where his father was proprietor of Husabost. His appointment as Sheriff Substitute of Kirkcudbright in 1872 was a mark of his comparative failure as an advocate in Edinburgh; but the office, if not a sinecure, at least permitted him the leisure to pursue other interests, in particular mountaineering and the study of Gaelic literature. Nicolson pioneered many of the climbing routes in the Cuillin of Skye in the 1860s and 1870s, and it is appropriate that the highest peak in the Cuillin should be named after him, *Sgurr Alasdair*. His collection of Gaelic proverbs was published in 1881. Many of these proverbs and sayings about landlords, factors and ground officers are interesting in the light of his appointment to the Royal Commision. Among these proverbial sayings was — "*Is treasa tuath na tighearna*" — a slogan that appeared on many a banner in the Land League demonstrations of the 1880s — "The tenantry (or peasantry) are stronger than the laird". Nicolson wrote:

"This is a remarkable saying to have originated among a race distinguished by their subordination to their natural chiefs and lords; it belongs to a time

70

when the rights of the clan and tenantry were real and believed in by themselves."

Then there was the remark, which became a proverbial saying, of the man who had been cheated by the factor and who exclaimed at the factor's funeral, shaking his fist at the grave — *"Na'm bu tig a' là dh'éireas tu-sa as a sin."* ("May the day never come that you rise out of there!"). Nicolson remarked that the Celts of Scotland had never in modern times maltreated much less killed a factor, steward or magistrate.

"They have often been treated unjustly, but they are neither so quick of tongue nor so unsparing of hand as their Irish brethren."

Nicolson helped in preparing a new edition of the Gaelic Bible along with his fellow-member of the Commission, Professor Donald MacKinnon, who was appointed to the newly-established chair of Celtic at Edinburgh University in December 1882, after Nicolson had declined an invitation to be the first professor. Sheriff Nicolson was a member of the Argyll Commission on education in 1865, and was responsible for compiling the section of the Commission's report dealing with the Highlands and Islands. It could be claimed for Nicolson that none of the other members of the Napier Commission knew the Highlands and Islands so well as he did.[2]

Donald MacKinnon, the recently appointed Professor of Celtic at Edinburgh University, was to occupy the chair until his death in 1914, when he was succeeded by W.J. Watson, rector of Inverness Royal Academy. In Watson's *Rosg Gàidhlig* there are two contributions from the pen of Professor MacKinnon, the first about his old village school in the island of Colonsay, where he was born and brought up, and the other about proverbs, in which he refers in flattering terms to the collection made by Sheriff Nicolson, his collaborator in the new edition of the Bible. MacKinnon would probably have been a fisherman were it not that Lord Colonsay, a judge of the Court of Session and a brother of Sir John MacNeill, helped him to study at Edinburgh University, where he took a first-class degree in mental philosophy.

The Secretary of the Royal Commission, Malcolm MacNeill, had also a link with Colonsay, his father being laird of the island and a brother of Lord Colonsay and Sir John MacNeill, who was the first chairman of the Board of Supervision for Poor Relief. Educated at Eton and Sandhurst, he was well-connected. He was a relative of Lady Gordon-Cathcart, proprietrix of South Uist and Barra, he was a cousin of the Queen's private secretary, who became the third wife of the Duke of Argyll. Like his uncle, Malcolm MacNeill was to become head of his department, the Local Government Board, and gain a knighthood.

Perhaps, after these biographical details, it would still be worthwhile to quote from the Glasgow magazine, *Quiz*, in which there appeared pen portraits of the Commissioners, when they were sitting in Glasgow:—

"The chairman, Lord Napier, is a benevolent looking old gentleman" (he was 64), "with a dreamy pair of eyes and a slight burr in his speech. Sir Kenneth MacKenzie is a half sailor-looking man of dark complexion speaking with the slightest possible suspicion of an aristocratic lisp. Sheriff Nicolson has rather a solemn face and his closely-shaven cheeks give him an almost theatrical appearance. His accent is decidedly nasal and the eyeglass pressure on his nose exaggerates this characteristic. The refined face and bald head of Lochiel suggest more the Lowland gentleman than the Highland chief. Mr Fraser Mackintosh might be a venerable professor, while Professor MacKinnon is a stout, good-humoured, smiling gentleman with a strong Highland accent, suggesting the keeper of a mountain hotel, and the Secretary of the Commission would pass for a soldier with his heavy moustache."

Preliminaries to Hearings

Before the Commissioners started on their tour of the crofting districts, proprietors, factors and crofters were asked to submit statements in preparation for the hearings. Many of these statements were published in an appendix to the Report, while others were read out by the witnesses when giving evidence, and some never saw the light of day, languishing today in the Scottish Office files in the Record Office. Among these last is one from a Lewisman, Angus MacPhail, who had been an inspector of schools, had lived in India and South Africa, and died at an early age a few weeks after writing his letter to Lord Napier. Among other comments on the crofters' condition he strongly criticised one aspect of religious life in the Hebrides. He condemned:

"the dread Calvinism, whose ministers delight in the dark and the mysterious and stamp out, with the vehemence of a narrow conception of men and life, every form of amusement as profane and the work of the Devil."

The letter is not all in this strain and contains valuable suggestions for the amelioration of the crofters' conditions.

The proprietors were also asked to make returns, giving details of numbers of crofters, stock, acreage and rents, which were duly published in an appendix to the Report. That these returns, like many other agricultural returns in other lands and in other times, were not fully reliable is suggested by some entries in the "Remarks" column. In Glendale in Skye, 45 of the crofters refused information and similarly in the parish of Tongue in Sutherland. In Lewis the factor experienced considerable difficulty in obtaining information and in one township the crofters drove off the surveyor who was trying to measure their crofts. The returns of stock on the Kilmuir estate (and probably also on many other estates), were made up from information received from the tenants, who would be reluctant to give figures exceeding their entitlement according to the souming of their crofts. The chamberlain of Lewis, William MacKay, wrote to the Commission more than once about the impossibility of completing the returns in time as it was equivalent to carrying out a census and a survey of the island. The proprietrix, Lady Matheson, would not give permission to employ extra staff and he asked for authority to enlist the services of two surveyors and their assistants, the expense incurred to be reimbursed by the Commission. Eventually, the Treasury approved payment of expenses at the rate of 3d per crofter, the sum paid for the Matheson estate of Lewis amounting to £36 15s 3d.

The preparation of the crofters' evidence was later to be the subject of acrimonious discussion in the press. The Whig and Tory newspapers had given publicity to the fact that friends of the crofters ("agitators" in the eyes of the friends of the proprietors), had gone round the crofting districts ahead of the Royal Commission and there were allegations of Irish influence. These allegations may have arisen out of the visit, earlier referred to, by two self-avowed propagandists — John Murdoch, the doughty champion of the crofters, and Edward MacHugh, a native of Tyrone and an Irish Land Leaguer. This visit to the crofters took place the year before the Commission was appointed. John Murdoch devoted part of his retirement to championing the downtrodden in Ireland, where he had served as an exciseman, as well as in Scotland; but he was above all a patriotic Scotsman and true Gael. Because he was invariably dressed in the kilt he was known as *Murchadh an Fhéilidh* (Murdoch of the kilt) and was highly regarded by the crofters, but the proprietors and factors tried to blacken his reputation because of his association with Irish Land Leaguers. It was thus not unnatural that the crofters' agitation in 1882-83 was blamed on Irish influence, as if there was no underlying cause for grievance.[3]

Preparation of Evidence

Between the appointment of the Commission and the commencement of the hearings, John Murdoch and Alexander MacKenzie visited many of the crofting districts. Murdoch, when giving evidence before the Commissioners in Glasgow, referred to the *Scotsman's* attack on himself and others as "cowardly and unscrupulous agitators who had manipulated the crofters' evidence"; and he defended his actions, maintaining that in many cases crofters were unable to draw up their statements and sometimes were afraid to do so. This last allegation was confirmed by another witness at Glasgow, the Rev. Murdo MacAskill of Greenock, who succeeded Dr Kennedy at Dingwall in 1884. He was of the opinion that according to the Lewis crofters' evidence they had little to complain of. But he understood that estate officials had gone round among the people beforehand, threatening them with serious consequences if they complained about any of the officials. Murdoch himself went "in a very hurried manner" over Lewis, Loch Broom, Assynt, part of the Reay country, Arisaig, Tobermory and Salen in Mull, Morvern and Islay. In Moidart, Murdoch persuaded the crofters to send representatives to the Royal Commission to show how well they were treated by their landlord, Lord Howard of Glossop. Alexander MacKenzie, giving evidence in Inverness, admitted that he had gone round in advance through the whole of Skye, part of North and South Uist and Benbecula, and all the north and west mainland from Thurso to Lochcarron, but maintained that he had not written or dictated a single statement and had warned the crofters against exaggeration, advising them not to use Irish Land League terms or phrases. MacKenzie claimed that he had invariably urged the crofters to make their own statements, bad grammar and all, which, he said, would be more likely to impress the Commissioners. He himself had two books published in 1883, *The Highland Clearances*, in February, before the Commission's hearings began, and *The Social State of the Isle of Skye in 1882-83* in October.

In Lewis, in addition to John Murdoch, the president of the Lewis branch of the Highland Land Law Reform Association was active in touring the townships to give advice. He was a Stornoway business-man, Alick Morison, son of one of the notable "Men" of Lewis, Sandy Morison, rope-spinner and fish-curer in Stornoway. Alick Morison had rather a chequered career: he had been declared a bankrupt at the age of 30 in 1881, but after his father's death the following year he had thrown himself with enthusiasm into the movement for land law reform. His speech to the Commissioners at the Stornoway hearing contained, according to one newspaper, a few catchwords and rhetorical phrases and nothing more.

There were many cases where the delegate for a crofting township was actually a townsman, chosen by the crofters because he was better able to express their feelings and opinions and would not be under the fear of victimisation. Such a delegate was John MacDonald, a Mor-vern man who worked as a shop assistant in Glasgow but whose father had been evicted from Drimnin years before. MacDonald became the Secretary of the Ardnamurchan, Morvern and Sunart Association in Glasgow and lambasted the "grasping landlords" of Morvern in letters to the *Oban Times*. He helped to prepare the formal statement and gave evidence as one of the delegates for the crofters of Lochaline at the Commission's hearing in the crowded Free Kirk there. Another delegate from Glasgow who represented a crofting community was Angus Sutherland, the Glasgow Academy schoolmaster, one of the men of that city to take up the crofters' cause through the Federation of Celtic Societies (of which he was Secretary), the Skye Vigilance Committee, and the Glasgow Sutherland Association. A native of Helmsdale, he gave evidence at the hearing there on behalf of the people of Loth and Kildonan.

At Isleornsay in Skye the Free Church minister, the Rev. Finlay Graham, actually told the Commissioners that the documents given in from the several townships in Sleat were prepared by the parish minister and himself. "We thought," he said, "that we had a duty to perform in preparing the people for the Royal Commission and did the work together." To this statement Lord Napier replied: "We are very much obliged to you". In the report of the Royal Commission, the question of the validity of the evidence was examined, in particular with regard to outside intervention in the preparation of statements. The Commissioners admitted the right of sympathisers to assist in such a task. Their examination of witnesses, who were sometimes very thoroughly grilled, enabled them to test the reliability of the evidence. On the whole, they were impressed by "the evidence from even the poorest and least-educated class", among whom there were "many examples of candour, kindness and native intelligence, testifying to the unaltered worth of the Highland people".

Route of Commission

In all, the Commissioners visited 61 places, starting with the Braes of Portree on May 5, 1883, and finishing at Tarbert, Lochfyne on December 26, 1883. The itinerary was based on the use of a naval yacht, the *Lively*, on which the Commissioners and newspaper correspondents were accommodated. After sittings at 11 different places in Skye and Raasay, the *Lively* took the Commissioners over to the Western Isles, where sittings were held in Castlebay, Lochboisdale, Benbecula, Loch Eport and Obbe in Harris, before taking a trip out to St Kilda. It was a rough crossing and most of the passengers were sea-sick. Their arrival, unannounced, at mid-day on Saturday, June 2, was a tremendous surprise for the St Kildans, who were at first worried about the intentions of the visitors. In the afternoon, however, all gathered in the church, where the minister, the principal witness, opened the meeting with a prayer in Gaelic. After the brief sitting, the Commissioners toured the island, distributing comestibles, according to the *Scotsman* (which may have meant sweets or gingerbread, regarded as a delicacy in the Hebrides in those days, or even a loaf of bread, which the St Kildans seldom tasted). From St Kilda the *Lively* crossed over to Lewis, where the Commissioners sat at Miavaig in Uig, Breascleit (after which the Commissioners made a short excursion to the Callanish stones), Barvas and Ness before going round the Butt of Lewis to Stornoway. Just before entering Stornoway harbour, the *Lively* ran aground on the submerged Chicken Rock, half-a-mile from Chicken Head, on the evening of June 7. The *Lively* was evacuated without panic by a passing steamer, the *Mary Ann* of Glasgow, bound for Oban with a cargo of herring, and without serious loss except for some of the returns relating to Caithness. The wreck of the *Lively* caused an alteration of the Commission's time-table. As it happened, news of Lord Napier's mother's death was telegraphed to him on the same day and he left for the south immediately, Sir Kenneth MacKenzie taking over as chairman at the Stornoway hearings, after which the Commission decided to adjourn for three weeks, resuming at Lerwick, almost a month behind schedule, on July 13.

After Shetland and Orkney, the Commission, using a chartered vessel, the *North Star*, visited places on the north and west coasts from Bettyhill in Sutherland to Lismore, which was reached on August 13, when, as the charter of the *North Star* had expired, the hearings broke off. They were resumed on October 4 at Lybster, and from there the Commissioners travelled south by train, with stops at Helmsdale, Golspie, Bonar Bridge and Dingwall. Inverness, where there was a three-day hearing, was reached on October 12, Glasgow on October 19, and Edinburgh on October 22. Finally, on December 26, there was a brief session at Tarbert, Loch Fyne, attended only by Lord Napier, Sheriff Nicolson and Professor MacKinnon, specifically to inquire into the fishing industry on the west coast. Despite pleas for sittings in Islay and elsewhere, the Commissioners finished their tour at Tarbert.

Their meetings had been held in a variety of venues — most often the local church, either the Established Church or the Free Church, although on the island of Lismore it was the Baptist Church; sometimes in the local school; on a few occasions in the Sheriff Court House, at Portree, Lerwick, Kingussie and Glasgow; on three occasions in the Volunteer Drill Hall, at Stornoway, Kirkwall and Bonar Bridge; once in a hotel, at Lochboisdale, and once in a Temperance Hall, at Tobermory. Sitting through a hot summer's day in a crowded schoolroom or courtroom and listening to evidence, first in Gaelic and then in English, must have been very trying for the Commissioners. At Scarinish in Tiree on August 8, the atmosphere became so stifling that it was decided to adjourn outside; but just then joiners arrived and proceeded to take out the windows, a task they performed with such vigour that Sheriff Nicolson had to remind them they were not "Disestablishers". On two occasions only was Lord Napier compelled to cut short the sittings — once at Bonar Bridge, where a local farmer, George Anderson, Kincardine, so annoyed the audience by his remarks that they started hissing and after a warning again hissed him so much that Lord Napier adjourned the hearing; and once in Glasgow, where John Murdoch, after almost three hours of evidence, became so offensive that three of the Commissioners, MacKenzie, Cameron and Fraser Mackintosh, left the courtroom and, finally, when Murdoch said to Lord Napier, "Do not let Sheriff Nicolson fall asleep as I have something for him," Lord Napier closed the meeting.

Evidence of Witnesses

The evidence, amounting to four large volumes and running to 3,375 closely printed pages, has provided a great number of writers on crofting with a rich variety of source material. Indeed, the Report and the evidence accompanying it have been called the "Domesday Book" of the Highlands and Islands. The Commission had been appointed "to inquire into the condition of the crofters and cottars in the Highlands and Islands of Scotland, and all matters affecting the same, or relating thereto"; and the Commissioners interpreted their mandate in the broadest sense imaginable. The story of clearances in the 1850s could be considered relevant to the crofters' grievances; but in the case of those who recounted the Sutherland clearances, it was more a question of putting the historical record right. Not that this aim was achieved by having a secondhand account of what happened; but the Commission's hearings had the effect of opening up disputes of long ago and it was possible for proprietors or factors or their adherents to make reply either at a later hearing or by a letter to the Commission or to the press. Thomas Sellar, son of Patrick Sellar, whose name was linked in the public mind with the worst Sutherland clearances, actually made application, through his lawyers, to appear at the Edinburgh sitting to defend his father's name. A summary of the grievances has already been given in the opening chapter and what follows is a selection of the evidence of the various classes of witnesses — crofters, factors, proprietors, ministers, shopkeepers, townsmen sympathisers. It is a sign of the great changes that have taken place in the past century that not a single woman appeared as a witness, although two of the greatest landowners of estates with crofters were women — Lady Matheson of the Lews and Lady Gordon-Cathcart, owner of Barra, South Uist and Benbecula.[4]

At the outset, in the Skye hearings, tempers ran high among crofters and factors and were with difficulty controlled by Lord Napier, who throughout proved a competent chairman. On the very first day, at the Braes, after the lunch interval, the first witness, Angus Stewart, the crofter delegate from Peinnchorran, sent a letter to the Secretary of the Commission:—

"Sir,
During the interval, our Factor cursed me to the face.

Angus Stewart."

The factor was the famous Alex. MacDonald, *Alasdair Ruadh*, the factor for six estates in Skye and nicknamed by the Radical press "the uncrowned king of Skye".

The Glendale Martyr

Generally, the crofters gave their evidence in a straight-forward manner and answered questions put to them intelligently and politely. Mis-statements of fact did occur as the witnesses were sometimes relating events which happened years before, but the opportunity was given to factors or proprietors to correct them later. For example, John MacPherson, the "Glendale Martyr," as he was called after his term of imprisonment in Edinburgh, in the course of a very long examination made allegations about the eviction of ten or twelve families from Waternish to make room for deer, a statement bound to arouse the sympathy of his hearers but later denied by Captain Allan MacDonald, who declared there was not a word of truth in it. MacDonald explained that the island of Isay in Loch Dunvegan had been let by his father to ten or twelve fishermen from Glendale to develop the cod and ling fishing, at an annual rent of so many fish per year; but after a few years they went back to Glendale as there were no peats on the island, and it was re-stocked with sheep and cattle. All this had happened about forty years before, but a few years ago Captain MacDonald himself had put eleven fallow deer there along with the cattle, which MacPherson had represented as the reason for the so-called eviction. It will be recalled that MacPherson's release from the Calton Jail in Edinburgh coincided with the commencement of the hearings in Skye, and that he was given a hero's welcome at Portree where he arrived just in time to give his evidence at the Glendale hearing. Speaking in Gaelic (which was translated by the Portree lawyer and banker, Dugald MacLachlan), MacPherson began:—

"I would ask, my lord and gentlemen, that I would not be blamed for telling the truth — for I got 61 days' imprisonment already for telling the truth and asking for justice."

After his lengthy statement, he answered lucidly and eloquently,

JOHN MACPHERSON, GLENDALE.

albeit with occasional exaggeration, the questions put to him by the Commissioners, who treated him with respect as befitted a man who already enjoyed a national reputation.

Another Skye witness who impressed the Commissioners was

Donald MacQueen of Bracadale, who gave his age as over ninety, but according to Sheriff Nicolson, "there are historical facts which prove that he was over a hundred." MacQueen had conducted a prayer meeting in the Free Church just before the Commissioners were to meet there, and had invoked Divine help and guidance for the Commission. His evidence, part of which related to the ancient practice of transhumance, taking the cattle to the summer shielings, he gave in a sonorous bass voice. He could read without spectacles and none of his faculties, except his hearing, was impaired. Two other patriarchs who gave evidence, but in their case far from their native parishes, were James MacDonald (81) and John MacKay (83), who recounted at the Edinburgh hearing the sad tales of the eviction of their parents during the Sutherland clearances.

Many of the crofters, like John MacPherson, gave their evidence in Gaelic, and even in translation they have a certain ring about them which would be alien to the Lowlander. Charles MacLeod of Arnish in Raasay, where the new proprietor, Mr Wood, had turned the island into a sporting estate, boldly declared:

> "It is with the view of getting deliverance from bondage that we have come here today. The Israelites before us were in bondage but there is One above who heard the sighing of those in bondage and fixed the time for their deliverance."

Landlords and Farmers

A number of proprietors and tacksmen gave evidence, some of them more outspoken in their criticism of the crofters and their leaders than the most extreme crofter spokesmen were about them. Dr Nicol Martin of Husabost, aged 83, remarked of the Glendale crofters:—

> "The crofters are getting indolent and lazy besides. Look at this winter: they did nothing but go about with fires on every hill and playing at sentinels to watch for fear of the sheriff's officer coming with warnings to take their cattle for rent."

And he concluded:—

> "I would give £500 today if all the crofters on my place went away."

Donald MacDonald, Tormore, a farmer who had been factor both at Glendale and on Lord MacDonald's estate, was no less forthcoming. He said of the evidence of Peter MacKinnon, crofter and postmaster, Lephin:—

> "His evidence must be taken for what it is worth, and it is quite worthless."

He named the chief instigators of "the rebellion in Skye and the west" as:—

"John Murdoch, MacHugh, the Irish Land Leaguer, and last but not least (and certainly if the others have to answer for a lot of sins he has to account for a great many more) — he has a broad back and a very thick hide — his name is Dean of Guild MacKenzie."

The Free Church came in for some scathing denunciation from tacksmen. Donald Cameron, Glenbrittle in Skye, described the Free Church as "the Fenians we have in Skye".

Another farmer, Thomas Purves of Rhifail in Strathnaver, giving evidence at Inverness, described the first witness at Bettyhill, the Free Church minister, as —

"perhaps the most bold and unscrupulous of the clergy in our district".

When he was asked if he had any animus against the Free Church, he replied:

"I have a great animus for I say the Free Church teaching and the Free Church clergy are the cause of half of the evils that affect Sutherland."

And he added, for good measure:—

"This Commission is going to make matters worse."

Few of the proprietors made a personal appearance before the Commission, preferring to send in statements or be represented by their factors or chamberlains. One who did appear at Inverness was Duncan Darroch, who had bought the estate of Torridon in 1872 and had transformed it. He was very proud of the good relations between himself and the crofters and he believed, as others were to come round to believing later, that the only hope for the Highlands was to clear off the sheep or at least restrict sheep-farming, for which he would substitute cattle-raising and deer. Duncan Darroch of Torridon was not the only proprietor to receive praise for the management of his estate. The Earl of Dunmore, the only peer of the realm who could speak fluent Gaelic, was proprietor of South Harris; nearly all the witnesses from there spoke in favourable terms and the only complaint came, oddly enough, from the Free Church minister, a man of over seventy years of age, about the prohibition of angling:—

"It is very unnatural that old and young should not be allowed to cast a hook into a standing loch or stream to catch a trout without being pursued by an officer of the Law."[5]

Other proprietors who received praise at the hearings were Lachlan MacDonald of Skeabost because of his sympathy for the crofters, although even he had to answer criticism from some of his tenants: Edward Wood of Raasay, despite his eight gamekeepers and his ten thousand rabbits; John Fowler of Braemore, for whom the Lochbroom minister, the Rev. John MacMillan, had nothing but commendation; Sir Alexander Matheson of Ardross and Lochalsh, whose estate management was frequently contrasted with that of his uncle, the late Sir James Matheson of the Lews; Lord Howard of Glossop, proprietor of Lochsheil; Colonel Balfour of Balfour Castle in Orkney; and two members of the Commission, Sir Kenneth MacKenzie of Gairloch and Cameron of Lochiel.

Some factors also came in for approbation. John MacDonald, factor for Sir John Campbell-Orde in North Uist, was described by Alexander Carmichael in his account of "Grazing and Agrestic Customs of the Outer Hebrides" (which was printed in the Appendix to the Report) as —

"a man endowed with more excellencies of head and heart, without faults, than ordinarily falls to the lot of men."

William Gunn, factor on the Coigach estates of the Countess of Cromartie (who was also Duchess of Sutherland) was spoken of by the Free Church minister as —

"a man who, I believe, would not do an injustice . . . an excellent man and a gentleman."

Napier Campbell

In addition to those with a direct interest in the land — the crofters and cottars, the proprietors, the factors — there were not only ministers but fishcurers and merchants (to use the dignified term for shopkeepers in the north), who also had contacts with the crofters. Then there were also the sympathisers in the towns, in Portree, Inverness, Stornoway, Dingwall, Glasgow and Edinburgh. One of those in Stornoway who supported the crofters' demands was a solicitor, Napier Campbell, who had been involved in conflict with the Lewis establishment several times during his career. He had been asked by the local Highland Law Law Reform Association to prepare a statement for the Commission and had submitted it to the Association beforehand. It contained some sentences in condemnation of Sir James Matheson, Sheriff MacDonald of Stornoway, and Donald Munro, former chamberlain of Lewis, who had been dismissed from his office after the so-called Bernera Riot of 1874. Munro had heard from one present at the preliminary reading of the statement about its contents and complained to the Commission that they were defamatory. When Napier Campbell appeared before the Commission, he was several times interrupted and Sir Kenneth MacKenzie, acting chairman, and his fellow Commissioners adjourned for twenty minutes before intimating to Campbell that they were not prepared to accept his statement. The official version of Campbell's evidence is severely condensed in comparison with the newspaper report of the day's hearing. Napier Campbell refused to be silenced, pointing out in a letter to the Commission that much of his statement had already been leaked to the press and that he was prepared to defend any challenge as to the accuracy of his statements. He finally had his statement, only slightly altered, incorporated in the Appendix to the Report, where it takes up over ten closely printed pages. It is possible to judge of the severity of his criticism of the Lewis establishment from the following excerpts. Of Sheriff MacDonald, who had held office for 28 years prior to 1871, and the Sheriff Clerk, Colin Leitch, he said:—

> "Neither of those gentlemen appeared to me to maintain the position and dignity of their respective offices, in face of arbitrary power."

Regarding the former proprietor, Sir James Matheson, he credited him with being "a great man, a public benefactor, a resolute pioneer of progress, the architect of his own colossal fortune, most hospitable and sometimes profusely benevolent" but "peculiarly accessible to flattery" and with an estate policy which Campbell characterised as "tortuous, subtle and aggressive" in pursuit of "territorial aggrandisement and despotic power, so absolute and arbitrary, as to be almost universally complained of". To describe Donald Munro, the former chamberlain, Campbell wrote, he would have to resort to comparison with Bismarck for his iron rule and far-reaching diplomacy and with King Theodore of Magdala, surrounded by "terrified prisoners and trembling subjects, pursuing even to the bitter end his measures of revenge, tyranny and oppression."[6]

Eviction of Witnesses

Some of the witnesses at the Commission's hearings complained during the time of waiting for the Report that they had been victimised by their lairds or factors for giving evidence. Alexander Allan of Aros, who owned most of Tobermory, evicted two of the Commission witnesses, Angus MacInnes and Donald Colquhoun, ostensibly for other reasons but without doubt because they had given evidence critical of the management of Allan's estate. In Orkney, General Burroughs, proprietor of Rousay, removed two of the Digro delegates, James Leonard and James Grieve, from their crofts and from the houses they had built themselves. General Burroughs, who had been described as "unchristian, unrighteous, unjust and oppressive", had himself been a very difficult witness at the Kirkwall hearing and had refused to give an assurance of security to men whom he regarded as "inimical" to him. "Is the property mine or is it not? Am I to keep discontented people?" As for guaranteeing the witnesses' security, he was quite forthright. "I am not prepared to do so. It is contrary to human nature." Burroughs received an anonymous letter threatening death if he evicted the two tenants. It was couched in semi-literate style and the juvenile writing prompted the police authorities to suspect the son of one of the men threatened with eviction. He was detained along with another boy for several hours, precognosced by the Procurator Fiscal and then released. No charges were brought and General Burroughs made the most he could out of the threat hanging over him without in any way diminishing his unpopularity in Orkney.[7]

The London *Times* gave some publicity to the case of four South Uist men, one from Loch Eynort and the other three from Stoney-bridge, who were said to have been evicted because of being witnesses before the Napier Commission. Actually, although the four were active members of the H.L.L.R.A., none of them gave evidence to the Commission but they were considered by the factor, Ranald MacDonald, as ringleaders in what he termed the "agitation". The H.L.L.R.A. branch had been started at Stoneybridge after the Commission's visit and as an immediate consequence some of the crofters and cottars took possession of the island of Calvay in Loch Eynort. This was typical of the "land raiding" which took place in the years following the Commission, the people taking what they considered was theirs by right. The Stoneybridge case received national publicity and the men, who were later imprisoned on a charge of deforcing a sheriff officer, were to become known by what was then an accepted practice in the Radical press as the "Stoneybridge martyrs".

Report of Commission

The publication of the Commission's Report on April 28 was over-shadowed in the Highland press by the death of the noted preacher, Dr Kennedy, Dingwall, tributes to whom filled columns of the black-edged newspapers. The Royal Commission acknowledged the evidence of a strong body of opinion behind the notion that the small tenants of the Highlands and Islands had inherited an inalienable title to security on their farms, although it had never been sanctioned by legal recognition and long since repudiated by the proprietors; and the Commissioners felt that a claim to security of tenure could not be seriously entertained, and that to grant to "the whole mass of poor tenants" security of tenure would only perpetuate social evils of a dangerous character. They were however prepared to give security to those crofters paying a rent of at least £6 a year who would accept improving leases; in a dissenting report, Fraser Mackintosh advocated a lower limit of a £4 rent, as otherwise the bulk of crofters would be unable to benefit by this provision. About cottars, who existed in profusion on some estates, all the Commission could suggest was that they should be recorded on the books of the estate, pending the introduction of remedies which would "gradually transfer and disperse this class of people". A proposal to recognise the setting-up of communal townships with constables to ensure that regulations were enforced was only a majority decision, the two Highland lairds, MacKenzie of Gairloch and Cameron of Lochiel, entering their dissent, the former in "most emphatic language". The idea of a rural commune, as many called it, is supposed to have emanated from the brain of Lord Napier, who had been impressed by the communal life of Indian villages. Alexander Carmichael's paper on agrestic customs in the Hebrides, published in an Appendix to the Report, must also have left a favourable impression so far as the communal life of the Hebridean township was concerned.

The general consensus of opinion about the Report was most critical. The crofters and their friends, although appreciative of the recognition of their grievances and the recommendations for improvement of communications, fisheries, educational provision and administration of justice, felt that in regard to land tenure it did not go nearly far enough. Proprietors, factors and economists were even more severe in their criticism. The professor of political economy in Edinburgh University, Joseph S. Nicolson, called it "an ill-adjusted concourse of compromises and concessions", although he admitted that the weakness of the Report was due to failings "that lean to virtue's side, consistency being sacrificed to benevolence". Lochiel, in a letter to Sir William Harcourt, the Home Secretary, in December 1884, maintained that Lord Napier himself had told him often that he did not believe his proposals would be adopted, so long as the cold hearts of the House of Commons continued to pay regard to political economy, a science for which he professed utter contempt. Harcourt dismissed the proposal for communal townships as a "fantastic and foolish scheme". Only the *Northern Chronicle* in Inverness gave the Report a modicum of praise, not because of the proposals abovementioned but because, in regard to security of tenure and compulsory acquisition of "the land for the people", the Report would disappoint

"the unscrupulous people who misquote and pervert Scripture, while they teach robbery and wrong, and try to make the crofters as lawless and disreputable as the Fenian Irish".

The Napier Commission had definitely helped to awaken the

people of the Highlands and Islands from the torpor which had prevailed for so long. With the extension of the franchise in 1885, the crofters were to have an overwhelming majority in succeeding elections and soon realised the power which they could wield. The Portree factor, Alex. MacDonald, was of the opinion that the worst influence in the land agitation was the Royal Commission, which had "raised extravagant hopes and enabled the people to tell baseless stories in support of baseless claims". Malcolm MacNeill, Secretary of the Commission, in a confidential report he made to the Secretary for Scotland in 1886, confirmed this view as widely held by factors and proprietors about the Napier Commission and its "baneful influence". Certainly, the Highlands and Islands were never the same again and the Napier Commission marks a watershed in crofting history.

Notes

1. A statue of Lochiel in Highland garb stands at the east end of Fort William in the open space in front of the Alexandra Hotel.

2. Sheriff Nicolson, in his article, "The Cruise of the Lively" in *Good Words*, described the singing of the psalms in the St Kilda church, with a precentor giving out the line, as "simply delightful". He himself enjoyed a certain fame as a minor bard. The visitors' book at Sligachan Hotel, which he used as a base for his mountaineering expeditions, contains, in addition to a record of his climbs, light-hearted verses, his last entry shortly before his death still being quoted in Skye:—

   > "Jerusalem, Athens and Rome,
   > I would see them before I die,
   > But I'd rather not see
   > Any one of the three
   > Than be exiled for ever from Skye."

3. Murdoch was a regular target for attacks on his character in newspapers supporting landlords because of his connection with Ireland. He had spent much of his working life in Ireland and made no secret of his support for the Irish National Land League and the Home Rule movement. The *Scotsman*, which could indulge in vitriolic language that would be considered libellous if used today, made specific allegations about Murdoch's visit to Canada and the United States in 1879-80, ostensibly to raise money for the ailing *Highlander* newspaper, from Scottish emigrants and descendants of Scottish emigrants. During that visit, Murdoch had appeared on the same platform as Parnell, the Irish Nationalist leader; and 2,000 dollars had been paid to Murdoch partly because of his support for Irish Home Rule and partly as *solatium* for Parnell's refusal to share the same platform with Murdoch. (He had been taken aback by Murdoch's appearance in the kilt and his speeches in Irish Gaelic.) The question of the source

of this financial assistance was in dispute. According to the *Scotsman*, the donation had come from the Fenian Skirmishing Fund, which, it was claimed, was tantamount to accepting money which had been subscribed by those who condoned Irish terrorism. Murdoch, who was strongly opposed to Fenianism and was a believer in non-violence, was compelled to defend himself against the scurrilous attacks on his character in letters to other newspapers as the Edinburgh editor refused to publish them. A collection of Murdoch's writings, edited by James Hunter and entitled *The People's Cause*, was published for the Crofters Commission in 1986 to mark the centenary of the Crofters Act.

4. John Murdoch praised the Dowager Countess of Dunmore, who had started the Harris tweed industry, but not the Earl of Dunmore, whom he blamed for the poor condition and the torpor of the people in Harris. The earl had, in a letter to the secretary of the Gaelic Society of Inverness, accused men familiar with Gaelic of "feeding the flames of discontent among the ignorant and uneducated" and with "urging them to rebellion and crime" (*Scotsman*, January 24, 1884).

5. An unusual display of the new attitude of crofters' defiance of authority gained wide publicity in the press a few weeks after the start of the Napier Commission's hearings. Cargoes of fish were about to be landed at Strome Ferry, the railway terminus at that time, after midnight on Saturday, June 2, when the local people prevented unloading and maintained their blockade until Sunday midnight, having assaulted the Chief Constable and a small force of police during the day. The authorities took a serious view of the Strome Ferry riot and ten of the upholders of strict observance of the Sabbath Day were sentenced to four months' imprisonment despite the jury's recommendation for utmost leniency.

6. For evidence of Munro's conduct in the Burgh of Stornoway which justified Napier Campbell's denunciation, see the articles, "In Search of Lewis", by James Shaw Grant in the *Stornoway Gazette* of 1987 and 1988.

7. The extraordinary vendetta waged by Burroughs, who had commanded the 93rd (Sutherland) Highlanders in India at the time of the Mutiny, is the subject of W.P.L. Thomson's *The Little General and the Rousay Crofters* (1981).

CHAPTER 4

REFORM AGITATION

Federation of Celtic Societies

The agitation of the 1880s in favour of land law reform started mainly in the cities. The Federation of Celtic Societies, formed in 1878, soon became so involved in crofter affairs that the Inverness Gaelic Society in 1880 decided not to send any delegates to the annual meeting of the Federation, partly because it had become political rather than literary but partly also because general meetings of the Federation were all being held in Glasgow instead of in rotation in the major towns and cities. Highland and Gaelic societies continued to discuss Highland affairs. At a meeting of the Glasgow Highland Society in November, 1880, Angus Sutherland, the Glasgow schoolmaster, delivered a lecture on evictions concluding —

> "Every Highlander is a born agitator because he has suffered directly or indirectly from landlordism".

When trouble erupted in Skye over the dispute between the crofters and the proprietor of the estate of Kilmuir in the north end of Skye, a meeting of the council of the Federation of Celtic Societies was held in the Christian Institute, Glasgow, on May 6, 1881, and a motion was passed unanimously in support of the Kilmuir crofters —

> "threatened with eviction from the homes which have belonged to them and their forefathers from time immemorial because they refuse to pay an impossible rent".

It was in Glasgow also that the Skye Vigilance Committee was formed. It was significant that its formation in 1881 occurred after the Easter Monday demonstration of the Irish Land League; and the critics of the champions of the crofters were not slow in pointing out the link with Ireland, which was then the scene of murder and agrarian outrages. The Irish Land League demonstration took place in the City Halls, where a large audience of Irishmen and Scottish sympathisers heard an eloquent address by Charles Stewart Parnell, "the uncrowned king of Ireland". After Parnell had spoken, John Gunn MacKay, a shop assistant in Glasgow and later a shopkeeper in Portree, made the "impassioned speech" already referred to in support of a resolution to the effect that in view of the threatened evictions on Kilmuir estate the meeting of Irishmen should pledge itself to give support to the Highland crofters "whatever forms the struggle might ultimately assume".[1] He was seconded by Henry Whyte, "Fionn", the bard, a native of Easdale in Argyll and Glasgow correspondent of the *Oban Times*; and the resolution was carried unanimously. The Skye Vigilance Committee, which was formed thereafter on May 15, had as its organisers both John Gunn MacKay and Henry Whyte and also Angus Sutherland, John MacDonald of Morvern, and others, who declared their intention of assisting the crofters with counsel to act on constitutional lines.

It was, as has been stated, the Skye Vigilance Committee which approached Cameron of Lochiel, M.P. for Inverness-shire, and Dr Charles Cameron, M.P. for Glasgow and proprietor of the Radical *North British Daily Mail*, to take up the cause of the Kilmuir crofters and raise the matter in Parliament. Lochiel, as might be expected, declined but Dr Cameron consented and gave nationwide publicity to the rack-renting policy of the Kilmuir proprietor, Captain Fraser, who was forced to grant a reduction in rents. The Portree correspondent of the *Scotsman*, then the establishment newspaper *par excellence*, put the worst possible interpretation on the activities of the Vigilance Committee. He wrote:—

> "Members of the Irish League are in regular correspondence with some of the Kilmuir tenantry and arrangements are being made by the Leaguers for holding 'indignation meetings' in Skye."

Two of the men most active in Glasgow at the time on behalf of the Kilmuir crofters were Henry Whyte ("Fionn"), the secretary of the Skye Vigilance Committee, and Angus Sutherland, a member of the committee and secretary of the Federation of Celtic Societies — neither of them a native of Skye. Like many other Highlanders and, indeed, Lowlanders and Englishmen and Welshmen, they sympathised with Gladstone's Irish policy involving reform of the land laws but they, like Gladstone, did not condone the murders and outrages which still continued after the passing of Gladstone's Irish Land Act of 1881. This act gave Irish tenants the rights known as the "3 F's" — (1) Fair Rents, to be fixed by a Land Court; (2) Fixed Tenure, so long as the rent was paid; (3) Free Sale of the tenant's interest in the holding, which meant that the tenant would be compensated for his house and for any improvements he had carried out. The terms of the Irish Land Act were considered by many crofters and their sympathisers to be worthwhile gaining for the Highlands and Islands of Scotland and served as aims to be achieved.

The Annual General Meeting of the Federation of Celtic Societies at the end of 1881, which was held in Perth and attended by over 1300 delegates from all over the country, had as chairman Dr Charles Cameron, the Glasgow M.P., who ranged over a number of subjects in his presidential address but laid particular emphasis on the crofter question. But it was John Stuart Blackie who received the greatest applause for his speech in moving a resolution in favour of reform of the Scottish land laws. The speech was typical of the Edinburgh professor — joking, exaggerating, scathing, digressing, and the meeting closed with three cheers for Professor Blackie. It was the last convention of the Celtic Societies which focussed attention on the crofter question as in 1882 the crofters' cause was taken up by other bodies. The Ben Lee dispute in Skye, which erupted in the Battle of the Braes on April 19, 1882, spurred the Skye Vigilance Committee in Glasgow to set up a fund to be called "The Highland Crofter Defence Fund", and soon afterwards a meeting of Edinburgh Highlanders in Darling's Hotel agreed to start a similar fund to defend the Braes men then in jail and assist their families. Already, on July 12, 1881, the Dublin branch of the Irish Land League had decided on a grant of £50 to the crofters "fighting against landlord tyranny in the Isle of Skye."

London and Edinburgh Associations

Sympathy for the Skye crofters was shown throughout the country in letters to the press and also in public meetings. On May 5, 1882, a mass meeting of Glasgow Highlanders was held in the Grand National Halls, which were crowded by an audience estimated at 3,000. Over twelve Highland societies were represented by delegates, and various resolutions were passed unanimously, criticising conditions in the crofting area and demanding reform. Before the meeting was held, the committee responsible for arranging the meeting distributed throughout the city a pamphlet containing the reply to the Lord Advocate by Kenneth MacDonald, the Inverness lawyer who was defending the Braes men awaiting trial on charges of deforcement and assault. A fortnight later, the London Inverness-shire Association sponsored a meeting to consider crofters' grievances. The chairman was Dr Roderick MacDonald, president of the Gaelic Society of London, later to be M.P. for Ross and Cromarty, and the main speaker was the ebullient Professor John Stuart Blackie. Several resolutions were passed and it was agreed to send a petition embodying the resolutions to Charles Fraser Mackintosh, M.P. for Inverness Burghs, for presentation to Parliament. Fraser Mackintosh was one of those who supported Donald MacFarlane in the debate on crofting conditions in the House of Commons on August 4, 1882, when the Scottish M.P.s, Dr Cameron, Sir George Campbell, Dick Peddie, failed to convince the Lord Advocate, J.B. Balfour, of the need for a public inquiry. Another meeting, held in London in February, 1883, was convened by Lord Archibald Campbell, son of the Duke of Argyll. To the main resolution of the meeting, which was to appoint a deputation to proceed to Skye with the object of inducing the crofters to respect the law, a rider was moved — "and that Her Majesty's Government be asked to take immediate steps for redressing the grievances of the Highland crofters and cottars". The rider was moved by T.C. Hedderwick, a barrister who later became M.P. for Wick Burghs, and seconded by "a young man of magnificent proportions, the glow of whose eyes, the ring of whose voice, bespoke the true mountaineer" (according to the Rev. Donald MacCallum in his biographical history of the Crofters' War, *Highland Patriots*). The young man was James Murray, a son of the manse born in Lewis, and it was his brother Donald who asked those in favour of the rider, which was ruled out of order, to meet outside after the official meeting ended.[2] From this nucleus the Highland Land Law Reform Association was formed, with Donald Murray as its first secretary and Donald Hume Macfarlane, then M.P. for County Carlow in Ireland but later M.P. for Argyllshire, as president. The rather lengthy title of the new association, copied from the title of the similar English association, was adopted as more accurate than that of the similar body in

PROFESSOR J. STUART BLACKIE.

Ireland, but right from its inception, the association's critics referred to it as "the Land League", which in time became the universal form in popular use and in 1887 the Annual Conference adopted the "Highland Land League" as the official title.

By the spring of 1883, when the Government announced the appointment of a Royal Commission under Lord Napier to inquire into "the conditions of the Crofters and Cottars in the Highlands and Islands", the three bodies which amalgamated in 1887 as the Highland Land League were functioning independently. In addition to the

Highland Land Law Reform Association set up in London, there was a body with a similar name and similar aims in Edinburgh. The Edinburgh Highland Association also took an active interest in crofters' affairs. An enthusiastic crowded meeting in Edinburgh on February 9, 1883, under the chairmanship of the famous Radical, Duncan MacLaren, endorsed the aims of the Edinburgh H.L.L.R.A. and adopted motions in favour of a Royal Commission and a thorough reform of the land laws. The Edinburgh body, which amalgamated with the Edinburgh Highland Association in 1884, was dominated directly and indirectly by Free Church ministers, who regarded the London body as encroaching on their particular sphere of influence.

Sutherland Association

The Sutherland crofters were independent of both the London and Edinburgh associations. Sutherland people regarded the clearances of the early part of the nineteenth century in their county as the most savage of all, and their memories were stirred by the renewed interest created by the publication of Donald MacLeod's *Gloomy Memories* by Alexander MacKenzie of Inverness along with his own account of the Highland clearances. The Sutherland crofters were organised at first in small groups. The first was formed as a result of threatened evictions at Gartymore and other small townships near Helmsdale. The crofters had taken their sheep off the hill grazing but some of them refused to give a written promise never to put their sheep back on the hill. Eight of them received notices of eviction in 1882. The crofters were defended by a Tain solicitor, MacLeay, and the notices were withdrawn. Out of this trouble an association was formed, with John MacKay, civil engineer, Hereford, as president, Angus Sutherland, the Glasgow schoolmaster, as vice-president, and Donald Bannerman, Bual, and John Fraser, Gartymore, joint-secretaries. One of the early propagandists, Joseph MacLeod, author of *Highland Heroes of the Land Reform Movement*, confessed years later that, to overcome the apathy prevailing at that time, he would visit a village and deliver a speech but even if there was no audience he would send a full report to the newspapers, with the result that other villages would invite him to speak. In August, 1882, there was held at Helmsdale a meeting at which the main speaker was Angus Sutherland, whose speech sparked off the formation of other branches. Sutherland's message was "Organize, organize, organize". The main work of organizing was undertaken by John MacLeod of Gartymore, later to be M.P., and when the various groups became a federation in 1885 there were 21 branches and 1540 paid-up members. From time to time the Sutherlandshire

Association (as it was called) was to follow a course independent of the two large bodies based on London and Edinburgh.

Napier Commission

One of the first steps taken in aid of the crofters was in the preparation of evidence to be submitted to the Napier Commission, beginning its sittings in May, 1883, at the Braes near Portree. The two editors, Alexander MacKenzie and John Murdoch, toured the crofting areas, advising the crofters how to prepare their statements. The hearings of the Royal Commission, which lasted from May to December, had a most powerful effect in promoting the participation of the crofters (and, it should be added, the cottars) in land law reform organizations. At a mass meeting in Fraserburgh in August, 1883, of west coast fishermen engaged in the herring fishing, it was unanimously resolved to start land law reform associations in the various parishes on their return home. At the end of 1883, the H.L.L.R.A. of London published three pamphlets for distribution to the public generally, to schoolmasters in particular, and to crofters and cottars. In the pamphlet addressed to the public, reference was made to "the dismal desolation of many a fertile strath" and "a harrowing record of cruelty and oppression", but the emphasis was on peaceful and constitutional methods. Schoolmasters were encouraged to use their influence in promoting "the social emancipation of the people among whom their lot was cast". The crofters were enjoined to "earnest effort" and "well-directed agitation" in favour of changes in land laws which would lead to (1) a durable tenure, (2) fair rents, fixed by a land court, (3) due compensation to tenants for any improvements, (4) re-allocation of land for production of food for man instead of for sporting purposes, (5) a scheme to enable tenants to become owners. In addition, it was pointed out that, with the forthcoming extension of the franchise, crofters would have the vote for the first time and should return to Parliament men who were interested on their behalf. They were encouraged to form district branches, as "God helps those that help themselves". The pamphlets for the crofters were printed in Gaelic as well as English and on December 19, 1883, John MacKenzie, a local manager at Uig on the Kilmuir estate, reported to the factor, Alex. MacDonald of Portree, that copies of the circular had been sent to all the crofters and others who had appeared as delegates before the Royal Commission. One of the first districts to form a branch was Glendale in Skye, where the crofters had been holding regular "indignation meetings" to discuss their policy towards landlord and factor since February, 1882. Rules for branches were drawn up by the central headquarters in London, to which members' annual subscriptions of one shilling were remitted.[3] Lachlan MacDonald of Skeabost, referring to cases of intimidation on his estate of Bernesdale — scattering of corn crops, cutting of herring nets at night to influence crofters reluctant to join the League — stated that some crofters paid their subscriptions as insurance against destruction of property. Damage of this kind was perpetrated by over-enthusiastic youths and young men and was condemned "in the strongest terms" at the branch meeting.

Branch Meetings

Branch activities varied from place to place. At Stoneybridge, in South Uist, a red flag was hoisted to call the people together when a communication arrived from the H.L.L.R.A. in London, and the people proceeded to engage in actions in defiance of estate regulations. The Rev. James M. Davidson, parish minister of Stenscholl in the north end of Skye, had on his arrival in the parish been impressed by "the moral cowardice of the people", still affected by their memories of the reign of terror during the clearances. Three years later, after the visit of the Royal Commission, the mood of the people had changed considerably. He described the meetings of the Highland Land Law Reform Association as having all the effect of a debating or mutual improvement society:

"The crofters began to think for themselves, and the periodical meetings of the Association afforded opportunities of expressing their views. This some do with creditable fluency and it may be noted that not a few come with their speeches written."

Reports of the meetings were sent to newspapers favourable to the crofters, the *Oban Times*, the *Invergordon Times*, and later the *Scottish Highlander*. Writing in the last-named, the South Shawbost correspondent claimed in the summer of 1885:

"We are learning by degrees to work out our own salvation and since we joined the H.L.L.R.A., we have been taught courage and to take it upon us to send accounts to the newspapers."

Thereafter followed a lengthy account of the dispute with a neighbouring farmer over a grazing of which the crofters claimed possession. Meetings were usually held in the local church or school and were often opened with prayer, delivered by some one like Rory Bàn MacLeod of Bayble in Lewis, a leading elder in the Free Church, or like John MacPherson of Glendale, endowed with a gift of eloquence. Seldom was a meeting held without someone quoting from the Bible as if to add conviction to his argument. Joseph MacLeod, whose *Highland Heroes of the Land Reform Movement* appeared in 1917, entitled his first chapter "Land Reform Justified: The Bible and the Land Question", and gave a list of appropriate texts:—

The earth is the Lord's and the fulness thereof. — Psalms, 24, 1.

Remove not the old landmark, and enter not into the fields of the fatherless. — Proverbs, 23, 10.

The husbandman that laboureth must be first partaker of the fruits. — Timothy, II, 2, 6.

Woe unto them that join house to house, that lay field to field, till there be no place, that they may be placed in the midst of the earth. — Isaiah, 5, 8.

Political Agitation

The Highlands and Islands were not the only parts of Britain where the people were engaged in agitation in the 1880s. It was a period of great social distress, the period of the "Great Depression" of the nineteenth century, the period when the word "unemployed" was first used, the period which saw the birth of the Scottish Labour Party, the Scottish Home Rule Association, the Social Democratic Federation, the forerunner of the Communist party.

February, 1884, when Sir Alexander Matheson intimated his intention to resign his seat in Parliament, saw the commencement of Henry George's campaign in the Highlands and Islands, including meetings in Portree and the Braes.[4] The "Prophet of San Francisco" did not have much success in Skye but in the south his campaign led to the formation of the Scottish Land Restoration League. At his meeting in the City Hall, Glasgow, on February 18, 1884, the author of *Progress and Poverty* urged his audience to —

"proclaim the grand truth that every human being born in Scotland has an inalienable and equal right to the soil of Scotland — a right that no law can do away with, a right that comes direct from the Creator who made earth for man and placed him upon the earth."

These words echo the phrases and the sentiments of the preamble to the American Declaration of Independence but George was going far beyond the claims of 1776. Nationalisation of the land was advocated by him, and its protagonists were strengthened in their beliefs by his denunciation of land ownership as it then existed. Many a time in the next decade, the slogan "The Land for the People" was used as a rallying cry and appeared as a motto on the banners at Land Law Reform demonstrations, although Henry George himself did not win many adherents for his single-tax policy (of increasing taxation on land until the whole value of land would be taken for public benefit). Immediately after the City Hall demonstration the Scottish Land Restoration League was formed at a meeting presided over by John

Murdoch, and this body adopted Henry George's views completely, advocating a land tax of six shillings in the pound as a first step towards taking all the ground rent for the public revenue. Scottish Land Restoration League candidates, including John Murdoch, stood in Glasgow constituencies in the election of 1885 but received only a handful of votes.

The Radicals who composed the left wing of the Liberal party were led by Joseph Chamberlain, whose views at that time were regarded by the Conservatives as "socialistic". His attack on the House of Lords, which threatened to obstruct the measures of Gladstone's Liberal Government, won him the applause of the still-unenfranchised mass of the people.

> "Lord Salisbury" (the leader of the Conservatives) "constitutes himself the spokesman of a class — of the class to which he himself belongs, who toil not neither do they spin" . . .

1885 was the year of the franchise reform, introduced by the Liberals to extend the franchise to all male adult householders, a move which gave the vote to the Irish small tenant and the Scottish crofter for the first time. The Franchise Bill was held up by the Lords until a bill providing for redistribution of seats was promised. The crofters, waiting for the report of Lord Napier's Commission (which at last came out at the end of April, 1884), were naturally in favour of the Liberals' franchise reform, and from this time onwards the crofter question became inextricably linked with franchise extension. When a by-election was announced for Ross and Cromarty the crofters and cottars, still without votes, became enthusiastic supporters of Dr Roderick MacDonald, who stood professedly as champion of the crofters against the official Liberal candidate, Munro-Ferguson. MacDonald, a native of Skye, was one of the founders of the Highland Land Law Reform Association of London and had been asked to stand for Parliament by Donald Murray, secretary of the Association, in order to prepare the ground for the general election which was due to be held in the following year. As might be expected, he finished bottom of the poll in the by-election in August, 1884, but was easily victorious at the general election in 1885 when the electorate was five times larger.

Dingwall Conference

The Dingwall Conference, organized by the London Highland Land Law Reform Association, was held just after the by-election of August, 1884. It brought together delegates from branches of the association to consider and approve the stated aims of concerting united action throughout the Highlands and Islands at the forthcoming general election, appointing a consultative political committee for the selection of suitable candidates, and considering the propriety of starting an independent reform newspaper. Dingwall, the county town of Ross-shire, the town of which Gladstone's grandfather, Andrew Robertson, had been provost, was far away from the main crofting area but, as a railway junction, was a convenient place for a rendezvous for delegates from north, south and west. The conference marked a significant change in the crofters' agitation for reform. The London H.L.L.R.A., through the suggestion by Donald Murray that Dr MacDonald should intervene in the Ross and Cromarty by-election, had shown the way to prepare the ground for the general election when the crofters would be able to vote for the first time. Resolutions were passed unanimously in preparation for the election and it was agreed that no candidate would be acceptable in a Highland constituency who would not agree to the programme adopted by the conference.

The Dingwall Programme (or Manifesto) included the following:— (1) The introduction of a bill in Parliament suspending the power of a landlord to evict crofters and cottars; (2) legislation on the lines of the Irish Land Act — fair rents to be fixed by a Land Court, free sale of improvements, and fixed tenure so long as the rent was paid; (3) representation to be made to Mr Gladstone for implementation of the recommendations of the Royal Commission; (4) approval of a proposal for compulsory enlargement of townships and formation of new townships; (5) recommendations of the Royal Commission about education, fisheries and communications to be put into effect; (6) a ban on factors or estate agents acting as procurators-fiscal; (7) modification of the game laws to allow tenants to kill game on their grounds; (8) the establishment of a newspaper devoted to land reform; (9) a protest against the Lords' delay over the Reform Bill.

Among the speakers were the chairman, Dr G.B. Clark, president of the London H.L.L.R.A., D.H. MacFarlane, M.P., C. Fraser Mackintosh, M.P., Sir George Campbell, M.P., Dr R. MacDonald, Rev. Donald MacCallum, Waternish, Skye, Rev. Mr Cumming, Melness, Sutherland. There does not seem to have been any representative of the Edinburgh H.L.L.R.A., which was in the process of negotiation with the Edinburgh Highland Association about amalgamation. That there was some rivalry between the London and Edinburgh bodies at first was natural; both staged mass demonstrations in Lewis in the month of October, 1884. Hundreds of men marched from all over the island of Lewis to hear speeches for the London H.L.L.R.A. demonstration on reform, including critical remarks about the previous demonstration, at which one of the main speakers was a landlord's son, the Liberal M.P., Munro-Ferguson. When the Edinburgh amalgamation was completed, Donald Murray, the secretary of the London Association, wrote to the *Scotsman*, pointing out that the London and Edinburgh bodies were "distinct and separate associations".

Amalgamation

In September, 1884, the Edinburgh Highland Association began the moves which culminated in its amalgamation with the Edinburgh Highland Land Law Reform Association by the end of the year. A statement was issued which the *Ross-shire Journal* hoped might "put a stop to London demagogy and socialism". It reiterated the crofters' demands for concessions similar to those contained in the Irish Land Act and pressed for the formation of more branch associations. At the demonstration organized in Stornoway on October 2 in favour of the Franchise Bill and land law reform, speeches were given by the newly-elected M.P. for Ross and Cromarty, Munro-Ferguson, Dr Rainy, Principal of the Free Church College in Edinburgh, and other ministers. In the next few days, during which Principal Rainy opened a new church at Carloway, branches of the Edinburgh association were formed at Ness and Shawbost, in addition to the branches of the London association already established. At the first Annual General Meeting of the combined Edinburgh Highland and Land Law Reform Assocation (as it was called at first), held in the Free Church Assembly Hall on December 18, it was claimed that there were 30 branches spread throughout the crofting counties. Free Church divines predominated in the discussion on the resolutions but there were also addresses by Munro-Ferguson, M.P., Duncan Cameron, the young son of the owner of the *Oban Times*, John MacPherson, "the Glendale Martyr", the Rev. Donald MacCallum, parish minister of Waternish in Skye. The meeting was held during the early period of the Skye military expedition and many felt strongly about the dispatch of an armed force, the first to that part of Scotland since the Jacobite Rebellion of 1745-46. At the end of the meeting, a vote of thanks to the chairman was moved by Principal Rainy and the benediction pronounced by the Rev. Murdoch MacAskill of Greenock. When the Liberal Government was defeated in June, 1885, during the budget debate by a snap combination of Conservatives and Irish Nationalists, Gladstone was glad to resign and hand over the reins of office to the Marquis of Salisbury, who formed a "caretaker" Government until the new electoral registers would be ready. All this time the crofters and cottars were waiting for implementation of the recommendations of Lord Napier's Commission, whose report had been published in April, 1884, and agitation continued to grow apace, stimulated by the presence of candidates seeking votes. No Conservative had any chance of winning an election in the crofting counties and indeed the Conservatives had only a feeble representation in Scotland generally in the 1880s and later, until the Liberal split over Irish Home Rule brought in the Unionists who combined with the Conservatives. Among the so-called crofter candidates, standing as Liberals against official Liberals, were Dr Roderick MacDonald in Ross and Cromarty, Donald Hume MacFarlane in Argyll, Dr Gavin Clark in Caithness, Angus Sutherland in Sutherland, who had all taken leading parts in Land Law Reform Associations, the first three in the London association. The crofter candidates were labelled by the *Scotsman* as "carpet-baggers", and when the H.L.L.R.A. annual conference was held at Portree in September, 1885, it was described as "organized for the sole purpose of trying to secure the election of the carpet-baggers".

Portree Conference

Portree, the "capital" of Skye, provided a peculiarly appropriate setting for the meeting of crofters and their supporters. Although the timing of the conference prevented the attendance of many men who were at the east coast fishing, their numbers were partly made up by representatives of various Socialist and near-Socialist organisations in the south, such as the Scottish Land Restoration League, which stood for Henry George's single-tax policy: some of its members were soon afterwards to join in founding the Scottish Labour Party. Dr Clark, the candidate for Caithness, who was chairman of the executive committee of the London H.L.L.R.A., was himself in favour of nationalisation of the land and was later to be prominent in the International Working Men's Association. Throughout the meetings at Portree the emphasis was however on land law reform in the Highlands and Islands, and one of the resolutions expressed approval of six men "pledged to vote for a satisfactory scheme of land reform" — the four candidates mentioned above, MacDonald, MacFarlane, Clark, Sutherland and, in addition, W.S. Bright MacLaren in Inverness Burghs and Fraser Mackintosh in Inverness-shire.

The influence of the Scottish Land Restoration League was evidenced in the resolution denouncing the evils of the existing land system; it was moved by Stuart Glennie, a London barrister, and seconded by Angus Sutherland, the prospective candidate for Sutherland. Glennie was also successful with an amendment to the main resolution condemning the inadequacy of the proposed crofters' bill, adding words advocating "the restoration to the people of the whole area of the Highland forests, moorlands and hill grazings". It was accepted by Dr Clark, M.P. in the name of the committee formed by the Edinburgh and London associations to organise the conference.

Branches of the London and Edinburgh associations were represented by delegates from Stornoway, Barvas, Park, Leurbost and Knock in Lewis; North Uist, Benbecula, South Uist, Barra, Salen in Mull, Oban, Carnan (Kilninver); Ardnamurchan, Applecross, Gairloch, Kintail and Glenshiel, Plockton and Aird, Lochalsh, Lochcarron, Torridon; Alness, Mulbuie, Ardgay. The Sutherland association, which had staged its own demonstration at Golspie the previous week, was represented by Angus Sutherland from Glasgow and only a few delegates from Caithness and Sutherland. By far the largest contingent came from the Skye branches — Arnizort, Snizort, Mininish, Sconser, Bernisdale, Kilmaluag, Garrafad, Valtos, Braes, Glendale. For the demonstration on the day after the conference, a field on the Home Farm, Portree, had been made available by John MacKay (the farmer who had figured prominently in the Ben Lee dispute), with the approval of the factor, Alex. MacDonald. Many from the outlying districts like Dunvegan and Glendale walked through the night. The Portree contingent marched north to meet the Staffin and Valtos men from Kilmuir, who carried banners bearing slogans — "*Ceartas* (Justice)" and "*Ri Ghuallaibh a Cheile* (Shoulder to Shoulder)". When the Braes and Sconser men arrived, led by three pipers, the Braes men had English slogans — "Ben Lee for Ever" and "The Land for the People" while the Sconser men used both Gaelic and English — "Down with Deer Forests" and "*Is treasa tuath na tighearna* (The tenant is stronger than the laird)". The procession moved from Portree Square to the field to start the meeting at noon. It went on until 7.30 p.m., with only one shower about two o'clock to damp their spirits. Over thirty speakers addressed the assembled delegates and supporters; and the meeting closed with a song from the Skye poetess, Mary MacPherson (*Màiri Mhór nan Oran* — Big Mary of the songs) which was greeted with rapturous applause.

Newspaper Competition

The general election of 1885 was not held until the end of November and the beginning of December (elections were held in different places at different dates in those days) and led to fierce competition among the newspapers. Competition had already existed at the time of the by-election of 1884 between the *Inverness Courier* and the *Ross-shire Journal* representing the official Liberal point of view and the *Invergordon Times*, which championed the crofters, also supported by the *Oban Times*. Other newspapers which championed the crofters included the *Aberdeen Free Press*, the *Dundee Advertiser*, the *Dundee Courier* and the Wick-based *Northern Ensign*. The *Scotsman* and the *Glasgow Herald*, with much more than a local readership, represented the offical Liberal and Conservative points of view and were rivalled by the Glasgow-based *North British Daily Mail*, owned by the Radical M.P., Dr Cameron, the weekly edition of which sold over 230,000 copies. Dr Charles (later Sir Charles) Cameron was born in Dublin of an Irish mother and a Scottish father, both of whose parents came from Inverness. After studying at the universities of Dublin, Berlin and Vienna, he succeeded his father as newspaper proprietor. In addition to his support for the crofters, he sponsored parliamentary bills for abolishing imprisonment for debt, the franchise for women, and reforms in the legal code. He topped the poll in Glasgow at the election of 1874 and represented a Glasgow seat until 1895. The people of Inverness, to judge from the number of newspapers, all politically aligned, must have been one of the most politically-conscious communities in the country. At one time in the 1880s there was a newspaper coming out every day of the week except Sunday. The *Inverness Courier*, representing the old Whig establishment since 1817, came out twice a week

DR CHARLES CAMERON, M.P.,
PROPRIETOR NORTH BRITISH DAILY MAIL.

and for a short period three times a week. The next oldest newspaper, the *Inverness Advertiser*, which was started in 1849, was a rival of the *Courier*. It ceased publication in December, 1885, just after the election. The *Highland News* was started in 1883 as the organ of the Highland Temperance League under Philip MacLeod as editor and proprietor but from 1887 was edited by John MacLeod, a strong

101

champion of land law reform and M.P. for Sutherland from 1894. The *Scottish Highlander* first appeared in July, 1885. It was financed by Fraser Mackintosh, and its editor, Alexander MacKenzie, the "Clach", in addition to giving loyal support for the proprietor's candidature, commented extensively on Highland affairs. There was one Conservative newspaper, the *Northern Chronicle*, started in 1881 as a result of the efforts of Charles Innes, the lawyer, and ably edited by Duncan Campbell, who regarded the rôle of the paper as protector of the farming interests. The election campaign contributed greatly to the success of the Inverness papers, the circulation sometimes increased, however, by the distribution of free copies. The *Northern Chronicle*, which averaged 6,500 copies in 1885, printed 8,400 copies on October 21, 1885, and 8,600 copies on November 25, 1885. Alex. MacKenzie, editor of the *Scottish Highlander*, claimed that 25,000 copies had been sold in the first six weeks of the paper.

H.L.L.R.A. Activities

The work of the H.L.L.R.A. was not confined to electioneering and conferences. The Crofters' Aid Fund, which was set up to assist in the legal defence of crofters charged with breaches of the law and in the support of prisoners' families, continued to attract subscriptions from sympathisers, rich and poor. A list published in January, 1887, contained donations from Donald MacFarlane (£20), Charles Fraser Mackintosh (10 guineas), from J.C., "a sufferer for the cause" (£3), Miss MacP., "capriciously evicted" (£2). Separate funds were started from time to time, for the Tiree prisoners in the summer of 1886, for the tenants of Skibo in Sutherland, for the crofters of Garrafad in Kilmuir, Skye. Even before 1885, the London H.L.L.R.A. was paying a regular weekly wage of £1 to crofters to act as propagandists — John MacPherson, "the Glendale Martyr", James Leonard of Rousay, who had been evicted after giving evidence to the Napier Commission at Kirkwall, and Michael Buchanan of Barra, who, although a little over forty years of age, had travelled the world. All three were eloquent speakers and no doubt found their duties, which involved travelling around to address sympathetic audiences, pleasant and satisfying, while their hearers were strengthened in their resolve to uphold the cause.

The election in the summer of 1886 which followed Gladstone's defeat over the Irish Home Rule Bill resulted in a victory for Salisbury and the Conservatives but the crofter counties were still represented by crofter candidates except Argyll, where the Conservative laird, Col. Malcolm of Poltalloch, won the seat from D.H. MacFarlane, whose conversion to Roman Catholicism and support for Irish Home

Rule weighed heavily against him in a predominantly Presbyterian constituency. (In the next general election in 1892 however MacFarlane turned the tables on his opponent and crowned his political career by gaining a knighthood in 1895.) During the six years of Salisbury's ministry, the land law reform agitation took some time to die down and the military expeditions sent to Tiree, Skye, Lewis and Sutherland led to an escalation of agitation rather than a decline in the first few years.

The Ministers and the Reform Agitation

It is difficult to assess the extent of influence of the ministers in the crofters' agitation for reform. Ministers from almost every parish in the crofting areas appeared before the Napier Commission in 1883 or sent letters to the Commission giving their views on the problems of the crofters and, as might be expected from men of their vocation, expressing their sympathy for the crofters without criticism of "landlordism" as many of the lay witnesses did. The Free Church itself was denounced by two witnesses, both farmers, Donald Cameron of Glenbrittle in Skye and Thomas Purves of Rhifail in Sutherland. According to the former, "the Gaelic and the Free Kirk and the want of education are the curse of Skye". According to the latter, "the Free Kirk teaching and the Free Kirk clergy are the cause of half the evils that affect Sutherland". It was the Free Church which was responsible for most of the edu-

PRINCIPAL RAINY, FREE CHURCH COLLEGE, EDINBURGH.

cational provision in the Highlands and Islands before the Education Act of 1872; and the official statement presented by Principal Rainy and the Rev. J. Calder MacPhail for the Highland Committee of the Free Church in December, 1883, referred at length to the benefits of their church's educational policy. At the end of their statement, the authors mentioned the feeling held throughout the Highlands that "acts of great oppression had been committed with impunity and without redress". This belief, they argued, tended to create

> "a spirit of suspicion and defiance and suggests a resort to illegal methods to protect them from danger which the law is known to be powerless to avert".

It was not long before the Edinburgh Highland Land Law Reform Association was actively engaged in establishing branches in the crofting areas, with Free Church ministers taking a leading part, hoping to induce the crofters to eschew violence and act on constitutional lines. At the by-election in Ross and Cromarty in August, 1884, the ministers actually favoured the Conservative and the official Liberal candidate rather than the crofter candidate. In Sutherland, where there were two crofter candidates standing at the general election in 1885, Angus Sutherland, the Glasgow schoolmaster, a crofter's son, and the Marquis of Stafford, son and heir of the Duke of Sutherland, who put forward an extreme Radical manifesto, some well respected Free Church ministers like Dr Gustavus Aird of Creich and the Rev. John Murray of Clyne, regarded as champions of the crofters, were strongly criticised for not supporting the crofter's son instead of the duke's son. By 1886, although there were certain exceptions like Dr Gustavus Aird of Creich, the Sutherland ministers and many other ministers throughout the country were becoming cooler in their support of the crofters, because of the contacts of some of the land law reformers with socialists.

Some Free Church ministers were in the embarrassing position of owing the grant of a building site for the church to the generosity of the proprietor. For this reason, both the Rev. John MacPhail of Kilmuir and the Rev. Joseph Lamont of Snizort avoided outright criticism of William Fraser of Kilmuir, who otherwise received almost universal condemnation. One case where the proprietor was faced with open antagonism by the Free Church minister was at Rousay in Orkney. The Rev. Archibald MacCallum, born in Glasgow but with West Highland connections, supported the crofters against the proprietor, General Burroughs, with whom he carried on a bitter feud. MacCallum, who became an alcoholic, was forced to resign from his Orkney charge and also from his charge at Knock parish church in Lewis. None of the ministers was so critical as the Rev. Hector Cameron, Free Church minister of Back near Stornoway. At the communion service at Barvas on the west side of the island in September, 1887, he launched an attack on members of the Highland Land League for not subscribing more liberally to the Sustentation Fund of the church for, he claimed, they had plenty of money for drink. The Free Church ministers' opposition to emigration was, according to hostile critics, based on fears for their stipends, which were financed not from teinds as in the Established Church stipends but from the Sustentation Fund, dependent on voluntary contributions.

Church of Scotland ministers gave little support for the agitation but there were a few notable exceptions. Most prominent of all was the Rev. Donald MacCallum, a native of Craignish in Argyll, minister of Hallin-in-Waternish in Skye from 1883 to 1887, who was a professing Christian Socialist. He had a very small congregation and seldom had even a dozen hearers for his sermons, many of which reflected his political views. He threw himself into the struggle for land law reform and travelled all over Skye and many parts of the mainland. His popularity as an orator induced the men of Tiree, after the military expedition of 1886, to call him as minister. He stayed only two years, leaving for the parish of Lochs in Lewis, where some of the Free Church members deserted their church and joined the parish church in order to give MacCallum a call. When in Skye, he was arrested, at the same time as John MacPherson of Glendale, and charged with "inciting the lieges to violence and class hatred". He spent the weekend in Portree jail but was released on bail and was never brought to trial. A monument to him was erected in the year he left for Lewis from Tiree. It stands in the Moss district and bears the inscription "Tur McCallum. Bas no buaidh. Death or victory." The Rev. J.M. Davidson, minister of the *quoad sacra* parish of Stenscholl, was brought up on Speyside, and was astounded when he first came to Skye at the "moral cowardice" of the people and welcomed the transformation created by the Napier Commission and the Highland Land Law Reform Association. Later, he offered hospitality to MacHugh, the Irish advance agent for Henry George, and to Duncan Cameron of the *Oban Times* in his manse at Stenscholl on the estate of Kilmuir. Another champion of the crofters in a Church of Scotland charge was the Rev. Angus MacIver of Uig in Lewis. The parish church in Uig had been empty for years, and there was a large glebe, on which squatters cast envious eyes. A number of the Free Church congregation joined the Church of Scotland and invited a Free Church minister from Glasgow, a native of the parish, the Rev. Angus MacIver, to be their minister. He accepted the call, came back to Uig but kept the glebe. He was prominent in the mass demonstration in Stornoway in October, 1884, and remained loyal to the crofters' cause despite attempts by Lady Matheson to persuade him to desert them. Another Lewis minister of the Established Church, the Rev. Ewen Campbell of Lochs, was strongly criticised for his evidence before the Napier Commission in 1883, when he suggested rather flippantly that it would be useless to create holdings on the boggy, rocky, barren soil of Lochs parish, adding that it would be far better for these poor people "to send for the 42nd to shoot every mother's son that would be put there". He had some sympathy for the crofters although he blamed them for encouraging overcrowding by permitting cottars and squatters, and his only solution (natural enough from one born in Nova Scotia), was emigration.

Songs and Poems

Reference has been made earlier to the part played by the Gaelic bards and singers in the 1870s in the societies of Glasgow, Edinburgh, Inverness and other towns and cities. The 1880s brought a burgeoning of the societies' activities and a large crop of songs and poems, only a few of which reached the level of the post-clearance period. The Psalms of David were given preference at some crofters' meetings, the most notable occasion being the mass demonstration in Stornoway in October, 1884, when several thousands joined in singing the first four verses of the 46th psalm. As has been stated, by far the most prominent figure in the sphere of Gaelic song in the 1880s was a woman, Mary MacPherson. Born in Skeabost, the daughter of John MacDonald, she was first known by the Gaelic patronymic, *Màiri nighean Iain Bhàin* (Mary, daughter of fair-haired John). She married a shoemaker in Inverness, Isaac MacPherson, who died in 1871. After his death, she spent some time in prison for what she called a "misdemeanour"; and this experience left her with a sense of grievance, which is perceptible in but does not dominate her poetry. It was when she was over fifty years of age that she took to composing songs, and during the 1880s she attached herself to the crofters' cause, singing songs of her own composition at Highland societies' gatherings. A big woman physically, she became known as *Màiri Mhór nan Oran* (Big Mary of the Songs), and it was she who provided a fitting climax to the day-long speechifying at the Portree Conference of the H.L.L.R.A. in 1885, when she sang one of her own songs. She is best remembered today for her songs of Skye like *"Eilean a' Cheo* (Isle of Mist)" or *"Soraidh leis an Àit'* (Farewell to the place)" or *"Nuair bha mi òg* (When I was young)"*. Another poet and song-writer closely associated with Land League agitation, John MacLean, the Tiree bard, who wrote humorous satires, is now best remembered for his love songs. Most of the song-writers of the 1870s and 1880s came from Argyll or the islands — Lewis, Skye, Tiree. Professor John MacLeod was a native of Assynt in Sutherland and after a distinguished academic career returned to Assynt for reasons of health and took an active interest in the Stoer branch of the H.L.L.R.A. The song he composed in praise of the shieling at Culkein near Clashmore is full of nostalgic recall of youth.[5] The first and last verses are given below. In the first he describes the shieling, and in the last he asks members of Parliament to restore to the people the land where the shielings used to be.

Airigh a' Chulchinn

Nam eirigh na gréine cuir fàilt' air a' bheinn,
Bu bhoidheach an airigh am braigh Chulchinn,
Na h'uiseagan 's na smeoraich cho ceol-mhor a' seinn,
'S na flùran a b' àluinn le 'm fàile 'ga inns'.
    O mar a bha 'nuair a bha sinn òg
    A' mireag air an airigh le manran is ceol.

Sibh-se tha cho fiosrach am Parlamaid na tìr
Thoraibh dhuinn na h-àirighean 's na mullaichean
    's na frith;
Is theid mi-fhèin an urras dhuibh mar dhuine 's fhaide chì
Gu'n dannsadh sinn 's gu'n seinneadh sinn, "gu ma fada beò
    an Rìgh".

A good deal of satirical verse in English saw the light of day in the newspapers favourable to the crofters. The week after the battle of the Braes, a parody of Tennyson's poem, "Charge of the Light Brigade", appeared in the *Oban Times*. The first verse gives the flavour of the satire.

"Half a league, half a league,
Four abreast onward.
All in the valley of Braes
Marched the half-hundred.
Forward, Police Brigade,
In front of me, bold Ivory said,
Into the valley of Braes
Charg'd the half-hundred."

James Simpson, a young shop manager in Glasgow, was a native of Achrinisdale near Brora in Sutherland, and was credited with the authorship of a clever parody of Burns's satire, "Holy Willie's Prayer", which contains a stinging attack on the Duke of Argyll. There was little common to Scotland's most powerful landlord and Burns's sanctimonious old sinner except that each believed that God was on his side but Simpson uses the original to make some telling phrases, as in the verses overleaf.

Holy Geordie's Prayer

Oh, Thou who in the heavens dost dwell
And seest my crofters all rebel
Just lend thy ear until I tell
    My story, too,
And if it seemeth meet, I quell
    Their curst ado.

And smite MacPherson of Glendale
And curse MacCallum, son of Baal.
Who quote Mosaic precepts stale
    To prop their cause
And teach the crofters how to rail
    Against my laws.

And bless the Peers, thy servants true,
Long may they fill the bench and pew.
And give them grace to rent and feu
    The sacred soil.
And chief among Thy chosen few
    Lord, bless Argyll.

Unification

At the Land Law Reform conference held at Bonar Bridge in Sutherland in September, 1886, the first steps were taken towards the unification of the various associations into one organization, the Highland Land League, a title similar to its Irish counterpart and the official name from the time of the Oban conference in 1887. At the annual general meeting of the London Highland Land Law Reform Association in June, 1886, Donald Murray, secretary of the Association since its inception, had expressed his wish to retire because his recent appointment as secretary of the National Liberal Club entailed such a schedule of engagements that it would leave him with little time to carry out efficiently his duties as secretary of the Association. In his report, he revealed a deficit of £49.10.9 in the general fund and a balance of £195.13/- in the Crofters' Defence Fund, a sum reflecting the steady flow of contributions from the public and a lull (temporarily, as it happened), in the prosecution of crofters and cottars. Murray, agreeing reluctantly to continue as secretary of the Association, which had 160 branches, suggested that the time had come for closer union with the Edinburgh and Sutherland Associations. At the Bonar Bridge conference Angus Sutherland, the M.P. for Sutherland, felt that it would be premature to proceed with negotiations for union. John MacLeod of Gartymore, representing the Sutherland Association, also favoured postponing a decision until the following year, and proposed that in addition to the three associations present at Bonar

Bridge the Federation of Celtic Societies should be included. Mac-Leod pointed out that the Sutherland Association had over 3,000 paid-up members and that union would mean £150 going annually into the general fund.

Discussion of the name of the new united organization produced suggestions such as Celtic League and Celtic Union, but in the end the conference decided on Highland Land League. The words "League" and "Leaguer" had been used in a pejorative sense by landlords, factors and anti-crofter newspapers for many years as if the main object of the reform associations was the violent overthrow of law and order on the Irish model. The aims of the Highland Land League, according to the resolution passed at Bonar Bridge, were to restore to the Highland people their inherent rights to their native soil, to resist the depopulation of the Highlands, to abolish the game laws, to amend the laws relating to sea, loch and river fishing, and restore to the people their foreshore rights, aims representing vague aspirations, still largely unfulfilled. The union of the three associations of London, Edinburgh and Sutherland, was approved reluctantly by the Sutherland delegates. From 1887 onwards, the annual conferences set the scenes for clashes between the different factions. The issues of Irish Home Rule and the proposed disestablishment of the Church of Scotland, which divided the Liberal party, also contributed to splits in the Highland Land League. At any rate, the Highland Land League, which in its origins had opposed the Liberal establishment, in time became part of that establishment and the Liberal tradition continued in the crofting counties down to the present day.

Notes

1. John Gunn MacKay had connections with both Sutherland and Skye. His father was a native of Rogart and his mother was a native of Bracadale, districts which had been subjected to savage clearances. MacKay himself was born at Lochalsh, where his father was schoolmaster, and was brought up in Skye. He went to Glasgow in 1870 to learn the drapery trade and was sacked by his employers after his outburst at the Irish Land League meeting, only to be reinstated soon afterwards. He was responsible for collecting 45,000 signatures to a petition to Parliament about crofters' conditions. He returned to Skye at the end of 1885 to start up on his own as a draper, and in November 1886 earned nation-wide publicity by his letter addressed to the *Inverness Courer* and the Scottish Secretary, denouncing Sheriff Ivory as a "judicial monster". He was arrested and put in jail but was never brought to trial. He later became a member of the newly-formed County Council for Inverness-shire and chairman of the county Liberal Association, declining on health grounds an invitation to stand for Parliament. He contributed articles to various newspapers on clan history and

the tartan under the pen-name of "MacAoidh" and produced a booklet, *History of the Highland Garb*. An interesting account of "J.G." (as he was familiarly known) is to be found in a series of articles by "Domhnall Donn" (Dr T.M. Murchison) in the *Stornoway Gazette* of August, 1974.

2. The father of Donald and James Murray was the Rev. Donald Murray, Free Church minister of Lochcarron in Wester Ross, formerly at Knock near Stornoway in Lewis. Both sons were active in the crofter movement: Donald became the first secretary of the London H.L.L.R.A. and James editor of the *Crofter* monthly. James died prematurely, partly as a result of overwork, and his funeral at Sandwick near Stornoway was attended by a huge crowd of mourners. The first M.P. for the Western Isles, after the constituency was created in 1918, was Dr Donald Murray, formerly Medical Officer of Health for Lewis, a near relative of the Lochcarron minister.

3. A copy of the branch rules of the London H.L.L.R.A. is included in the Appendix.

4. The Rev. Norman MacLean, son of the Braes schoolmaster, tells in his book, *The Former Days*, of Henry George's reception at a meeting in the Braes school. A charismatic figure, he had kept his audience enthralled until, in answer to a question, he criticised Peter for blaming Ananias, stating that Jesus would not have acted in such a way. Up stood an elder of the Free Church, who addressed the audience in Gaelic, claiming that this man from America would have them believe that he was a better man than the Apostle Peter, and then stalked out of the school, followed by all except the chairman and Henry George.

5. This is not the only song in praise of the shieling, which was part of the crofting practice of transhumance, keeping the cattle on the summer grazing to rest the township inbye land. In some cases, the summer grazings had been taken from the crofters or were situated miles from the crofts. The responsibility for the herding and milking of the cattle was undertaken by the township girls, who lived in small huts and busied themselves with making butter, cheese and crowdie, and carrying pails of milk to their homes. In the evenings they would welcome visits from the youths of the township and then would follow songs, music and youthful dalliance. The bards who composed these songs never seem to have experienced or had forgotten the midges and the rain which could made life miserable in the Highlands and Islands. A valuable account of some Lewis shielings is given in Donald MacDonald's *The Tolsta Townships* (1984). Two papers on the songs and poems of the crofters' agitation have been published in the *Transactions of the Gaelic Society of Inverness*, "Poetry of the Clearances" by Dr Sorley MacLean in vol. xxxviii (1962) and "Gaelic Poetry of the Land Agitation" by D.E. Meek in vol.xlix (1977). There are also two contrasting accounts — "Bards of the Movement" by Rev. Donald MacCallum in James Cameron's *The Old and The New Highlands and Hebrides* (1917) and "Gaelic Poets in the Lowlands and Highlands" by Derick Thomson in his *An Introduction to Gaelic Poetry* (1974).

CHAPTER 5

MILITARY EXPEDITION TO SKYE

Agitation in the Islands

It was not until the summer of 1886, more than two years after the publication of the Report of the Napier Commission, that the Crofters' Holdings Bill, which pleased nobody, became law. In the meantime crofters, encouraged by the prospect of reform in their favour, withheld their rents at the Whitsunday term of 1884; and at meetings of the Highland Land Law Reform Associations, sweeping claims were made and resolutions were passed, demanding "the land for the people", resolutions which were interpreted by the factors and Sheriff Ivory as "socialistic and destructive of society". It will be recalled that at the first conference of delegates from the various branches of the Highland Land Law Reform Associations, held at Dingwall in September 1884, among the resolutions passed was one in support of crofters' candidates at the next election, when the crofters would be able to vote. October 1884, with the men back from the Irish and east coast fishings, meant the recommencement of agitation in Skye and Lewis, this time on an unprecedented scale. At a meeting of over a thousand Skye crofters at the Quirang, a resolution was passed unanimously against the Kilmuir factor:

> "That we hereby resolve to pay no rent, nor have any dealings of any kind with Mr Alex. MacDonald, as factor for Major Fraser, on account of his gross misrepresentation of us before the Lord Advocate as well as for his many acts of tyranny and his backing of other unscrupulous characters who oppressed us in every conceivable way for many years; and that Major Fraser be requested to appoint a gentleman having at least a reputation for honour and integrity and having a practical knowledge of agriculture to be his factor; and that a copy of this resolution be sent to Major Fraser and the Lord Advocate."

This strongly-worded indictment could have come from the pen of Valtos schoolmaster, William MacKenzie, of whom Fraser had written to MacDonald that until the teacher was away from Valtos they could expect more or less trouble. The factor's meeting with the Lord Advocate had been as one of a deputation as far back as May 2, when MacDonald had refuted press allegations about "landlords' tyranny and oppression". According to the crofters, MacDonald had maintaned that those on whom notices to quit had been served had not been singled out because of Land League activities but only because of the

111

amount of their arrears. In Lewis, the deep-seated conviction in the rightness of their cause was reflected in the opening lines of the 46th Psalm, with which the vast assembly, singing in Gaelic, opened proceedings at the second of two mass demonstrations in favour of franchise and land law reform staged in Stornoway in October, 1884:

> 'S e dia a's tearmunn duinn gu beachd,
> ar spionnadh e 's ar treis.
> (God is our refuge and our strength,
> in straits a present aid.)

Resolutions were passed in favour of the franchise bill, the Highland Land Law Reform Association, legislation on the same lines as the Irish Land Act, and another pledged all those present to support a crofters' candidate at the next election.

Rumours

Garbled reports of the meeting appeared in the *Scotsman*, which throughout this period staunchly supported the landlords. The Lewis crofters were said to have decided on a "No Rent" policy, and the main speakers, the Rev. Angus MacIver of Uig and Alexander MacKenzie of Inverness, were portrayed as inciting their audience to breaches of the law. MacKenzie, who had advised his hearers to respect the law and at the end of the meeting had urged them to go straight home as if they were returning from a communion service, had actually been thanked by the local inspector of police for the part he played in ensuring that no untoward incident occurred. Although other newspapers favourable to the crofters, like the *Invergordon Times*, reported the same speakers as maintaining opposite views from those attributed by the *Scotsman*, it was the latter newspaper which had by far the widest influence in the south and particularly in official circles. Other newspaper reports, which seemed to indicate the imminent breakdown of the law in Skye and Lewis, were circulated by correspondents who naturally retailed rumours reflecting the political colours of their newspapers.

Copies of a handbill, which had presumably emanated from one of the embryonic Socialist groups in London, had been sent to the police authorities from the Home Office to enable them to check on its circulation. Its author seems to have had little knowledge of the Highlands:

> "Highlandmen! Crofters, cottars, delvers and others! Stand up like men before your oppressors! . . . Spare human life; kill no man except it be in self-defence; destroy the enemy's property . . . Roll rocks and boulders onto the railway lines, tear up the rails and do all other damage possible . . .

112

The oppressed toilers of England and the millions of disinherited people are watching your actions. Their hearts are with you in your battle for rights and liberty. God save the people!"

Although there is no evidence that this handbill was ever circulated (and it was not worth while circulating such a handbill in Skye or Lewis, neither of which possessed a railway), the authorities were again alarmed by false reports in the press that it was being distributed in both islands.

Another false rumour — that three men, James Urquhart, Uig Inn, Alexander MacLeod, farmer, Skudiburgh, and John MacKenzie, local manager, Uig, were to be forcibly carried to a crofters' meeting at Kilmuir to give explanations of their conduct — appeared in the *Inverness Courier* and *Scotsman* and was referred to by Sir William Harcourt, Home Secretary, in his speech in the House of Commons on November 14, when he announced the dispatch of a military expedition to Skye. Although there was no truth in the story and it was actually denied by two of the men in a letter to the *Inverness Courier*, it contributed to increased tension all round. Major Fraser, proprietor of Kilmuir, had asked the county authorities for additional police to be sent to Kilmuir in view of the report before it was denied. The Inverness-shire Police Committee, because of the apparent worsening of the situation, decided to send more police to Skye and to apply to the Home Secretary for a supply of 50 revolvers and 1,000 rounds of ammunition, with the necessary belts and pouches, for the protection of the police. The Home Secretary granted the request, adding that the small cutlass, a regulation issue at that time, was to be worn at night only or when rioting or serious public disturbance had taken place or was apprehended. The instructions may seem today slightly comic, but there was little doubt in the minds of those in authority about the gravity of a situation which called for such stern measures.

Sheriff Ivory

The person most concerned with the trouble arising out of the crofters' agitation and most insistent in his requests for military assistance was William Ivory, Sheriff of Inverness. The son of a Court of Session judge and, until 1880, leading the leisured life of a Highland Sheriff Principal on £700 a year, Ivory was called upon to act as the Government's executive officer responsible for the mainte-nance of law and order in Skye. A small man, 5 ft. 3 in. in height, with the abrasive character often found in men of his stature, he managed to quarrel with almost everyone he came in contact with, and worst of all with Chief Constable MacHardy of Inverness-shire — the two men were not even speaking to one another on the second military expedition in 1886. Sir Richard Cross, Home Secretary in Salisbury's "Caretaker" Government, which held office for a few months before the elections in November 1885, told his colleagues in the Cabinet that Sheriff Ivory was "quite unsuited for his place and ought to be got rid of"; but the Lord Advocate, who agreed with Cross, had to admit that it could not be done. When the second military expedition was in Skye in 1886, Cameron of Lochiel, in a letter to A.J. Balfour, Secretary for Scotland, blamed Ivory's "obstinacy and conceit," his "want of tact and judgement for making the task of controlling the crofters ten times more difficult," and hoped Ivory would resign his office, for which "he is quite unfitted, being in point of fact almost off his head". Balfour however stood by him, as he was almost bound to do at a time when Sheriff Ivory was denounced by John Gunn MacKay of Portree as a "judicial monster". One point in Ivory's favour, from the historian's point of view, may be mentioned here: he was most scrupulous in dealing with correspondence, and the Ivory Papers, now stored in the Scottish Record Office, fill five large boxes. Despite the stresses and strains of the 1880s, he managed to outlive most of his contemporaries and when he died in 1915 at the age of ninety he was "Father of the Bar".

Rout of the Police

The extra police whom the Chief Constable sent to Uig in response to Major Fraser's request, left Portree, nine of them altogether, on October 31, Hallowe'en, 1884, at 3 p.m., travelling by two "machines" as far as Glenhinnisdal Bridge, the march between the estates of Lord MacDonald and Major Fraser. They then went on foot towards Uig, and about 150 yards from Uig Inn they were met by a crowd of about 200, who asked the police why they had come. When Superintendent Aitchison and Inspector MacDonald answered that it was to keep the peace, they were told that in Uig the people never broke the peace. The crowd, in flagrant contradiction of this claim, then rushed on the policemen with yells and drove them back along the road to Portree, shoving and kicking them as they went. This incident induced Sheriff Ivory to make another appeal to the Lord Advocate for a gunboat and marines, a request which the Government reluctantly granted in the light of the sensational newspaper reports already referred to. Although the Sheriff and the police authorities described the Uig incident as a deforcement and asked for the prosecution of those reponsible, the Lord Advocate decided not to initiate proceedings against the Kilmuir crofters, as he was of the opinion that the people had opposed the police only because they were regarded as agents of the landlords, the County Police Committee being composed almost entirely of landlords. His decision was due also to a desire not to exacerbate the already-excited feelings of the people about the police; but it was naturally deplored by Sheriff Ivory and Alex. MacDonald and did little to increase the crofters' respect for the county authorities.

Portree Telegrams

One aspect of the clash between the police and the men of Uig on Hallowe'en, 1884, was not allowed by Sheriff Ivory to be forgotten. Two telegrams, signed "Friends Portree," had been sent from Portree Post Office on October 30 to crofters at Uig, warning them of a detachment of police bound for Uig, and one of them concluded: "Meet them and turn back and drive them past the Hinnisdal." Other telegrams, also signed "Friends Portree," were sent to Kilmuir and Glendale a fortnight later at the time of the arrival of the military expedition. Two of these last telegrams were definitely sent by Dugald MacLachlan, Sheriff Clerk Depute at Portree since 1866, agent of the Caledonian Bank, and a man who made no secret of his sympathy with the crofters, having acted as intermediary on their behalf at the time of the Braes dispute. MacLachlan admitted writing the later telegrams; one of them, addressed to the secretary of the Staffin branch of the H.L.L.R.A., Archibald MacDonald, Garrafad, whom he told to burn all letters at once, appeared to the authorities most incriminating. But, when challenged, he stoutly denied writing the earlier telegrams. According to Sheriff Ivory, who had insisted, in contravention of Post Office regulations, on seeing the originals, the handwriting of those inciting the Uig crofters to resist the police was that of MacLachlan, and he asked the Sheriff Clerk of the county to dismiss MacLachlan. This request the Sheriff Clerk refused, as also did the Lord Advocate, when Ivory approached him. The Liberal Government fell in June 1885, however, and the Tory Government which came in under Salisbury was more amenable to suggestions of this kind so that Sheriff Ivory, who pursued his prey like a terrier, was able to persuade the Tory Lord Advocate to dismiss MacLachlan.

Arrival of Expedition

The military expedition, so fervently and so long desired by Sheriff Ivory, arrived at Portree on Sunday, November 16, 1884, two days after a seven-hour debate in the House of Commons, during which the Home Secretary, Sir William Harcourt, announced his decision to authorise the expedition. Harcourt, who confessed to a deep sympathy and regard for the crofters, whom he had come to know and

115

admire in twenty years of sailing on the coast of Skye and other islands, had obviously taken his decision only with great reluctance; and he confessed to more anxiety over the Skye troubles than over the Irish "Dynamitards." In a letter written ten days before the debate to the Marquis of Lorne, who had blamed "canting and blasphemous ministers" for the agitation, Harcourt pointed out that all classes of men sympathised with the crofters. "I have been begged by the landlords," he wrote, "when asked to send troops to Skye, not to send

SHERIFF IVORY AND OFFICIAL PARTY APPROACHING PORTREE, 1884.

Highland troops. What a damning admission!" He went on to criticise the "ruthless and grasping avarice" of the Highland proprietors, "unequalled elsewhere," and confessed to a wish to resign office "in order that the landlord party might themselves have the handling of the frightful evils they have themselves created."[1] The reports of threats and violence, culminating in the clash between crofters and police on 31 October at Uig in Skye, had at last induced him to yield to the requests of Sheriff Ivory and the Inverness-shire Police Committee. But at the same time, in announcing the dispatch of an expedition, he included in his speech an appeal to the Highland proprietors to make some sacrifices to solve the questions confronting him.

The expeditionary force, the first sent to Skye since the time of the Jacobite Rebellion, comprised a troopship, H.M.S. *Assistance*, two gunboats, the *Forester* and the *Banterer*, with 350 marines and 100 bluejackets, and MacBrayne's steamer, the *Lochiel*, carrying the Sheriff, the Sheriff Clerk, the Chief Constable and a body of police drawn from the mainland districts of the county. Before its arrival, counsels of moderation were imparted to the crofters, by telegram and by letter, from leading members of the H.L.L.R.A. in Inverness, Glasgow and London. At a meeting at Uig on Saturday, November 15, the day before the expedition arrived, pacific speeches were

116

delivered by John MacPherson of Glendale, who nevertheless claimed that the only remedy for their grievances was to give the people the land which God gave and created for all, and by Duncan Cameron of the *Oban Times*, who played a prominent part in Skye affairs during the next month. It was also agreed at the Uig meeting to send a deputation to Sheriff Ivory to assure him that anyone charged with an offence would surrender at Portree for justice. MacPherson and Cameron, as delegates from the meeting, had an interview on board the *Lochiel* that same evening with Ivory. Although he informed them that he would forward their resolutions to the Home Office, he had waited so long and so avidly for the expedition that he would not undertake to call it off, the expedition being then on its way north.

On Monday, November 17, the expeditionary force made its first foray from Portree, the small flotilla sailing round the north end of Skye to Uig Bay. There they met with a quiet reception from the local inhabitants. The Rev. James Davidson, minister of the *quoad sacra* parish of Stenscholl, had ridden over from Staffin to assure Sheriff Ivory of the peaceful intentions of the crofters. Sixteen newspapers' correspondents from the south, with two artists representing the *Graphic* and *Illustrated London News*, were there for the much-heralded confrontation of troops and crofters and must have felt some disappointment when things passed off quietly, particularly the *North British Daily Mail* reporter, whose paper, only two days before, had carried sensational headlines — "Threatened General Rising of Crofters" and "Dunvegan Men on the March to Uig". For the rest of the week the *Mail's* report from the scene of operations was headed (hopefully perhaps) "The Revolt in Skye," but in the following week the standard headline was merely "Affairs in Skye". The newspaper reporters, who followed the expeditionary force in two waggonettes (Duncan Cameron of Oban riding sometimes on the Stenscholl minister's horse), experienced a great deal of difficulty in sending their dispatches, generally of considerable length, to their offices in the south, either through Uig or Portree Post Offices. To be first with his telegrams was the aim of each reporter; and on one occasion Cameron was offered a seat in the waggonette in exchange for riding horseback, the reporter who had evinced such generosity, Ross of the *Northern Chronicle*, then riding off hell-for-leather to Portree with his dispatches for head office.[2]

Mrs Gordon Baillie

It was during the first week of the expedition that John MacPherson, the "Glendale Martyr," as he was everywhere known, was made the recipient of a sword, presented by Mrs Gordon Baillie, an English sympathiser with the crofters. It was sent on ahead of Mrs Gordon Baillie, who in a letter to John MacPherson asked him to accept the sword, which had belonged to her grandfather, as a token of her appreciation of his gallant struggle against the oppressors of the people.[3] She concluded her letter: "All England watches your struggle against tyrants, landlords and hard-hearted factors. God save the cause!" Mrs Gordon Baillie arrived in Skye a few days later in the company of R.P.B. Frost, secretary of the English Land Restoration League, who addressed the crofters of Glendale and other districts of Skye. Mrs Baillie, who was also accompanied by an elderly lady and a young male secretary, gave out to reporters that it was her intention to write a novel about the sufferings of the Skye people. That she was a woman of considerable charm there is little doubt, as may be surmised from the report of an interview with her in the *Aberdeen Journal*:

> "Large brown sanguine eyes beamed lustrously from beneath a profusion of fair hair, falling in curls over her forehead — eyes that are penetrative and keen till they have got something to fasten on that amuses her fancy, when instantly the corners pucker, and a burst of merry laughter is the result."

It transpired, after her visit to the Highlands and Skye, that she had left without paying any of her bills. Three years later the mystery of her identity was revealed when she was convicted of several charges of fraud and sentenced to five years' penal servitude in 1888. The real name of this accomplished adventuress, as the *Scottish Highlander* termed her, was Mary Ann Bruce Sutherland, daughter of a Dundee washerwoman. She had been an evening-school teacher and an evangelist at one time or another and had travelled in England and on the continent before her first conviction for fraud in 1872. Her companion in Skye, the Socialist Frost, father of one of her five illegitimate children, was given an eighteen-month sentence at the same court on similar charges.

Marines on the March

Alex. MacDonald, factor for most of the Skye estates, had hoped that the military expedition would assist the civil authorities in the vindication of the law by backing up sheriff officers in the service of summonses which had not been delivered because of deforcements in the Braes and Glendale earlier in the year. But the Lord Advocate, J.B. Balfour, had made it clear to Sheriff Ivory that the Home Secretary would not permit the employment of the troops for such a purpose. In the circumstances, Ivory decided on a policy of marching the marines through the disturbed areas as a display of strength. Uig, part of Major Fraser's Kilmuir estate, had been the first place chosen for the marines to show the flag, on Monday, November 17. At the end of the week, on Friday, November 21, the troopship *Assistance* dropped anchor in Loch Dunvegan opposite Colbost and disembarked 100 marines and 15 policemen to march over to Glendale, where a company of soldiers was to be billeted in Hamara Lodge. Accompanying the force was the Sheriff of Inverness, William Ivory, with a copy of the Riot Act in his pocket in case of trouble. At the crest of the hill, unseen by the troops, a crofters' meeting was being held, presided over by John MacPherson. As the marines approached, they heard a cheer ring out from the six hundred crofters, not as a greeting to them but in appreciation of a speech just delivered by Frost, the English Socialist, who had told his audience that patience in waiting for the Government to introduce legislation might cease to be a virtue. Frost, by representing himself as the representative of the *Pall Mall Gazette*, had been entertained on board the *Lochiel* by Sheriff Ivory, who was shocked by the sight of the English agitator, wearing a magenta tam o' shanter and addressing the crofters.

The marches of the marines had little effect in damping the spirits of the crofters, who continued to flock to their meetings to hear the orators from the mainland. But in the absence of any disturbance, the Admiralty and the Home Secretary agreed by the beginning of December on the withdrawal of the bulk of the marines, detachments of soldiers to be left at strategic points in the disturbed areas — 15 at Staffin Lodge, 15 at Hamara Lodge, 10 at Uig Hotel, 10 at Dunvegan Hotel, 10 at Portree. There the marines were to remain until the expedition finally left Skye at the end of June 1885. When Ivory and MacHardy, the Chief Constable, decided at the same time to reduce the number of extra police who had been drafted in from the mainland and dismissed the *Lochiel*, the steamer in which the police had been quartered, Harcourt saw in their action a desire to save the county authorities from more expense while still leaving the national exchequer responsible for the maintenance of the marines. The Home Secretary was particularly incensed as Sheriff Ivory had not consulted him or the Lord Advocate over the withdrawal of the steamer and the police; and in turn he threatened to withdraw all the troops from Skye, a threat which Ivory foolishly countered by arguing that, for their own safety, the police would have to be withdrawn also. Neither threat, it need scarcely be added, was carried out.

As there was little or nothing for the marines to do in their outposts, it was natural that in time there developed a friendly relationship between them and the Skye people. When the marines left Uig in June 1885 they received a farewell message, couched in the most friendly terms, from the local crofters, shopkeepers and other residents in Uig, stating that the marines had shown the kindest interest and good feelings towards them. The marines at Staffin seem to have shown an even kinder interest in the women folk of the district as, according to William Nicolson of Marishader, speaking at a meeting in Staffin after the marines had left, "They gave more of their time to the god of love than to the god of war".

"No Rent" Campaign

But although marines and crofters fraternised, there was still plenty for the authorities to worry about, particularly when a "No Rent" campaign began to gather force. On Monday, December 1, a meeting was held in Glendale, presided over by Duncan Cameron of the *Oban Times*. Cameron was almost certainly responsible for the wording of the Glendale meeting's resolution on December 1, declaring the inability of the crofters of Glendale to pay their rents at the next term and accompanied by petitions from each township giving reasons for their inability to pay. During the next few days, in advocating this form of a "No Rent" policy, Cameron addressed meetings, along with John MacPherson of Glendale and the Rev. Donald MacCallum, at Edinbane, the Braes, Kensaleyre and Uig, at which last meeting he was introduced to the huge gathering as the prospective candidate for Inverness-shire. The resolutions at Cameron's meetings showed that the determination of the crofters not to yield to the factors had not been weakened but, if anything, strengthened since the expedition had arrived.

Deforcements

Attempts to serve summonses for non-payment of arrears while the marines remained in the island were no more successful than in previous years. Major Fraser of Kilmuir had suggested to Alex. MacDonald, the factor, that the military expedition's presence might be utilised to serve summonses of removal on men he listed as "badly disposed," who like nearly all their neighbours were in arrears and therefore liable for such a summons.[4] Fraser had also decided to offer an olive branch to the crofters in the form of a 25 per cent reduction (or "abatement," as he termed it) in the rent, which served to reinforce the crofters' conviction that they had formerly been overrented. A sheriff officer from Portree, John Lamont, attempting to serve summonses was, however, deforced in Kilmuir on 26 December, and a month later three Kilmuir men were arrested and tried in Portree Sheriff Court. One of the accused was Norman Stewart, "Parnell," of Valtos, who successfully defended himself at the trial against the

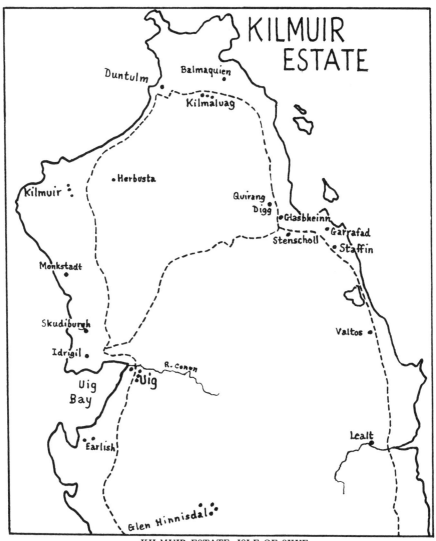

KILMUIR ESTATE, ISLE OF SKYE.

charges of mobbing and rioting, bringing witnesses forward to testify to his efforts to prevent violence during the deforcement. Sheriff Ivory indiscreetly sent to the *Scotsman* a copy of his confidential report on the case to the Lord Advocate. In this report, which was published in February, a month before the trial, Ivory stated:

"We apprehended Norman Stewart, alias Parnell, the leading ringleader of the mob and the principal promoter of the former lawless proceedings in the district."

This libellous statement, for which Ivory could not claim the privilege accorded to him in the document if it had been kept confidential, was made the basis of a claim for damages by "Parnell," with the backing of the newly-established Crofters' Rights Vindication Fund; and the Sheriff, in June, 1887, had to suffer the humiliation of losing the case and paying £25 damages to the Valtos crofter. The four policemen who effected the arrests after a lengthy chase had been rewarded by Sheriff Ivory for what he called their "special and meritorious services" by the presentation of a small silver pendant, intended to be attached to their watch-chains; but his gesture of generosity was not welcomed by the Chief Constable and was greeted with ridicule in the press.

Another deforcement occurred at Glendale on December 30, a few days after the Kilmuir deforcement. As the Skye sheriff officers were unwilling to serve summonses, one had been brought from Inverness, Daniel John Grant; but he suffered the same fate as Lamont. His method of serving the first summons by throwing it into the door of a widow's house in Holmisdal in Glendale was resented by her son, Peter MacKinnon, who collected his neighbours by sounding a horn, the usual procedure in Glendale at that time; and the sheriff officer and his two "concurrents" (one of whom had formerly been a policeman at Dunvegan and was very unpopular with the local people), were driven five miles back along the road to Dunvegan. Later, the deforcers were taken into custody without any disturbance and given mild sentences by Sheriff-Substitute Speirs at Portree. Kenneth MacDonald, Town Clerk of Inverness, who acted as defence lawyer in this case, as in many similar cases, led no evidence in order, as he put it, to shorten the time of the court; he put forward pleas of guilty on a reduced charge for two of the prisoners and asked for verdicts of "Not guilty" for the others. MacDonald maintained that the authorities (i.e. the Crown Office) had not taken a serious view of the offence or they would not have remitted the case to be dealt with summarily in the local court. Sheriff Speirs was an amiable individual, much put out by having to act as a judge in such difficult times, and he accepted the defence lawyer's representations. His lengthy homily to the Glendale accused did not please his superiors nor did it have any noticeable effect on his audience.

"Now, I know you have your agitation, and whether right or wrong, I do not pretend to know, you have your grievances. Lots of grievances no doubt would never be brought to light if not for agitation, but let me remind you that these agitations and these meetings are very apt to turn into lawlessness in the end" —

and much more in the same vein.

John MacPherson and the Sheriff

It was when the arrest of the Glendale deforcers was being effected on January 29 that Sheriff Ivory and John MacPherson engaged in a conversation which was later to be reported in almost every Scottish newspaper. MacPherson had asked the Sheriff to come up the road to see the fence at Waterstein, about which complaints had been made. But it was very wet and Ivory had said: "Well, John, if His Majesty upstairs would give us dry weather, I might go." Ivory seemed to have been in one of his rare jocular moods as he went on to say that God had made some parts of the earth "very good" and others (presumably in Skye) "deuced bad". When John MacPherson ventured to question the authority which Sheriff Ivory took upon himself in ordering arrests, the Sheriff claimed that he had the authority to kill every man in Glendale, adding that if he did not have powder and shot enough there in Glendale, "there is plenty in England which is at my disposal." The Rev. Donald MacCallum, in a letter to the *Oban Times*, gave full publicity to what he called "the profanity and idiotic conversation" of Sheriff Ivory, whom he characterised as "a profane, reckless creature". Ivory thought for a time about suing MacCallum but refrained.

By this time, John MacPherson and the Rev. Donald MacCallum were constantly in demand as speakers at Land Law Reform meetings. Latterly, MacPherson was paid a regular £1 a week (plus expenses) by the H.L.L.R.A. MacPherson's eloquence and humour seldom failed to make an impression on his audience, whether he spoke in Gaelic or in English. According to MacCallum,

"His Gaelic prayers at the opening of all our meetings, made by this lovable man, were well worth hearing, even if one went all the way to Glendale for nothing else."

The *Pall Mall Gazette*, the day after MacPherson, the Rev. Donald MacCallum and Duncan Cameron all addressed a meeting in London on behalf of the crofters, gave the report of an interview with MacPherson, of whom the writer (the future Lord Milner) wrote:

"No one can look at the fine head and honest, engaging face — a little careworn perhaps but with a bright gleam of intelligence in the eyes and the play of humour lighting up the features, — without feeling irresistibly attracted by this genuine son of the soil."

It may be added that MacPherson was a cousin of Neil MacLeod, the Skye bard, and brother-in-law of Professor Magnus MacLean, the eminent scientist and author of *The Literature of the Highlands.*

Service of Summonses

The two trials referred to above — those of the Valtos and Glendale deforcers — did not prevent further deforcements, at Waternish on March 27 and at Kilmuir on April 1, 1885. The sheriff officer deforced on both occasions was Daniel Grant, who, as has been stated, had been brought over to Skye from Inverness as the local sheriff officers were unwilling to act. The service of a summons required not only a sheriff officer but also a concurrent as witness to the service. Even to procure a concurrent for the Inverness sheriff officer proved most difficult and, in the cases of Glendale and Braes summonses, impossible. Alex. MacDonald, whose duty as factor it was to make arrangements for serving summonses, found himself foiled at almost every turn but continued to struggle on manfully in the execution of his duties. "This is no time for cowards or men who wish to shirk their duty", he wrote, in reference to the reluctance of the Kilmuir ground officer, Ewan Campbell, to act as a concurrent. Both MacDonald and Sheriff Webster of Lochmaddy in North Uist considered that the effect of the two deforcement trials, at which Norman Stewart, "Parnell," had been acquitted and the Glendale men had received "trifling punishments," had "rather encouraged lawlessness than otherwise", and had made matters "ten times as difficult to manage". Sheriff Ivory himself, in a letter to the Lord Advocate in March and, again, in a report to the county Commissioners of Supply in April, maintained that the Isle of Skye was in a more disturbed state than before the expedition arrived.

The county authorities had from the first been hampered by the Home Secretary's insistence that the marines must not be used for the protection of sheriff officers and police in the service of civil summonses unless disorder or violence was imminent or expected. Sheriff Ivory and Alex. MacDonald could certainly point to previous deforcements and to resolutions passed at Land Law Reform meetings as reasons for expecting disorder or violence at the service of summonses. But the Home Secretary and the Lord Advocate were adamant that the county authorities should use more police as protection for the sheriff officers in the execution of civil summonses, the marines being called upon to help only with the arrest of anyone who had attacked or assaulted the police. According to Major Fraser of Kilmuir, it was widely held in Inverness that Harcourt's attitude had neutralised the effects which landlords and factors had hoped would accrue from the expedition. Ivory's frustration in April 1885 was such that in one letter to the Lord Advocate he threatened to disclaim all responsibility for the consequences as little or no attention had been paid to his views; and he went so far as to suggest again to the county Police Committee that if the Government would not permit the marines to be used in protection of the sheriff officers, the county should also refuse to allow the police to do so. The Home Secretary, who was most irascible by nature, was furious on hearing of Ivory's suggestion. Writing to Cameron of Lochiel, he declared that the Highland landlords were bent on self-destruction and that he would not use troops to —

> "become the bum-bailiffs of Major Fraser and the Police Committee of Inverness . . . if the Highland landlords choose to have a rent roll which drives their people into insurrection, they must spare part of it in order to keep down the rebellion they have caused — at all events Her Majesty's Government will not do it for them".

Stalemate

By May 1885 a stalemate had been reached, and arrangements were made for the withdrawal of the marines, which took place in the last week of June. Proprietors and factors, unable to exact payment of arrears by serving summonses, could only anticipate that the volume of arrears would grow as a result of the crofters continuing to withhold their rents at the Whitsunday term, encouraged by rumours that the Government would arrange for cancellation of all arrears as in Ireland. While the crofters, following the advice proffered to them by their friends in Inverness and in the south, had on the whole refrained from breaches of the law, their resistance to factors, landlords and police had hardened since the arrival of the expedition. Whether the marines could have been used to greater advantage from the Government's point of view is a moot point. Sir Richard Cross, the Home Secretary in Salisbury's Conservative Government, which held office from the end of June to the elections in November, was of the opinion that the expedition had been quite useless. Writing in September 1885 to the Duke of Richmond and Gordon, the first Secretary for Scotland in modern times, Cross refused to consider a military expedition to Lewis, where violent scenes had been reported:—

> "I certainly do not wish to bring back marines if it can possibly be avoided. The late Government brought them, paraded them about, did nothing with them and sent them away . . . It is their course of action which makes our own so difficult now."

Notes

1. Queen Victoria replied to a letter of Sir William Harcourt of November 24, 1884, stating that it would not do to encourage the crofters in their "wild and impossible demands, the result, to a great extent, of Irish agitators' preaching of sedition" (A.G. Gardiner, *Sir William Harcourt*, I, 523).

2. On the Sunday after the arrival of Sheriff Ivory and the expedition in Skye, according to the *Scotsman*, the minister at Uig preached a sermon on the text, 1 Kings, 10, 22: "Once in every three years came the navy of Tharsish bringing gold and silver, ivory and apes and peacocks", (*Scotsman*, Dec. 19, 1884).

3. The sword which was presented to John MacPherson is now in the possession of Mrs Norman MacPherson, Glendale, and was displayed by his grandson, Dr Charles D. Ferguson, Lochcarron, when he unveiled a memorial cairn to the "Glendale Land Leaguers" in 1970. A highly-coloured account of Mrs Gordon Baillie's visit to Skye and other episodes of the Crofters' War may be found in the Rev. Norman MacLean's *The Former Days*, cited above.

4. The list of "badly disposed" tenants, named by Major Fraser as suitable for removal, contained men from different townships:— John MacLeod, Earlish; John MacLeod, "Gladstone", Idrigil; Donald Matheson, Feaull; Charles MacDonald, Balmacquien; Archibald MacDonald, Garrafad; Charles MacArthur, Elishader; Donald Matheson, Elishader; Wm. Nicolson, Marishader; Norman Stewart, "Parnell", Valtos; Murdo MacLean, Lealt.

CHAPTER 6

GRAZING DISPUTES

Island Grazings

One of the most common causes of landlord-tenant confrontation in the 1880s was the question of grazings which had at one time belonged to crofters and had passed into the hands of tacksmen or farmers. This was the issue in the Braes and Glendale disputes in Skye and similarly in Lewis, where crofter tenants attempted to claim possession of grazings in different parts of the island. The earliest challenges came from the people of Uig on the south-west side of Lewis, the land of the MacAulays, at one time a powerful clan. In the nineteenth century it was notable for its farms and sporting estates, the creation of which had involved clearances and the loss of grazings. By successfully rebelling in 1874 against the Lewis estate management and bringing about the downfall of the domineering factor, Donald Munro, the

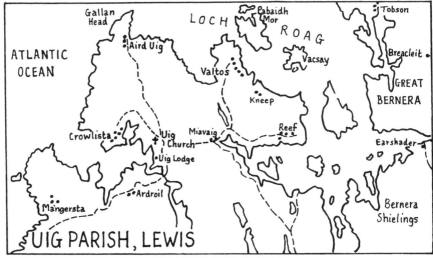

UIG PARISH, ISLE OF LEWIS.

Bernera crofters had set a precedent for other crofter tenants to follow. The parish of Uig, one of the most extensive in Scotland, had an indented coast-line and numerous off-shore islands, some of them mere skerries but others inhabited or used for grazing sheep or cattle. Even before the Napier Commission provided an opportunity for the

127

crofters to ventilate their grievances, the tenants of Valtos and Kneep began to copy the Irish practice of boycotting neighbouring tacksmen, forcing the removal of domestic servants and refusing to work for them on any terms. From a small tradesman, who refused to attend crofters' meetings, they also withdrew their custom. In February, 1883, they announced their intention of withholding their rents until they were given more land and rumour had it that they intended to take possession of a neighbouring tack. The Napier Commission visited Uig at the beginning of June when Murdo MacLean, Valtos, and Donald Matheson, Kneep, recounted to the commissioners the story of the loss of their island grazings as far back as 1827 in the time of the Seaforths.

After the Napier Commission hearings there ensued a period of waiting first for the Commission's report, which came out at the end of April, 1884, and afterwards for the implementation of the recommendations of the report. In the summertime, agitation tended to die down, only to revive with renewed strength in the autumn. In both the Braes and the Glendale disputes, the initiative seemed to have come from the men who had been at the east-coast and Irish fishings. In Lewis, it was the young Royal Naval Reservists who were most prominent in the agitation. Lewis navymen were very highly regarded by the Admiralty. In 1888 Surgeon Lieutenant Roper of the gunboat, H.M.S. *Jackal*, described the men of Lewis as well-built, powerful, healthy-looking and exceedingly intelligent; and in 1890, after an inspection of the R.N.R. trainees in Stornoway, the Duke of Edinburgh declared that they were the finest body of men he had ever set eyes upon. There were generally about 1000 reservists in Stornoway during the summer engaged in their four weeks' training, in return for which they were entitled, when trained, to £6 a year and a suit of clothes. In addition, about 500 young militia men went through to Fort George near Inverness in summer for training. The by-election in August, 1884, in Ross and Cromarty, provided an opportunity for Dr MacDonald, a champion of the crofters, to make himself and his views known to the public, although he had no hope of winning a seat in Parliament until the franchise was extended to include the crofters. The growth of agitation was marked by the staging of the two mass demonstrations in Stornoway, one on October 2 and the other on October 16, and both attended by hundreds of men, young and old, from townships all over the island.

Valtos Deforcement

When William MacKay, chamberlain of the Lewis estate, went to Uig for the rent collection on September 29, 1884, a large crowd gathered at Miavaig House, where MacKay was to receive the rents; and a band of young men arrived, carrying two banners, which they set up in front of the house. One banner bore the words "Down with Landlords" and the other "*Is treasa tuatha na tighearna* (The tenant is stronger than the laird)". A man came forward and presented a paper containing a list of requests, including a demand for more land (but at the old rent), and the removal of squatters. Next day, when the chamberlain attended for rent collection at Glen Valtos, young men were again conspicuous and a few days later tenants of Tobson in Great Bernera placed some of their cattle on the small islands of Pabaidh Mór and Little Bernera, the grazings of which were let to James MacKenzie, tacksman of Linshader. In the middle of what threatened to become a developing confrontation, Lady Matheson, proprietrix of Lewis, who had returned to the island in mid-September after an absence of two years, appeared at Miavaig with three friends to whom she wished to show the new shooting lodge. When she heard of the trouble between chamberlain and tenants, she

LEWS CASTLE, STORNOWAY, 1888.

declared herself prepared to investigate their grievances. Of the crofters invited to Uig Lodge to meet Lady Matheson, all but one declared that they had no stock on the tacksman's island grazings and that they were willing to pay their rents but that the young men would not allow them. "How many young men?" asked Lady Matheson. "About 150", replied the spokesman. He received a surprising answer — "Why did you not fight your way through them?"

The farmers whose island grazings were taken over by the crofters or their sons decided on the same policy as that adopted in Skye by the proprietors — vindicating the law (as they claimed) by raising an action of interdict. This was begun by James MacKenzie of Linshad-

129

er, tenant of the island grazings of Little Bernera and Pabaidh Mór, on November 29, 1884, and similarly by Alexander MacRae of Ardroil, tenant of the island grazings of Vacsay and Vuia Mhór.

An attempt to serve notices of interdict in December by George Nicolson, a messenger-at-arms from Edinburgh, was thwarted by a group of young men, who obstructed Nicolson by barring his entry to the first three houses he visited in Valtos, assaulted him and his concurrents with stones and clods, and chased them back to Miavaig. This deforcement happened when the military expedition was operating in Skye, and the Lord Advocate and Home Secretary, who had taken so long before sanctioning the use of military force to assist the civil authorities, informed Sheriff Macintosh, Sheriff Principal of Ross and Cromarty, when he requested military assistance, that a gunboat would be placed at his disposal. On Christmas Day 1884 (which at that time was just an ordinary day for the people of the Hebrides), the gunboat *Seahorse* steamed into Loch Roag and anchored off Miavaig. On board were county officials, Sheriff Macintosh, Chief Constable Munro, Procurator Fiscal Ross from Stornoway, Superintendent Cameron from Tain, a small party of police, and, in addition to the ship's crew, a force of 75 Marines. Superintendent Cameron had only recently left Lewis after many years' service and was strongly opposed to the use of force at the outset, arguing that a quiet approach would be more likely to induce the wanted men to surrender.[1] With the Marines and police still on board, Cameron walked from Miavaig to Valtos, where he was met by a group of older men, who expressed their regret for what had happened. The 9 wanted men quietly surrendered when their names were called and were marched to Miavaig, from where they were taken aboard the gunboat. All were young, the ages ranging from 17 to 28, and at least 4 were in the R.N.R., wearing the reservist's uniform. All were from Valtos except Murdo MacDonald and Peter Matheson, who hailed from Kneep.

After the prisoners were safely on board the gunboat, the Marines were sent ashore and marched through the township in a display of military strength to intimidate any with feelings of reprisal. The generally peaceful attitude of the local people was typified by the request of some young men to see over the warship; and when they were invited aboard they brought some freshly-caught fish as a present. After sailing round the Butt of Lewis, the *Seahorse* arrived in Stornoway on a Sunday, and large, silent crowds watched the prisoners being marched off to prison. The next morning they were liberated on bail. Their case came up on February 6 but through delays and adjournments Sheriff Black of Stornoway gave his decision on February 21, sentencing John MacAulay, Valtos, one of the youngest accused, to 50 days' imprisonment, Donald Morrison, Valtos, one of the oldest accused, to 40 days, Peter MacDonald and Malcolm Matheson, both of Valtos, to 30 days, and the two Kneep men, Murdo MacDonald and Peter Matheson, to 10 days, while the charge against Kenneth MacLean, Valtos, was dropped. Both the Sheriff and the Procurator Fiscal, William Ross, were severely criticised in the press for their handling of the case. Even the *Scotsman*, which normally took the landlords' side, was forthright in its condemnation of the "inexcusable carelessness" and "great want of discretion" on the part of the Sheriff and Procurator Fiscal. In cross-examination of the Rev. Angus MacIver, a witness for the defence, Black told him that it was "the parson's duty to persuade the people to give up their occupation of the tacksman's grazings and pay their rents", adding that the Lewis crofters were "a shocking bad lot". His summing-up was described as an "extraordinary harangue" and lasted almost three hours. On appeal, the sentences were quashed and an order for the liberation of the prisoners was granted by Lord MacLaren on March 6. The people of Uig were by no means induced to change their policy so far as the occupied grazings were concerned and kept their stock on the islands they had seized.

Township Bulls

The next move came from the landlord's side. It was decided by the Lewis chamberlain, William MacKay, to attempt the removal of crofters' cattle from the islands of Pabaidh Mór and Little Bernera, let to James MacKenzie of Linshader, and Vacsay and Vuia, let to Alexander MacRae of Ardroil, both tenants having obtained inter-dicts against the crofters. A steamer, the *Norseman* of Glasgow, was chartered, and on May 5, 1885, arrived off the shore of Uig with MacKay in charge of a small landing party — two gamekeepers, a river watcher, two shepherds from Linshader farm and a crofter from Callanish, who was said to be willing to do anything for money. Operations started well to the south of Valtos, at the farm of Mealista, the tenant of which, John Mitchell, had attempted as far back as January to raise an action of interdict against the crofters of the nearby township of Brenish but, failing to appear or be represented, had lost his case and had to pay costs and damages. On the island of Mealista, the crofters of Brenish had pastured the township bull and MacKay decided to remove the bull, which proved a simple operation. The *Norseman* then steamed north to Pabaidh Mór, the island grazing of James MacKenzie of Linshader, and removed nine cattle and nine sheep on to the steamer. By this time the alarm had been raised and Valtos and Kneep men set off in boats to intercept the chamberlain's raiding party, which had proceeded to the island of Vuia Mhór, in order to remove the bull belonging to the people of Aird Uig, a township near Valtos. Not only did the Valtos men prevent the seizure of the bull and recover the animals taken from Pabaidh Mór but they took in tow one of the *Norseman's* boats and its occupants, the sheriff officer, John Fraser, and seven assistants, all the way to near Valtos. There they were released and their boat, which had been carried a quarter of a mile inland, was retrieved only with difficulty.

The trial of the deforcers was fixed for September 22 but the accused ignored the summonses. Before that date, an attempt was made on August 28 by the Lewis estate officials to transport cattle from Reef farm, the tenant of which was James MacKenzie of Linshader, to Pabaidh Mór. The cattle were being gathered on the shore at Reef by a strong body of estate employees and shepherds under William MacLennan, sub-factor, ten able-bodied men in all, when they were attacked by a mob consisting entirely of women. Brandishing sticks, rattling pails, and yelling, they prevented the embarkation of the cattle. The foremost among the women — Mary Smith, daughter of Murdo Smith; Margaret MacLennan, daughter of Alexander MacLennan; Ann MacIver, daughter of Murdo MacIver; Christina Morrison, daughter of Angus Morrison; Ann MacKay, wife of Hugh MacKay; Margaret MacIver, daughter of Widow Catherine MacIver (all of Valtos except the last, who was from Aird Uig) — at first ignored the summonses from the Sheriff Court. Once again, Superintendent Cameron of Tain was called upon to act as peacemaker, and he managed to persuade the men involved in the affair of May 5, 1885, to appear in court on March 6, 1886, the same day as that of the women's trial. Before the trial, the Valtos and Kneep men — Peter MacDonald, Malcolm Matheson, Donald Smith, Angus MacLeod, Norman MacIver, Murdo MacDonald, Murdo MacLeod, Allan Morrison, Donald MacLennan, William MacDonald — had taken an unprecedented step, writing to the Stornoway Sheriff a letter, in which they declared their willingness to appear in court provided the punishment was restricted to a fine. Whether the Sheriff's decision was influenced by this letter or by the pleas of guilty and the contrite expression of regret, or both, the sentences were undoubtedly light — a fine of 20/- or 18 days' imprisonment for each of the accused except Malcolm Matheson and Murdo MacDonald, who failed to appear, as a result of which the charges against them were dropped. The women, who also pled guilty, were sentenced on the same day — a fine of 5/- each or 3 days' imprisonment.

Dalmore and Dalbeg

Between Carloway and Shawbost on the west side of the Isle of Lewis lie Dalmore and Dalbeg, less than a mile apart, with their green meadows and silver sand reaching down to the Atlantic. Early in the 1850s, after the purchase of Lewis by James (later Sir James) Matheson, both villages were cleared. Dalbeg had the unusual distinction of possessing an inn, one of only three licensed premises in Lewis outside Stornoway at that time. There was a farm attached to the inn; and five crofters, Malcolm Morrison, John Maciver, Malcolm MacLeod, Kenneth Murray, Malcolm MacKay and their families, were removed to give more land to the innkeeper, Donald MacKenzie.

Three years after the Dalbeg clearance, the twenty families in Dalmore were evicted and their lands attached to the Dalbeg farm, MacKenzie's rent being raised from £55 to £100 per annum for the increased acreage. According to William MacKay, chamberlain of Lewis, writing in 1883, Dalmore was a most unhealthy place with hardly a healthy person in it, and the people, three years in arrears with their rents, were glad to leave. Three of the Dalmore families settled in South Shawbost, some in Carloway, some in Laxay on the other side of the island, while others emigrated to America. The South Shawbost crofters suffered doubly by the clearance of Dalbeg as not only were five more families thrust upon them but the part of their common pasture nearest to Dalbeg was also given to the farming tenant of Dalbeg without any corresponding reduction of the crofters' rents, although it was estimated that it was the best part of the South Shawbost grazing and could maintain one-third of the cattle of the township.

The Shawbost men were not long in following the example of the men of Valtos. In November, 1884, the dyke between their common grazing and that of Dalbeg was broken down. It had been built by order of the estate officials by the Shawbost people themselves, and they were held responsible for maintaining one half of it in good repair, while the farmer had to maintain the other half. But as the crofters were, naturally enough, reluctant to do so, the estate officials had added an extra shilling to the rent of each crofter. Before the dyke had been built, Donald MacKenzie and his son, who succeeded him as tenant of Dalbeg farm, used to seize the crofters' cattle or sheep and impound them, keeping them for two or three days until a fine was paid. With the breaking down of the dyke in 1884, John Sinclair, who had followed John MacKenzie in the tenancy of Dalbeg in 1875, resumed the practice of impounding the cattle and obtained from the Small Debt Court decrees for payment of damages caused by the trespass of the cattle. The dyke was repaired and broken down time and again. Sinclair had also to contend with trouble at the Carloway side of his farm, where a dyke had been erected between the Dalmore grazing and those of Garenin and Upper Carloway townships. For repair of the dyke on the Dalmore side, Sinclair engaged local men, much to the disgust of their more militant neighbours. On December

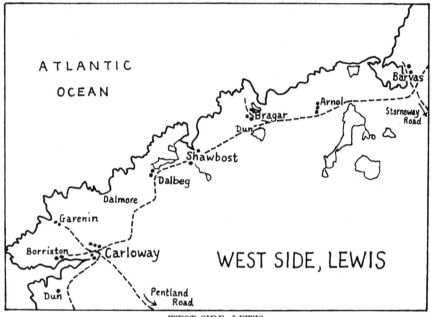

WEST SIDE, LEWIS.

15, 1884, the three men employed in rebuilding the Dalmore-Garenin dyke, Donald MacKenzie, Upper Carloway, Murdo Paterson, Park Carloway, and Donald MacDonald, Doune, ground officer, were approached by John MacLeod, Garenin, who threatened them that if they came back next day, even though the ground officer had seven men with rifles, they would not go home with whole skins. In consequence, the men did not return to work. MacLeod was later charged with breach of the peace by threatening to do bodily injury and fined 30s. or six days' imprisonment.

Some of the younger men began to resort to more reprehensible forms of protest against estate officials. The *Scotsman* of January 22, 1885, reported a "dastardly outrage" in the Carloway district, stating that "in no other part of Lewis is dyke-breaking so prevalent". Whether those who committed the "outrage" were from Carloway or Shawbost is not clear, but at some point between these villages, "where the ground slopes down precipitately", boulders had been

134

placed across the road in a "diabolical attempt" to wreck a carriage bearing back to Barvas H.M. Inspector of Schools, along with a member of the School Board and the clerk of the Board, both estate officials, after an examination of the evening school at Carloway. Whoever was responsible for the "dastardly outrage", more in keeping with events in Ireland at the time, the men of Shawbost were prepared to achieve their ends by more constitutional methods. At a meeting of the Shawbost branch of the Highland Land Law Reform Association on February 2, 1885, about 200 crofters and cottars gave unanimous approval to a resolution to the effect that

> "no concession by the landlord shall be satisfactory until Parliament shall interfere to legalise the proper requirements of the crofter."

On the Dalbeg grazing, trespassing by the Shawbost cattle and impounding of beasts by the farmer continued. On April 21, 1885, Sinclair, accompanied by a strong party of farm servants, rounded up thirty-three head of cattle on the disputed grazing. The Shawbost children in charge of the cattle did their best to prevent them being driven to the Dalbeg farm and as a result found themselves forced into the pound, an enclosure with walls six to eight feet high. There they were detained until their parents arrived and broke down the door at twelve o'clock midnight, when the children were "nearly dead with hunger and thirst and fear". The question of the enforced confinement of the Shawbost children in the Dalbeg pound was raised in the House of Commons by Charles Fraser Mackintosh, M.P. for Inverness Burghs, who was informed that the children had followed the cattle into the pound of their own accord and that Crown Counsel, following a report from the Stornoway Procurator Fiscal, had decided on no further proceedings. The farmer, Sinclair, however, sued the children's parents and obtained decrees for trespass and damage to the grazing by the cattle.

Shawbost Deforcement

Not all of Sinclair's decrees for payment were enforced without opposition. When John MacLeod, South Shawbost, refused to pay 9s. 10d., for which Sinclair had obtained a decree in the Small Debt Court, a sheriff officer arrived from Stornoway to poind his effects. The sheriff officer, William Ross MacLeod, accompanied by his concurrents, Roderick MacLeod, Laxdale, and Norman MacLeod, estate constable, were given a reception in South Shawbost which they would long remember. When they appoached MacLeod's house, they were deluged with "urine or other filthy liquid". MacLeod's wife, Effie, and other women, who gathered in support, brandished sticks and threatened to use them against the officer, who was compelled to retreat without poinding any goods. MacLeod and his wife, along with a Mrs Ann MacLeod, wife of Kenneth MacLeod, South Shawbost, were later charged in the Sheriff Court in Stornoway with deforcement of the sheriff officer and when they failed to appear on October 16, 1885, a warrant was issued for their arrest. It was not until February 2, 1886, that they were tried, John MacLeod and Mrs Ann MacLeod being each fined £1 or four days' imprisonment, while the charge against Mrs Effie Macleod was dropped.

The summer of 1885 was a poor one. A Lewis correspondent of the Inverness weekly, the *Scottish Highlander*, reported at the end of July bad weather for the past three months, the peats too wet to be gathered, and the cattle market at Stornoway so poor that many beasts were brought home unsold. A later report in the same newspaper from the Shawbost branch of the Highland Land Law Reform Association stated that the people had acquired courage since joining the Association, but with the young men away at the east coast fishing, the meetings had been adjourned "as the old people have not much life and have the fear of the factor and his officials before their eyes". During the summer, however, over 200 yards of the Dalbeg dyke were levelled to the ground. Men sent to repair the dyke found that overnight their tools had disappeared into the nearby Loch Raoinavat. An exception was made in the case of one Shawbost man, John MacLean, who, although regarded as working for the enemy, was excused as he had recently lost all his possessions when his house was burned down.

"Battle" of Dalbeg

After the passing of the Crofters Act in June, 1886, the Lewis people waited for the arrival of the newly-appointed Crofters Commission, which would fix fair rents and deal with the question of arrears of rent and other matters. Sinclair, the Dalbeg farmer, had still to contend with the Shawbost people's insistence on grazing their cattle on the disputed ground. On August 2, Sinclair's son, Hector, with one of the shepherds, John MacLeod, and a cowherd, Norman Martin, attempted to lead off some of the South Shawbost cattle, which were grazing on Aird Dalbeg, well beyond the ground claimed by the Shawbost people as theirs. This time they had to deal not with children but youths, Murdo MacPhail, Alexander MacLean, and John MacLeod, who were subsequently charged with breach of the peace and disorderly conduct. It was alleged that they had hooted and yelled at Sinclair and his assistants and had thrown clods and stones at the farmer's dogs to prevent them driving off their cattle. During the mêlée, the barefooted Shawbost youths were at a disadvantage, compared with their opponents with their hob-nailed boots, but they managed to prevent their cattle being impounded. In the Sheriff Court, the youths' spokesman, Murdo MacPhail, defended their action by stating that they had been informed by the older men in the village that the Dalbeg grazing had been taken from them thirty years before, but that, as there had been no reduction in the crofters' rents, they were therefore still paying for the grazing rights. Their arguments failed to convince Sheriff Black, who gave them a homily on the consequences of defying the law and imposed fines of 15s. on Mac-Phail and MacLean, the charge against MacLeod being dismissed.

This was the last case connected with the Dalbeg grazing dispute. In the following year, the ground to the west end of Loch Raoinavat was restored to the South Shawbost crofters, who also had their rents reduced and most of their arrears cancelled. Sinclair, who also lost part of his grazing on the Dalmore side, had his rent reduced from £102 to £90.

South Uist

Lewis and Skye were not the only districts where the authorities were alarmed at the threat of lawlessness. In South Uist the proprietrix, Lady Gordon Cathcart, whom John Murdoch described as "a good, kind, liberal woman, deeply concerned about her tenants", was the widow of Colonel John Gordon of Cluny in Aberdeenshire, who had been responsible for savage clearances in South Uist and Barra, formerly the properties of the chiefs of the MacDonalds of Clanranald and the MacNeills of Barra. Two years after her husband's death in 1878, she married Sir Reginald Cathcart of Killochan. By that time considerable sums had been expended on improvements — roads, reclamation, drainage, even some model houses; but her proposals for redistribution of land were frustrated by Ranald MacDonald, a native of Benbecula and factor at first for the Cluny estates in Aberdeenshire and latterly of the Cluny Hebridean estates of South Uist, Benbecula and Barra. Shortly after the visit of the Napier Commission in 1883 a branch of the H.L.L.R.A. was formed at Stoneybridge on the west side of the island with Alexander MacDonald, cottar ("deeply in debt" to the extent of £14.16.5 arrears on a rent of £1.11/-), as chairman, and Peter Walker (son of a crofter who had only £5.11/- of arrears on his rent of £9.15/-), as secretary. One of the first consequences of the formation of the branch was a raid by some landless squatters on Loch Eynort, about four miles from Stoneybridge, to occupy the small island of Calvay, where they planted potatoes two years running. There had been many instances in Skye, Lewis and

137

elsewhere of crofters placing their cattle or sheep on the grazing of a neighbouring farm, but digging a farmer's ground was seen by landlords as a serious breach of the law. Ranald MacDonald, the factor, acting with the Edinburgh agents of Lady Cathcart, Skene, Edwards and Bilton, decided to remove four of the ringleaders of the reform agitation which had erupted. Summonses of removal were sent to four tenants — Alexander MacDonald, chairman of the local branch of the H.L.L.R.A.; John Walker, father of the secretary of the local branch; Mrs MacRae, whose son, Donald, was one of those involved in the occupation of Calvay Island; Mrs Bowie, whose son, John, was described by the estate management as "objectionable" and, as manager of his mother's croft, had an overstock considerably in excess of the souming, while he "was foremost in the township to do all that the H.L.L.R.A. required of them". The local branch officials were not slow in following the example of Skye crofters threatened with eviction. After a meeting at Stoneybridge on April 5, 1884, a letter was sent to the London headquarters of the H.L.L.R.A.:

> "We are gathered here today some of the members of the Association for a certain purpose which has afflicted on us a severe trouble of mind but we trust in God and with your help that it will be all right with us soon."

After detailing the threats of removal at Whitsun (the term day), the letter concluded:

> "We are ready to prove that it is factors and ground officers who are illegally threatening to evict the Loch Eynort delegate and those selected by the people to be the leaders of this branch of the Association."

Some publicity was given to the Stoneybridge affair at the end of April in the London *Times*. Stuart Glennie, a member of the executive of the H.L.L.R.A., writing from the Athenaeum, accused the estate management of threatening to evict men who had given evidence to the Napier Commission, a charge which Mr Peacock Edwards, one of the Edinburgh agents, was easily able to rebut as none of the four men mentioned had appeared before the Commission. Lady Gordon Cathcart had given "most explicit instructions" that no person should be prejudiced for his evidence, and indeed three of the delegates who gave evidence were at that time on their way with their families to Canada, each family having received an advance of £100 and the cancellation of the past year's rent and arrears. Edwards also explained that in the Highlands and Islands a notice of removal was served in order to obtain payment of rent and pointed out later that in the period, 1878-83, when Lady Cathcart was in sole possession and control of the estate, there were 45 summonses but only 5 removals. There was little doubt however in people's minds generally that the reason for the summonses was active membership of the H.L.L.R.A. but actual removals were put off for the time being.

Things were quiet in the summer. Lady Cathcart's emigration scheme (criticised by Dr MacGillivray of Barra as "too liberal") was continued. In 1884 56 families from her estates in the Long Island (South Uist, Barra, Benbecula), received financial assistance to emigrate to Manitoba in Canada, but only one emigrant repaid his loan and Lady Cathcart was so discouraged by the failure of the scheme at the Manitoba end that after 1886 she abandoned her plans. In the autumn there occurred several incidents which the estate management considered tantamount to a breakdown of law and order. Telegraph wires were cut down, placed across the road under boulders to trap any vehicle. Fencing was pulled down, a gate smashed and a large quantity of clover and hay thrown into the ditches. Picks and shovels belonging to men working on the road disappeared overnight, presumably thrown into the loch, and a boat used by the factor completely destroyed. Most sensational event of the year, the minister's seat, the communion table, vestry, the pulpit Bible of the parish church at Howmore were found to be saturated with paraffin on the Saturday evening before Lady Cathcart was to attend divine service there.

As happened in Skye and Lewis, a "No Rent" campaign was started and at Martinmas few rents were paid in Stoneybridge or other townships in South Uist. Lady Cathcart, in a letter sent to all crofters on her Hebridean estates, catalogued the farms (mainly in Benbecula and Barra) which had been broken up to provide land for crofts, in addition to which the crofts vacated by emigrants had been made available for crofter tenants, and she expressed her pain over the recent seizure of lands at Stoneybridge. At the beginning of March, 1885, an attempt was made to serve notices of interdict on the 34 tenants in Stoneybridge and 8 tenants at Loch Eynort. A messenger-at-arms was employed (as the interdicts had been issued from the Court of Session) and served only 23 notices when he was stopped by a crowd of about 30 men, who assured him that no violence was intended, but being blocked before the door of a house, he declared himself deforced and departed. On April 10, Peter and Donald Walker, and their father, John Walker, appeared before Sheriff Webster in Lochmaddy Sheriff Court. The father was found guilty of breach of the peace and the sons guilty of obstruction. There had been some criticism of the mild sentences imposed by Sheriff Speirs in Portree, and reporting to Sheriff Ivory, Webster explained his lenient sentence on the ground that no violence had been used. He continued:

"As this was the first case in the district, I thought it consistent with my

139

duty to limit the imprisonment to 21 days, at the same time warning them about the future."

Sheriff Ivory's response is not recorded. When the Walkers emerged from prison, they were hailed by the Radical press as the "Stoney-bridge martyrs". After the prosecution of the men regarded as ringleaders, things quietened down, and although meetings were held under the auspices of the H.L.L.R.A., crofters had to wait another year for legislation.

Garrafad Park

It was on the east side of Kilmuir estate at Valtos that William Fraser, the proprietor, was first forced into a confrontation with his crofter tenants; and it was also on the east side that a challenge was made by the tenants of Garrafad, a small township near Staffin. The challenge came in the spring of 1884, when crofters generally, emboldened by the public sympathy and support for their cause, began to insist on their rights. The trouble in 1884 arose over an enclosed grazing of about 40 acres, Garrafad Park (also called Staffin Park). It had been enclosed about 1870, when Fraser almost immediately let the park to a farmer, Alexander MacLeod of Skudiburgh. MacLeod's farm, Sku-diburgh, was on the west side of Kilmuir estate and he used Garrafad Park for fattening sheep and cattle. He was considered by the crofters a bad neighbour and because the dyke separating the park from the crofters' grazing was not kept in good repair, the farmer's sheep or cattle often strayed on to the crofters' grazing and the crofters' cattle or sheep strayed on to the park grazing. The farmer's shepherd would drive them through the Kilmartin river into a pound, from which they would emerge weak and dirty, after a fine was paid.

One night in April, a portion of the dyke (about 60 yards) was knocked down, an occurrence which greatly alarmed proprietor and factor, who regarded it as an outrage, symptomatic of the lawlessness which was fast growing in Skye. Rumour in Portree had it that the Garrafad people intended to seize the grazing. Fraser suggested to MacDonald, the factor, that a reward of £5 be offered for information leading to the conviction of the "miscreants". MacDonald urged the local manager, John MacKenzie, formerly the policeman in the district, to give priority to employing watchers at night to prevent a repetition of the dyke-breaking and a herd to take note of cattle belonging to the Garrafad crofters trespassing. Rebuilding of the dyke he regarded as essential in order to prevent further trespass. A list of suspects named 9 youths, 3 of them from Garrafad, 3 from Brogaig and the others from neighbouring townships — Elishader, Marishad-er and Stenscholl, and it was sent to the Portree Procurator Fiscal.

Identification proved too difficult, however, to proceed with charges of malicious damage — much to the annoyance of MacDonald, who blamed the authorities for lack of support. During the month of June, MacDonald was sending letters or telegrams to MacKenzie almost daily on the subject of trespass by the Garrafad cattle and also on the importance of rebuilding of the dyke. The chief difficulty with regard to the rebuilding of the dyke was that John Lamont, the local mason, proved unwilling to undertake the job because of his fear of reprisals. The night after he had taken the contract, he had his windows broken and, despite warnings by the factor that he would not receive any more work on Kilmuir, he was resolute in his refusal to carry on with the job. With July there came an unexpected development: on the 5th of the month Fraser himself met the 18 crofter tenants of Garrafad. It was not an acrimonious affair and, according to the tenants, Major Fraser (as he was then styled) gave permission to the Garrafad tenants to drive their cattle through the park to reach the river until such time as another passage would be arranged. After the meeting landlord and tenants adjourned to Staffin Lodge, where, according to MacKenzie, the local manager, sentiments of peace and goodwill were exchanged over a dram of whisky.[2] Even with a herd in charge, 80 head of cattle could take some time passing through the park to drink and back again, feeding as they went, and the crofters made the most of the privilege which had been granted, while MacLeod, the farmer, complained bitterly about the excessive grazing, which diminished the value of the ground he had leased. As the summer went on, MacDonald became more and more convinced that notices of interdict would have to be served on the Garrafad tenants but he was faced with the problem which had troubled him before — finding sheriff officers and concurrents to serve summonses.

In the meantime, Skye seemed to be facing a growing tide of lawlessness, which led the Government at last to sanction the military expedition to the island. On different estates, meetings were held and resolutions were passed, declaring the crofters' refusal to pay rents until their grievances were redressed. On October 3, over 300 crofters and cottars from the Kilmuir estate met at the Quirang in a storm of wind and rain; and they passed among a number of resolutions one calling for the dismissal of MacDonald, the factor, and his replacement by "a gentleman of honour and integrity", MacDonald took justifiable umbrage at the wounding statements made about his character and, in particular, at a report that Archibald MacDonald, a shopkeeper in Garrafad, had accused him of having gone to London in September to ask the government to send troops to put down the crofters in Skye. He tried unsuccessfully to force the Garrafad shopkeeper, who was secretary of the local branch of the

H.L.L.R.A., to retract his statement, maintaining that his visit to the south had been for reasons of health. His critic denied using the words alleged by the factor and also declined to repeat his actual statement so that, despite a threatened claim for £1000 damages, the factor received no satisfaction. He was unsuccessful also in his attempt to resist the growing "No Rent" campaign by the deforcement of the sheriff officer, despite the presence of a large-scale military expedition. The growing confidence of the crofters in their cause was shown by their refusal to meet Major Fraser, who had invited them to a meeting at Uig on December 10. They maintained that Fraser, having granted them the liberty of passage through Garrafad Park, had failed to keep his word and without notice had raised an action of interdict against them.

The action of interdict against the Garrafad tenants was, however, raised in Portree Sheriff Court in July, 1885. It was drawn up in the names of Major Fraser and Alexander MacLeod of Skudiburgh, the tenant of the park, against the Rev. J.M. Davidson, the Church of Scotland minister of Stenscholl, and 18 tenants of Garrafad township. The inclusion of the minister's name he himself alleged in court was due to malice on the part of the farmer, MacLeod, who resented Davidson's acknowledged support for the crofters. The case was heard by Sheriff Speirs, who found surprisingly for the defenders, represented by the Inverness town clerk, Kenneth MacDonald. For the minister, whose horse used to graze in the park, it was argued that when the church was established in 1828, his predecessor had been granted, instead of a glebe, the right to use the crofters' grazing (part of which had been enclosed in Garrafad Park), and this right had never been withdrawn. The tenants were able to claim that they had been given permission by Major Fraser to drive their cattle to drinking water and that this permission had not been revoked. It was in the last week of December, 1885, that Sheriff Speirs issued his decisions, commenting favourably on the impression of frankness and truthfulness created by the witnesses, particularly the minister and Archibald MacDonald, and indicating that the action should not have been brought. MacDonald, as secretary of the local branch of the H.L.L.R.A., was able to deny that there had been any proposal at a branch meeting to break down the dyke and he also maintained that the intimidation of Lamont, the mason, whose windows were broken in, had been officially condemned and the perpetrators threatened with expulsion. Sheriff Speirs's decision in favour of the minister and the Garrafad tenants was, in February, 1886, overturned by Ivory, the Sheriff Principal in Inverness, whose decision was widely condemned, the *Scottish Highlander* claiming that he should be relieved of his office.

142

Major Fraser's attitude in the whole affair was in contrast with his conduct during the Valtos dispute. He seemed to adopt a more generous attitude but as in Valtos, where Norman Stewart (Parnell) was regarded as a ringleader in the agitation, Fraser blamed Archibald MacDonald for the trouble over Garrafad and in November 1886 tried to evict him for arrears of rent. His action failed, however, as MacDonald was able to prove that his shop was situated on the minister's glebe, not on Fraser's land. There was an interesting sequel to the story of the Garrafad Park dispute and the part played by Archibald MacDonald. Fraser sold Kilmuir estate in 1888 to Abinger Baird, who took a more enlightened view of the crofting situation and in 1893, among a number of transactions in favour of the small tenants, gave Archibald MacDonald the lease of Staffin Inn and lands, formerly held by MacLeod of Skudiburgh. MacDonald had as far back as 1881 tried to obtain the lease of the newly-built Staffin Inn and had actually travelled through to Nairn to interview Major Fraser about the matter. Fraser was favourably impressed by MacDonald, whom he described to the factor as "a very nice man" (although he later formed a different opinion). In the summer of 1893, MacDonald found himself in a similar situation to that of the tacksmen whom he had in the past so often criticised. The small Staffin Island was taken over by five cottars and MacDonald was compelled to apply for interdict against them. There followed the familiar deforcement of the sheriff officer, who was assaulted by a crowd of women, three of them being later fined £1 each.

Another champion of the crofters who was the object of criticism by cottars and a victim of their desire for land was the Rev. Donald MacCallum, who was at one time minister of Hallin-in-Waternish in Skye, then of Hylipol in Tiree, and latterly of Lochs in Lewis, where he was inducted in 1889. As Church of Scotland minister, he had a small congregation but a comfortable income and a large glebe. Some cottars from the overcrowded townships of Crossbost and Leurbost had threatened the minister in 1892 that if he did not put into practice his gospel about the people's right to the land they would take over his extensive glebe. This they did in the spring of 1893, marching to Keose and measuring off lots for themselves. MacCallum set off to Stornoway to consult with the Lewis chamberlain, who advised him to ask for police protection. The police however suggested that he should use the proprietors' and tacksmen's usual method of applying for interdict, which he was unwilling to do. Land raids (as such occupations of land were called), continued sporadically to be carried out by cottars, whose condition, in comparison with the improved status of crofters, led to frustration and defiance of the law.

The Clashmore Dispute

Across the Minch from Lewis on the mainland in Assynt, resistance to the authorities continued into 1888, and enforcement of the law was found to be impossible without the use of a military force. Ten years before, the seeds of trouble had been sown by the creation of a large farm at Clashmore in Assynt, 18 families being removed to much poorer land to make way for a tenant farmer, who in 1887 was a Mr Dunnett, hotel-keeper at Lochinver.

The first "disturbance" (to use the terminology of the authorities), occurred on April 21, 1887, when a sheriff officer, accompanied by a ground officer and two policemen, attempting to serve summonses for payment of rent arrears, suffered the humiliation of having his summonses burned and then being compelled, along with the ground officer and the driver of the "machine" from Lochinver, to go down on bended knees and promise never to return on the same errand. A month after the sheriff officer's deforcement, when Sandieson the Lochinver policeman (who covered the whole of Assynt), arrived to serve summonses on the deforcers, the men of the township were away at the peats but the women of Clashmore seized him, burned his summonses and threatened to dip him in the river should he ever return on the same errand. When the case of the men charged with deforcement was called at Dornoch Sheriff Court, only one of the accused, John MacKenzie, shoemaker, appeared. As the Sutherland constabulary comprised only 14 men, Sheriff Cheyne requested the assistance of a gunboat with marines to effect the arrest of the other three men. At MacKenzie's trial, the Duke of Sutherland made an unexpected appearance, to plead for leniency, which the Sheriff granted, sentencing the Clashmore shoemaker to fourteen days' imprisonment. A second attempt to serve the summonses on the other three by Sandieson the Lochinver policeman, on June 5 again failed. The first house at which Sandieson called was that of Hugh Kerr, who again happened to be away at the peats but quickly returned when informed of the policeman's arrival. Seizing him by the scruff of the neck, Kerr threw the policeman out of the house. Six women, led by Hugh Kerr's wife, belaboured the unfortunate constable, who was compelled to defend himself by swinging his belt about him.

Sheriff Cheyne was still hoping to obtain the services of a military force but considered the *Jackal*, at that time stationed off Barra to supervise the herring fishing, as too small for the purpose and suggested *Seahorse*, which was then engaged in the Skye expedition, and, if possible, as many as 70 marines. Two of the wanted deforcers, George and Hugh Matheson, surrendered during the summer but the third, Hugh Kerr, still defied arrest and for months lived the life of an outlaw, so that the press christened him "the Sutherland Rob Roy". It was not until December 20, 1887, that a military expedition was sent to Assynt. This followed the occupation of Clashmore farm by crofters' stock and the burning down of the farm steading on November 20. As the lease of the farm had expired and a new lease given to a Mr MacBrayne, the crofters felt strongly that this was the time to regain possession of the grazing that had once belonged to them. The gunboat *Jackal* crossed the Minch to Lochinver, from where a combined force of police and marines marched to Clashmore, served notices on 37 persons in Clashmore and made three arrests. A cordon of police was thrown round Clashmore in the hope of capturing Hugh Kerr but once more he managed to remain at liberty and continued to do so until August in the following year. Land League sympathisers were said to have given him £50 to help him to remain at large and, although he was for a time living rough in caves, he managed to visit Glasgow and Edinburgh and find casual work. Kerr was finally arrested near Dornoch in August after the police had been tipped off by someone who recognised him. Kerr had thought more than once of surrendering after his wife had been jailed for her part in the raid on Clashmore farm. She was released in August, 1888, in time for a reunion with her husband, who actually received a shorter sentence (3 months) than his wife.

The difficulties of the authorities in the case of Hugh Kerr and the Clashmore people were due at least partly to the remoteness and the inaccessibility of the place; and the military expedition's approach from the sea was in contrast to the experience of the county Procurator Fiscal, W. Sutherland Fraser, who in his eighty-seventh year, on December 16, 1887, drove all the 70 miles from Dornoch, returning along snow-covered roads four days later.

In the two years after the passing of the Crofters Act there was much talk about violence but, all things considered, the crofting community had not gained a great deal by the violence shown in their confrontation with the authorities. The conduct of the principals in the struggle was in marked contrast: Sheriff Ivory was a troublemaker while Sheriff Fraser was a pacific person. All the time, the Crofters Commission was carrying out its duties in a plodding manner and bringing about a better atmosphere in the crofting area. But it was the security of tenure granted by the Act which made it possible for the crofter to look forward in confidence. For the cottars and squatters, their problems still remained.

Notes

1. In April, 1884, Superintendent Donald Cameron had been presented with a gold watch and a purse of sovereigns in recognition of his service in Lewis

since 1872. He had acted with considerable courage in helping to defuse the situation at the time of the Bernera affair in 1874. His sympathy for the crofters stemmed from his experience as a child of four years of age when his family was evicted from Inverlael on Little Loch Broom. In the *Stornoway Gazette* of June, 1984, there is a full account of his career in Lewis, written by the wife of his grandson, Donald Cameron.

2. John MacKenzie had been the district policeman before William Fraser of Kilmuir persuaded him to become local manager. He was nicknamed "Jumbo" and was most unpopular on the estate, particularly after the fiasco of the Kilmuir petition. He was appointed factor of Kilmuir after the resignation of Alex. MacDonald.

CHAPTER 7

PARLIAMENTARY ELECTIONS

Elections before 1885

A century ago, parliamentary elections were vastly different from those of today. For one thing, no woman was allowed to vote and, for another, the mass of the men were excluded from the franchise. It was only after 1872 that the enfranchised few were able to vote by secret ballot but the ballot made no difference in most Highland county elections, in which there was no contest. The franchise before 1885 differed as between the burghs and the counties. There were two burgh constituencies in the crofting counties — Inverness Burghs, comprising Inverness, Forres, Fortrose and Nairn, and the Northern Burghs, comprising Wick, Cromarty, Tain, Dingwall, Dornoch and Kirkwall. By Disraeli's act of 1868, the franchise in burghs was held by all male householders and by lodgers who paid at least £10 a year in rent. In the counties outwith the burgh boundaries, the franchise was restricted to those who owned property worth at least £5 per annum or tenants who paid at least £14 a year in rent, a rent well above that of any crofter. Before the Third Reform Act of 1884, the shire electorates were very small — 1861 in Inverness-shire, 1720 in Ross and Cromarty, 1243 in Caithness, 325 in Sutherland, 3299 in Argyll, and 1704 in Orkney and Shetland.

Up until the 1880s the county elections were characterised by the unopposed return of the M.P.s, all of them Liberal and almost all landowners or the sons of landowners. In Ross and Cromarty, there was only one election between 1847 and 1884, during which period the seat was held first by Sir James Matheson of Achany and the Lews and later by his nephew, Sir Alexander Matheson of Ardross and Lochalsh.

Sutherland since 1852, with the exception of six years, had seen a representative of the family of the Duke of Sutherland returned unopposed at every election. Similarly, in Argyll, the Marquis of Lorne and Lord Colin Campbell, sons of the Duke of Argyll, held the parliamentary seat continuously from 1868, although the latter had to face a challenge in 1878 and 1880 from the Conservative, Colonel James Malcolm, younger, of Poltalloch. It was the same story in Caithness, where Sir John Sinclair was the fourth baronet of Ulbster in succession to represent the county in Parliament, and in Orkney and Shetland, where the parliamentary seat was for long part of the patrimony of the Dundases, the family of the Earls and Marquises of Zetland. The burgh constituencies saw elections more frequently. In the Inverness Burghs, Charles Fraser Mackintosh held the seat from 1874, when he defeated another Liberal, Aeneas Mackintosh of Raigmore; and in the Northern Burghs the wealthy John Pender (later Sir John Pender), a Scottish merchant who had won fame by backing the laying of the Atlantic telegraph cable, had been M.P. since 1872. The general picture was thus of the continued ascendancy of the landed families in the county constituencies, based on the very restricted franchise, and of Liberal supremacy in both counties and burghs.

Franchise Act of 1885

The Third Reform Act of 1885 brought about a vast extension of the franchise in the county constituencies and with it something akin to a revolution in the elections themselves. By Gladstone's Franchise Act, passed as a result of pressure by the Radicals in the Liberal party led by Joseph Chamberlain, all male householders and lodgers were entitled to vote. The 1885 Act, which had been held up for months by the Conservative majority in the House of Lords, increased the total electorate in the British Isles from three to five million, and had its most striking effect in the crofting counties of Scotland and also in Ireland, where it gave an impetus to the Home Rule movement which was to bedevil British politics for the next generation. In Argyll, the electorate was increased by over 200 per cent, in Inverness-shire by over 400 per cent, in Ross and Cromarty by nearly 500 per cent, and in Sutherland by nearly 880 per cent. The figures for Ross and Cromarty were 1720 in 1880 and 10,265 in 1885, when the Reform Act took effect, and for Sutherland 325 and 3,185 respectively. By contrast, the electorates in the burghs may be said to have had only a "natural increase" between the elections of 1880 and 1885 — 14.4 per cent in the Northern Burghs and 18.7 per cent in Inverness Burghs. The 1880s were years of political ferment, producing new parties and movements of protest. The promised extension of the franchise brought in some of these movements as allies for the crofters and their friends and encouraged them to increase their agitation for land law reform. The consequence was a revolution in Highland politics; and elections were never to be the same again.

By-election in Ross and Cromarty

There was considerable delay in implementing the Franchise Act of 1885, first because of the obstructive tactics of the House of Lords, which insisted on a Redistribution Bill before agreeing to pass the Franchise Bill, and later because of the necessity of drawing up a new electoral register. There was, however, a by-election in 1884 in Ross and Cromarty, which, although fought on the old electoral register, had the effect of a dress rehearsal for the general election of 1885. In 1884, the seat of Ross and Cromarty, which then included Lewis, was held by the Liberal M.P., Sir Alexander Matheson of Ardross and Lochalsh, whose uncle had held it before him since 1847. Sir Alexander, like his uncle, had amassed an enormous fortune by trading in opium and tea in the Far East, returning in his mid-thirties to Scotland and acquiring properties in Ross-shire. He had been created a baronet in 1881 when in his seventy-eighth year and he had let it be known early in 1884 that he would not be seeking re-election. Three candidates for the succession were soon in the field after the announcement of his intended resignation, and an election seemed a certainty for the first time in the county in over thirty years. The Liberals, who had held sway for so long, were challenged on two fronts, by a Conservative Ross-shire proprietor, and by a London Scot sponsored by the Highland Land Law Reform Association of London. The Liberals adopted as their candidate the young Ronald Craufurd Munro-Ferguson of Raith and Novar at a meeting held in Dingwall under the chairmanship of Sir Kenneth MacKenzie of Gairloch, who himself declined nomination, declaring that at fifty-two years of age he was too old to start a political career. (In 1885, when he stood at the general election for Inverness-shire, he was to be reminded frequently by his opponents of this remark.)

The Candidates of 1884

The Liberal candidate, although generally called Novar in the Highlands, was known in Kirkcaldy as Ferguson of Raith, his family having been prominent in that area since the early eighteenth century. With two great-grandfathers who were generals of renown, Sir Hector Munro of Novar and Sir Ronald Ferguson of Raith, it is not surprising that he was at first destined for a military career, going through Sandhurst and receiving a commission in the Grenadier Guards, but he had left the Army for the sake of entering politics. He was a young man of considerable talent. Sir William Harcourt, the Home Secretary, who met him at Lochalsh while on a yachting holiday, described him to the Prime Minister, Gladstone, as "a charming youth and withal very keen and intelligent". He was to have a long and successful career in politics, becoming in time Governor-General of Australia, Secretary for Scotland and gaining the title of Viscount Novar.

The Conservative candidate, Allan Russell MacKenzie, aged thir-

149

ty, had a background not unlike that of the Liberal candidate — an English public school, Harrow, and a commission in the Royal Horse Guards. His father, James (later Sir James) MacKenzie, son of an

Aberdeen hatter, had made his fortune as an indigo-manufacturer in India and on his return to Scotland had purchased an estate in Kintail from the MacKenzies of Seaforth. His son, as prospective M.P. for a Highland constituency, took an interest in the Gaelic Society of Inverness, and, as chairman of the Annual Assembly of the society in 1885, was to plead for the teaching of Gaelic in schools, although he himself had no Gaelic. He and his family came under much criticism in Ross-shire because of the conduct of their shooting tenant in Kintail, the "Yankee Nimrod", W.L. Winans, who had leases of seven of the best deer forests in the Highlands. His

DR RODERICK MACDONALD, M.P.

attempt to interdict a crofter at Morvich in Kintail, who had allowed a sheep to stray on to part of the deer forest, became known as the "Pet Lamb of Kintail" case and was used by MacKenzie's opponents to his detriment, even although he was sympathetic to the crofters and tried to cancel the American sportsman's lease. "Who let Kintail to the Yankee?" was the heckler's cry at MacKenzie's political meetings. He was to contest Ross and Cromarty twice but, as a Conservative and the son of a laird, he had little chance once the crofters obtained the franchise.

The third candidate in the field was Dr Roderick MacDonald, a native of Dunvegan in Skye, who after a period of teaching (including a short spell at the Free Church Ladies' School at Knock in Lewis), had qualified in medicine and had built up a lucrative practice at Millwall in London. A little over forty years of age, he had taken a leading part in the formation of the Highland Land Law Reform Association of London; and it was at the request of the Association secretary, Donald Murray, whose father had been Free Church minister at Knock, that he agreed to stand at the next election.

150

MacDonald was said to resemble the Prince of Wales (the future Edward VII) in appearance and in his polished manners. He was a fluent speaker in Gaelic and English but was regarded as "hopelessly dull" on the platform. The as yet unenfranchised crofters and cottars nevertheless invariably accorded him a rapturous welcome as he was standing professedly in their interest. In the days before payment of M.P.s, a parliamentary candidate required an independent income; and Dr MacDonald could be regarded as comfortably off with a coroner's practice in London worth £1600 a year. Before his death in 1894, he was credited with nine or ten directorships and he left an estate of £24,000. But his opponent, Munro-Ferguson, foolishly stigmatised him as a "penniless adventurer" (a remark he was later to regret) and the *Scotsman* referred to him as a "carpet-bagger candidate", ready to exploit the new opportunities made possible for aspiring politicians by the extension of the franchise.

Electioneering

The first visits of the three candidates to Lewis were reported very differently in the newspapers of the Highlands, reflecting their own political views. The Conservative *Northern Chronicle* of Inverness described the meeting of the Stornoway Liberals in February, 1884, as "uproarious" and attended by only a few "shop lads". But in the *Ross-shire Journal* and the *Inverness Courier*, both staunchly Liberal, John N. Anderson (later to be Provost of Stornoway) denied the report, claiming that seven J.P.s, including the chief magistrate of Stornoway, Matthew Russell,[1] several Free Church divines, the United Presbyterian minister and many other respectable persons engaged in a harmonious meeting, while he added the jibe that there were not enough electors at the Tory meeting to produce an uproar. The *Invergordon Times* had been adopted by the H.L.L.R.A. as the crofters' paper and its scathing criticism of the other candidates was characterised in the columns of the *Ross-shire Journal* as "blinded by partisanship, full of political rancour and degrading language". At one time, some of MacDonald's supporters bought 200 copies of the *Ross-shire Journal* and had them publicly burned in Dingwall, while another package of 200 copies was found floating in Stornoway harbour, suspicion this time falling upon the Stornoway Tories, whose electoral tactics had been attacked in a number of letters appearing in that particular issue of the Dingwall newspaper.

When Sir Alexander Matheson, instead of waiting for the full term of Parliament, unexpectedly decided to apply for the Chiltern Hundreds on August 5, 1884, a by-election fought on the old restricted register of voters at once followed and the three candidates ceased the preliminary sparring and began to fight in earnest. Dr MacDonald, who realised that his chances of success on such a restricted franchise were hopeless, decided to use the opportunity of appearing before the people who would be able to vote at the next general election. The crofter candidate, as he came to be known, arrived in Dingwall a few days after Sir Alexander's resignation, on Saturday, August 9, in preparation for his first meeting on the Monday at Alness, and put up at the Caledonian Hotel. On the Sunday afternoon, he was composing his speech in his hotel room, dressed in a kilt and with a bottle of whisky for inspiration, and as the day was rather warm he stood rehearsing his speech at a wide-open window overlooking the High Street. It was communion day at Ferintosh, and Dingwall was deserted so that MacDonald's booming voice could be heard distinctly in the street. Someone (MacDonald later suspected an old fellow-student), recognised the voice and mischieviously noted down some sentences, which appeared, much to the embarrassment of the orator, in the *Aberdeen Free Press* before the meeting at Alness. He was therefore from time to time accused by his rivals' supporters of being a Sabbath-breaker, a heinous offence in the eyes of some voters.[2]

Election Issues

Although the chief issue in the Highlands and Islands in 1884 was the crofting problem, neither the Conservative nor Liberal candidate did more than express vague and pious hopes that the grievances of the crofters would be remedied. The report of the Napier Commission, which had been issued at the end of April, had encouraged the crofters and their sympathisers to expect the Liberal Government to introduce a bill in implementation of the Commission's recommendations. In the summer of 1884, Gladstone and his Cabinet colleagues were faced with the refusal of the House of Lords to pass the Franchise Bill without some concession in the form of a Redistribution Bill. The *Scotsman* described the refusal of the Lords as "the most formidable crisis of recent times", and huge demonstrations in favour of the extended franchise were staged throughout the land, the Radical leader, Joseph Chamberlain, whipping up popular indignation with his rousing speeches. For the Tory candidate, however, the two main issues were the admission to Parliament of Bradlaugh, the agnostic Liberal M.P. for Northampton who had refused to take the oath as required by law and whose right to refuse had been defended by some, but not all, Liberals, and Gladstone's appointment of the Roman Catholic Marquis of Ripon as Viceroy of India.

The question of the disestablishment of the Church of Scotland was hotly discussed during the campaign of 1884, as also at the ensuing elections. The Free Church, dominant in the Highlands and Islands, had always, although critical of the Established Church of Scotland, felt strongly on this issue since the time of the Disruption of 1843. "Though we quit the Establishment", Dr Chalmers had maintained from the chair of the Moderator of the first Free Church General Assembly:

> "we go out on the Establishment principle; we quit a vitiated Establishment but would rejoice in returning to a pure one".

But by the 1880s the Free Church was split over this question. In the Highlands and Islands the people were overwhelmingly against Disestablishment; and the championship of Disestablishment by Principal Rainy ("Black Rainy" to many in the north and west) only strengthened that opposition.[3] The Tories made the most of a letter written by the much-revered Dr Kennedy of Dingwall just before his death, in which he expressed himself as more satisfied with the views of MacKenzie rather than Munro-Ferguson on the Bradlaugh and Disestablishment questions and went on to wish the young Conservative candidate all success. The Liberals did their best to undermine the influence of the letter, even going so far as to suggest that it was a forgery; but the Conservative *Northern Chronicle* gave it full publicity, ending its advice in Gaelic to voters: "*Bha fios aig Dr Kennedy air beachdan Chinntaile agus bha e làn toilichte leo* (Dr Kennedy knew the views of Kintail and was very pleased with them)". Munro-Ferguson maintained what would be called a non-committal standpoint, declaring at a meeting at Invergordon that he would support the party's decision on the question, but he was commended to voters by two other eminent Free Church divines, Dr Gustavus Aird of Creich and the Rev. Murdo MacAskill, who was to succeed Dr Kennedy in the Dingwall charge. Dr Aird declared:

> "If I had a thousand votes, I would give them to Novar. He is a most intelligent and deserving young man, whom it would be a credit for us to elect."

The meetings of Dr MacDonald were generally crowded with non-voters, who cheered him to the echo, although he could hardly be called a rousing speaker. The week before the election, he was assisted in his electioneering by one of his colleagues in the Highland Land Law Reform Association of London, D.H. MacFarlane, the M.P. for County Carlow in Ireland, who managed to arrange a yachting cruise to arrive in the Hebrides just before the election. MacFarlane was accompanied by two fellow-M.P.s, Richard Power, M.P. for Waterford and an Irish Home Ruler, and H.E. Gorst, one of the "Tory Democrats" and later a Liberal M.P., and also by John Stuart

Blackie, formerly professor of Greek at Edinburgh, still, as ever, a champion of the Highlanders and their language. Blackie, who joined MacFarlane's yacht, the *Santa Maria*, at Oban, maintained that the purpose of the cruise was non-partisan and that the speeches made at Stornoway, Portree and Glendale had been aimed at instructing their audiences.

But the *Scotsman* and other Whig and Tory papers were in no doubt that they advocated land law reform in support of Dr MacDonald. This was the first, but not the last, occasion when a yachting cruise was found to be an effective method of electioneering in the Hebrides.[4]

The result of the by-election in August, 1884, could have surprised no one except the most perfervid supporter of MacKenzie of Kintail — R. Munro-Ferguson (Liberal), 717; Allan R. MacKenzie (Conservative), 334; Dr R. MacDonald (Crofters), 248. The *Scotsman* interpreted the result as an emphatic defeat for Lord Salisbury's delaying tactics over the Franchise Bill, but a Liberal victory had never been in doubt. MacDonald might seem to have made little impact but his campaign had been aimed at the crofters, thousands of whom would come on to the voting register before the general election in the following year.

Duncan Cameron

The Skye expedition, which focussed the attention of the whole of Britain upon the island from mid-November, 1884, onwards, led to increased political agitation and provided the crofter candidates with plenty of opportunities for propagating their views. The most prominent of these at the time of the arrival of the expedition was Duncan Cameron, whose father was proprietor of the *Oban Times*. Cameron's initiative in interviewing Sheriff Ivory on board the *Lochiel* to try to persuade him that the expedition was unnecessary, brought him into favour with the crofters, even although the overture to the sheriff had proved fruitless.[5] Cameron's presence in the Isle of Skye has been attributed to a variety of motives — a genuine sympathy with the crofters' cause, a desire to increase the circulation of the family newspaper, and an ambition to enter Parliament. He was almost certainly responsible for the wording of the Glendale meeting's resolution on December 1, 1884, declaring the inability of the crofters of Glendale to pay their rents at the next term and accompanied by petitions from each township giving reasons for their inability to pay. During the next few days, Cameron addressed meetings, along with John MacPherson of Glendale and the Rev. Donald MacCallum at Edinbane, the Braes, Kensaleyre and Uig, at which last meeting he was introduced to the huge gathering as the prospective candidate for

Inverness-shire, the sitting M.P., Donald Cameron of Lochiel, having intimated his decision to retire.

Duncan Cameron's electioneering campaign, which was given prominence not only in the *Oban Times* but also in the national press, put the cat among the pigeons so far as the so-called Inverness clique was concerned. Charles Fraser Mackintosh had been M.P. for Inverness Burghs since 1874 but, along with his henchmen, Alexander MacKenzie, the "Clach", editor of the *Celtic Magazine* and later the *Scottish Highlander*, and Kenneth MacDonald, Town Clerk of Inverness, who had acted as counsel for the defence in a number of crofters' cases, he had decided that in future the shire constituency, with its large number of crofter electors, would be a safer seat for him than the burghs seat, which included Fortrose, Forres and Nairn as well as Inverness. But no public announcement had been made by him as for a time before the Redistribution Bill was published there had been talk of a separate constituency of the Western Isles, which would include Skye as well as the Outer Hebrides. (The Western Isles constituency was not to be created until 1918 and then without Skye.)[6] Such a constituency would ensure to a crofter candidate a certain victory at a parliamentary election. Fraser Mackintosh had, as a member of the Napier Commission, shown himself sympathetic to the crofters in their grievances and was accused by the *Scotsman* of setting himself up as "a sort of Highland Parnell". In May, 1884, just after the publication of the Napier Commission Report, Mackintosh had been asked at a meeting at Fairy Bridge near Dunvegan by John MacPherson and others to stand for the county seat but he had not accepted (or declined) the invitation. Later, he had assured his own constituents in the Inverness Burghs that he would again stand there as a Liberal candidate and even as late as October, 1884, he had intimated his intention of once more contesting the burghs seat. The publication of redistribution proposals in December, with no mention of a Western Isles constituency, and Duncan Cameron's manifesto, issued on New Year's Day, proclaiming his intention to "do battle for the crofters", forced Fraser-Mackintosh on the following day to inform the Inverness Burgh Liberals of his withdrawal from the burghs seat in favour of the shire seat. Cameron continued his electioneering for some time, mainly in Skye, but ultimately yielded to the persuasion of Donald Murray, secretary of the London H.L.L.R.A., who pointed out the dangers of a split vote, and on July 15, 1885, Cameron finally withdrew.

Prelude to Elections

The election of 1885 was a long time in coming as the new register of voters had to be prepared. Before the election came there had been a change of Government. In June, 1885, the Liberal Government had been surprisingly defeated by a combination of Conservative and Irish Nationalists in a vote on the budget. Gladstone, who had been mercilessly attacked over the failure of the British expedition to the Sudan (which led to the death of General Gordon), was only too glad to resign, and the Marquis of Salisbury headed a "Caretaker" Government until the dissolution of Parliament in the autumn. The preparation of the electoral register was not a straightforward task, especially in the Highlands. In the 1880s, registration courts were held at Inverness, Dingwall and other towns. Applications on behalf of crofters were invariably opposed by the Conservative agent and to a lesser extent by the official Liberal agent in cases where the names had been omitted from the lists drawn up by the Government assessor from information received from the factors, who, apart from genuine mistakes, omitted cottars (as distinct from crofters) and those in arrears. Fraser Mackintosh, in a letter to the *Times*, characterised the registration in Inverness-shire as "deplorable". The assessor's list contained nearly 9,000 names, but, through imperfect returns from owners and for other reasons, it was found that over 2,500 had been omitted. As the sheriffs would not authorise registration courts in the Outer Hebrides, about 1,000 claims, it was estimated, were not considered at all.

The conference of Highland Land Law Reform Association delegates in the beginning of September in Portree was in many respects similar to the pre-election conference of the main political parties today. There was none of today's television coverage but the press (friendly and hostile) reported speeches at great length, often *verbatim*. Although the timing of the conference prevented the attendance of many men who were at the east coast fishing, it was representative of a wide range of opinions and was considered a splendid success by the organizers. In addition to delegates from branches of the associations in crofting townships and cities in the south, there were representatives of Socialist or near-Socialist organizations, such as the Scottish Land Restoration League, which was to put up five candidates (including the former editor of the *Highlander* newspaper, John Murdoch), at the ensuing election in Glasgow and Greenock without success. Some of its members were soon afterwards to join in founding the Scottish Labour Party, Dr G.B. Clark, chairman of the executive committee of the London H.L.L.R.A., and prospective candidate for Caithness, was himself in favour of nationalisation of the land and was later to be prominent in the International Working Men's Association. But throughout the meetings, which included a "grand demonstration" of over 4,000 persons in a field near Portree, the emphasis was on land law reform in the Highlands and Islands. One of the

156

principal resolutions expressed approval of the candidature of six men "pledged to vote for a satisfactory scheme of land reform" — Charles Fraser Mackintosh (Inverness-shire), D.H. MacFarlane (Argyll), Dr Roderick MacDonald (Ross and Cromarty), Dr G.B. Clark (Caithness), Angus Sutherland (Sutherland) and W.S. Bright MacLaren (Inverness Burghs). These were the first official crofter candidates, to be reinforced soon afterwards by J. MacDonald Cameron, as prospective candidate in the Northern Burghs constituency.

Electioneering Cruises

Two of the crofter candidates whose constituencies were widely-scattered made effective use of their yachts in their electioneering — D.H. MacFarlane in Argyll and Fraser Mackintosh in Inverness-shire. It was in MacFarlane's yacht that Professor John Stuart Blackie and two parliamentary colleagues of MacFarlane had toured in the Hebrides at the time of the Ross and Cromarty by-election in 1884. In 1885, in his steam yacht, *Vanadia*, MacFarlane visited the islands in his constituency such as Lismore, Tiree, Coll, Mull and Iona, and also places remote from any rail-head such as Ardnamurchan. Donald MacFarlane was born in Caithness and emigrated to Australia when he was only eight years of age. After a successful commercial career in Calcutta, he returned to Britain and through his wife, the daughter of a Q.C., he became interested in Irish politics and joined the Roman Catholic Church. He entered Parliament as M.P. for County Carlow in Ireland in 1880 and was soon afterwards prominent in the House of Commons as a champion of the crofters in the Scottish Highlands and Islands. His decision to stand for a Highland constituency was attributed by the *Scotsman*, rightly or wrongly, to his fears of losing his Irish seat; but his chief interest was undoubtedly in the crofters' problems rather than in Irish Home Rule. His conversion to Catholicism brought difficulty for him in some parts of Argyll. The Rev. Neil Taylor, Free Church minister of Dornoch, in a letter to the electors of Argyll, referred to him as "a Papist and a pervert from Presbyterianism", unworthy of their votes. His religion, his support of Irish Home Rule, and rumours that some of his crew had been engaged in fishing from his yacht on a Sunday, did not prevent him from winning Argyll at the election against a Liberal Radical, John Stuart MacCaig, the Oban banker, who polled only 665 votes, and William MacKinnon of Balinakill, standing as an Independent, "a Protestant protester and Sabbath defender", who polled 2,852 votes, only about 500 fewer than MacFarlane's 3,336. Lord Colin Campbell, son of the Duke of Argyll, had been Liberal M.P. since 1878 but had decided not to contest the seat after his wife had secured a deed of separation on the grounds of cruelty. The Duke himself was almost apoplectic over MacFarlane's victory. Writing to Gladstone, he declared:—

> "We have had a thorough blackguard elected by the 'Crofters' — by sheer Bribery of Promises, one being to Fishermen that they should get all the Salmon as well as the Herring".

MacFarlane was to lose his seat the following year to a Conservative candidate, Col. Malcolm of Poltalloch, but regained it in 1892 and ended his political career as Sir Donald MacFarlane.

The yachting cruise of Fraser Mackintosh actually forms the subject of a book written by Hector Rose MacKenzie, son of Alexander MacKenzie, the "Clach", of Inverness. He accompanied Fraser Mackintosh on the cruise and later became a lawyer in Inverness. His account of the electioneering cruise appeared in the *Celtic Magazine*, edited by his father, and consists mainly of descriptions of the places visited, with only brief accounts of the election meetings. Fraser Mackintosh, having overcome the difficulty presented by the candidature of another crofter candidate, Duncan Cameron of Oban, was faced with opposition from an "official" Liberal candidate, Sir Kenneth MacKenzie of Gairloch, a much-respected landlord and one of the members of the Napier Commission but, as a landlord, not acceptable to most of the crofters except in his own country. He had stood as Liberal candidate in Inverness-shire in 1880, when he had been narrowly defeated by the Conservative, Donald Cameron of Lochiel, by 808 votes to 779. The third candidate for Inverness-shire was the Conservative, Reginald MacLeod, son of MacLeod of MacLeod. He had been private secretary to Sir Stafford Northcote, the Conservative leader of the House of Commons under Disraeli when he became Earl of Beaconsfield. MacLeod's chances in a constituency with a predominantly crofter electorate seemed remote. Even in the MacLeod country in Skye, the pressure of public opinion was such that three of his supporters at Talisker said that they did not want to pledge themselves in the canvass book, although they intended to vote for him.[7]

Fraser Mackintosh's cruise in his yacht *Carlotta* lasted from September 5 (just after the Portree conference of the Highland Land Law Reform Association) to October 2, 1885, and enabled him to visit the more remote parts of the mainland as well as almost all the townships in Skye and the Western Isles, although the weather was so stormy that the captain refused to take the yacht round the west side of Harris. At his meetings he was frequently heckled about his connection with Sir John Ramsden's estate of Alvie near Aviemore, where he had acted as legal adviser, and also with the estate of Mackintosh of Mackintosh in Lochaber, where he had been commissioner. Both the

Whig newspapers, the *Scotsman* and the *Inverness Courier*, gave publicity to allegations about evictions on these estates and kept up a running flow of criticism of Fraser Mackintosh, whom they regarded as a turncoat. The *Courier* was accused by him of propagating falsehoods and was at last forced to issue a rather lame apology for the allegations about evictions at Alvie. Copies of the *Courier*, containing these allegations marked with a cross, had been distributed free in Skye, but at Sconser they had been soaked in paraffin and burned. In the event, Fraser Mackintosh of Drummond (as he was designated) was returned by the voters at the top of the poll, with 3,555 votes, Reginald MacLeod surprisingly second with 2,031 and Sir Kenneth MacKenzie third with 1,897, the turn-out of electors being 80 per cent, a very high poll for a rural constituency.

The Radical Marquis

The Marquis of Stafford, eldest son and heir of the Duke of Sutherland, had represented the county of Sutherland as a Liberal M.P. since 1874 and had been returned unopposed at each election. In his first ten years as M.P., the Marquis of Stafford had never been heard in public either in or out of Parliament, but in the autumn of 1884 he toured the county, consulting with the Free Church ministers about the grievances of the people, and in October he presided at a huge demonstration staged in Golspie in favour of the Franchise Bill. From then onwards, either in order to conciliate those who were about to be enfranchised or from the prickings of conscience and a sincere desire to make amends for the actions of his ancestors and their officials, he became an advocate of land reform.[8] It was presumably at his instigation that his father, the Duke of Sutherland, sanctioned the publication of proposals intended to ameliorate the conditions of the crofters. They included an offer of 400 acres of grazing between East and West Langwell, formerly the property of George Dempster's family, but described as "moorland of very unpromising character" by John MacKay of Hereford, a wealthy sympathiser of the crofters. The proposals, if made five years earlier, would have been accepted by the crofters as worthwhile concessions but they were, as Disraeli said of the British policy in Ireland, unfortunately "too little, too late". The Marquis's conversion to Radicalism seemed to many too good to be true. At Bonar Bridge in June, 1885, he advocated the abolition of the House of Lords, peasant proprietorship, and nationalisation of the land — "out-Georging Henry George". When he addressed a meeting at Rogart in the following month, Donald Bannerman asked him if he would be able to

"withstand the influence of his father, the Duke of Sutherland, his uncle, the Duke of Argyll, and his cousins, the Marquis of Lorne and Lord Colin Campbell, and others of the aristocracy".

Although the Marquis replied hopefully, the crofters' leaders were not convinced. By this time, Angus Sutherland, the Glasgow Academy teacher, had been adopted as crofter candidate; and the county of Sutherland had the unusual situation of not merely having a contest but a contest between men of similar views — both Liberal and Radical and both pro-crofter. The Marquis's early electioneering tour of the county had not been fruitless. The ministers were favourably impressed by the apparently sincere desire on the part of the Marquis to bring about an improvement in landlord-tenant relations. At a meeting in Golspie in October, 1885, the Free Church minister, while congratulating Angus Sutherland, a crofter's son, on his pluck in coming forward, assured his audience that there was no man "more able to redress their grievances or forward their interests in the British House of Commons than the Marquis of Stafford". But the minister's support of his candidature was assailed by the supporters of Angus Sutherland as "clerical toadyism". Free Church ministers outside Sutherland who advocated his return were also criticised:

> "Who played the flunkey to the Marquis of Stafford and boasted that he had kept Mr Angus Sutherland from representing his native county? Why, the Free Church minister of Queen Street, Inverness."

The Queen Street minister, the Rev. A.C. MacDonald, supported the Marquis as "a most advanced Liberal, if not a fully-fledged Radical". At any rate, the Marquis's Radicalism and the support of the ministers brought him victory at the election by 1,701 votes to 1,058, and Angus Sutherland had to wait another year before becoming M.P. Stafford decided before the election of 1886 not to stand again, as he felt his position had become invidious, as the son of the landlord of most of his constituents. During the short Parliament of 1885-86, he introduced a crofters bill, which, although never debated, had some merit and was reckoned to have influenced the Government's bill. When he succeeded his father in 1893 as Duke of Sutherland, he offered the crofters a land purchase scheme which Alexander MacKenzie, the "Clach", described as "undeniably Liberal".

The "Carpet-baggers"

After the Civil War in the United States ended in 1865, there was a stream of glib-talking adventurers from the north seeking political careers among the newly-enfranchised people of the southern states. As their only property was in the personal goods carried in their carpet bags, they were christened "carpet-baggers". They have been called by a distinguished historian "a disgraceful horde of office and spoils seekers" who exploited their position and brought about chaos in the administration of the southern states. It may seem surprising that such a name as "carpet-bagger" should have been applied to the men who journeyed up from the south in the 1880s to stand as candidates at the elections on behalf of the crofters; but the newspapers of that period not infrequently indulged in vituperation and scurrilous innuendoes which would not be tolerated today. It was the *Scotsman* which first applied the term contemptuously to Dr Roderick MacDonald and Dr Gavin B. Clark, who travelled north in the spring of 1884 as prospective candidates for the constituencies of Ross and Cromarty and of Caithness respectively. The leader-writer of the Whig newspaper regarded such men with the greatest suspicion:

> "No greater misfortune could befall the Highland counties than that they should become the hunting-ground of candidates from London and elsewhere, who have absolutely no interest identical with them".

The H.L.L.R.A. conference at Portree in September, 1885, was regarded by the *Scotsman* as "organized for the sole purpose of trying to secure the election of the carpet-baggers".

In contrast to the spoils of office sought by the American carpet-baggers, the crofter candidates had little to gain and much to lose. Indeed, only men with a sufficient income could hope to contest an election in the Highlands and Islands at all. Once elected, those who had a home in London or in the south were able to attend to their duties in the House of Commons, in those days not so burdensome as today, and earn a living elsewhere, as there was no payment of M.P.s until 1912. As a crofter's son, a vice-president of the London H.L.L.R.A., chairman of the Gaelic Society of London, and later from 1886 treasurer of the Crofters' Defence Fund, Dr MacDonald had, contrary to the assertions of the *Scotsman*, an obvious community of interests with the crofter supporters. MacDonald's appearance as crofter candidate at the Ross-shire by-election of 1884 made his passage to Westminster an easy matter at the general election in December, 1885, defeating his opponent of 1884, the Liberal candidate, Munro-Ferguson, by 4,942 to 2,925 votes. The *Scotsman*, reporting the result, commented on the "melancholy fact" that nearly 2,000 "illiterate" votes were polled in Ross and Cromarty and that a large number of voters, unable to read English, in consequence "knew nothing of politics".[9] There was no Conservative candidate at the 1885 election, which may have increased Munro-Ferguson's total somewhat. Novar (as he was called in the Highlands) had changed his politics to some extent and vied with the Marquis of Stafford in his

Radical proposals. At his meeting in Ullapool at the Good Templar Hall on September 30, 1885, where he advocated the 3F's of the Irish Land Act (fixity of tenure, fair rents, and free sale of any improvements, such as a house), loans for fishermen to purchase larger boats, it is not surprising that he was afterwards carried shoulder-high to the Royal Hotel. But his welcome at Stornoway a fortnight later was quite the reverse, the police being summoned to escort him from the steamer at the quay to his hotel (which also was a Royal Hotel). Novar was fighting a losing battle from the start: he lost the support of the Free Church ministers who had spoken for him in 1884 by his voting for the admission of the agnostic, Bradlaugh, to the House of Commons. He returned to Parliament the following year as member for Leith and became private secretary to Lord Rosebery, rising to greater heights later in his career. Dr MacDonald was to retain the seat of Ross and Cromarty until he retired in 1892.

Caithness and the Northern Isles

Dr Gavin B. Clark, who was, with Dr MacDonald, the first of the London Scots on the scene even before the Franchise Bill was passed, had no family connection with the Highlands. The son of a Glasgow insurance agent, he had run away to sea at the age of thirteen but after some years before the mast qualified as a doctor, practising as a surgeon in Edinburgh and London hospitals. He was well-known in political and temperance circles, being editor of the *Good Templar* newspaper. He was also consul in London for the Boers of the Transvaal and was credited with having taken an active part in persuading Gladstone to grant independence to the Transvaal in 1881. His championship of the rights of national minorities led him to join the Scottish Home Rule Association, of which he became chairman. His views were what would nowadays be called "left-wing": he favoured nationalisation of the land, he was one of the leading lights in the First International, and he was vice-chairman of the Scottish Labour Party, formed in 1888. He was not put out by being called a "carpet-bagger" by the *Scotsman*:

> "The more the *Scotsman* abused him, the better he felt, as no greater enemy to the Highlands ever existed than that paper".

In Caithness, where he had been proposed as candidate in March, 1884, his opponent was also a Liberal, Major Sinclair, younger, of Ulbster, whose father, grandfather and great-grandfather had all been M.P.s for the county. Although a landlord's son and suffering from "want of knowledge" (as Dr Clark claimed), like the Marquis of Stafford and Novar, Sinclair put forward a number of Radical proposals — peasant proprietorship, enlargement of existing holdings, taxation of deer forests. The family tradition probably contributed more than his Radical views to his gaining 1,218 votes but still well behind the Liberal crofter candidate, Dr Clark, who received 2,110 votes.

The H.L.L.R.A. movement had in 1885 made little impact on the people of Orkney and Shetland, but they had been roused to a realisation of their condition by the visit of the Napier Commission, and the H.L.L.R.A. policy of opposition to landlords and their sons was paralleled in the Northern Isles, where the Earl of Zetland's son, the Hon. Cospatrick Dundas, standing as a Conservative candidate, was defeated by the Liberal, who favoured land law reform. Leonard Lyell was himself a laird but not a Highland laird (of Kinnordy in Angus) and nephew of the famous geologist, Sir Charles Lyell. Lyell was to hold the seat until 1900 and eventually gained a peerage.

Burgh Constituencies

The two burgh constituencies in the crofting area were both faced with elections between Liberal candidates but of different views. Described as a "carpet-bagger", the crofter candidate for the Northern Burghs (Wick, Dornoch, Tain, Dingwall, Cromarty and Kirkwall), John MacDonald Cameron, called himself "son of a poor man" and "one of themselves". At his opening meeting in the Temperance Hall, Wick, on October 12, 1885, he attacked the landed interest, still predominant in the House of Commons, and he advocated the election to the House of Commons of "men of intelligence and experience, men who are of the people and know their wants" — in other words, men like himself. Cameron had been brought up at Dornoch and at Saltburn near Invergordon, then at school in Perth. Starting as an exciseman, he became an industrial chemist, working in mines in India, Mexico and South America. A Gaelic speaker and native of the north of Scotland, he might have been expected to possess an advantage over the official Liberal candidate, John Pender of Minard Castle, who had held the seat since 1872, but Cameron triumphed only by a very narrow majority of 55, 923 against 868. Cameron was to hold the seat until 1900, when Pender (by then Sir John Pender) regained it as a Unionist.[10]

The Inverness seat (Inverness, Fortrose, Forres and Nairn), which had been vacated by Fraser Mackintosh, was contested by two Lowlanders, both Liberals — R.B. Finlay, Q.C., a man with a distinguished legal career ahead of him and W.S. Bright MacLaren, the Radical son of a Radical father, Duncan MacLaren, once called "the member for Scotland".

It was in Inverness, on the 18th of September, 1885, that one of the most notable speeches of the election campaign was delivered. Joseph Chamberlain, the Radical leader, had earlier in the week addressed a meeting in the St Andrew's Halls, in Glasgow, with thousands waiting outside for a sight of the famous orator and his audience listening with rapt attention for two-and-a-half-hours. Chamberlain had announced in the summer a Radical programme, the so-called "unauthorised Programme" — free schools, disestablishment of the Welsh and Scottish churches, payment of M.P.s, crofters' rights, the break-up of large estates into small holdings ("3 acres and a cow", as a Tory M.P. described it). His speeches attracted enthusiastic audiences but created embarrassment for the Prime Minister, Gladstone, and his colleagues in the Cabinet. In what his biographer called the "most passionate speech" of his triumphant campaign, at Inverness, he attacked the Scottish landowners with such venom that, according to Sir William Harcourt, "the red hair of Argyll must have been blanched". Argyll himself was shocked by the "outrageous falsehoods" of his former colleague, Chamberlain, at Inverness and warned Gladstone that "our Brummagem Elisha is determined to secure your mantle even before you have gone up to Heaven". It was in the Inverness speech that Chamberlain quoted the lines which afterwards became famous:—

From the lone shieling of the misty island
Mountains divide us and the waste of seas;
Yet still the blood is strong; the heart is Highland
And we in dreams behold the Hebrides.

Chamberlain's address, however did not altogether please the crofters' sympathisers, who complained that he had ignored them while "puffing up" the "landlord candidates", Munro-Ferguson of Novar and MacKenzie of Gairloch. He was given the freedom of Inverness and cheered by hundreds on the platforms of the railway stations on his homeward journey.

The main issue in the Inverness Burghs election was not crofters' rights but Disestablishment. The young Radical, MacLaren, had come out boldly for Disestablishment and Disendowment of the Church of Scotland while Finlay, who was against both, stated that he would not oppose either if the Scottish people expressed their opinion unmistakably. The Scottish Liberals at their annual conference had voted decisively for Disestablishment by 400 to 7 votes, Of the 87 Liberal candidates, only 9 were against, 48 were for, and 30 would vote for a Government measure. Gladstone, himself the M.P. for a Scottish constituency, Midlothian, was in a cleft stick as he knew the issue would divide the voters even more than the candidates. He was expected by Principal Rainy of the Free Church (a distant relative) to declare for Disestablishment, but at a crowded meeting in the Free Church Assembly Hall, he refused to pledge himself. Before the meeting, a petition against Disestablishment signed by 64 per cent of the electors of Midlothian had been presented to Gladstone, who had little alternative but to take the stand he did. In Inverness, the issue which Alexander MacKenzie, the "Clach", called a red herring, became the dominant issue by the time of the election. On November 23, 1885, the Sunday before the election, Dr George MacKay of the Inverness Free North Church (where he had been minister for forty years) at the end of his afternoon service spoke out strongly against MacLaren on the subject of Disestablishment. Finlay, who won the election by 1,709 to 1,546 votes, was to rise to the very summit of the legal profession in England, holding the office of Lord Chancellor during the First World War and becoming Viscount Finlay of Nairn.

After the 1885 Election

The elections of 1885 lasted almost a fortnight, beginning on Monday, November 24, and ending on Friday, December 4. While the elections were in progress, the hopes and fears of both parties rose and fell, but in the end the Liberals in Scotland won 61 seats against the Conservatives' 9 seats. This result produced a situation very similar to that following the general election of 1880, when the Liberals won 53 seats to the Tories 7. (The total number of seats in 1880 was 60, as against 70 seats in 1885 as a result of the Redistribution Act of that year.) The M.P.s who had stood as crofter candidates and are included in the total of 61 Liberals were five in number — Fraser Mackintosh (Inverness-shire), MacDonald (Ross and Cromarty), MacFarlane (Argyll), Clark (Caithness), Cameron (Northern Burghs). As Fraser Mackintosh pointed out in the House of Commons debate on the second reading of the Crofters Bill, the Marquis of Stafford had stood in Sutherland and as a land law reform candidate, and the new member for Orkney and Shetland was "heartily with them". In other words, the whole of the crofting area was represented by M.P.s who gave priority to the interests of the crofters, with the exception of Inverness Burghs.

The total numbers in the new House of Commons were not so predominantly in favour of the Liberals, who held 334 seats to the Conservatives' 248, a majority of 86, while the Irish Nationalists held 86 seats, one of them a constituency in Lancashire. These Irish M.P.s were the famous "86 of '86", who held the future of Parliament in their hands. Parnell, the Irish Nationalist leader, had been given to understand by Salisbury, the "Caretaker" Prime Minister, that the

Conservatives would bring in some measure of Home Rule for Ireland, and Parnell had actually advised Irishmen resident in Britain to vote Tory. But after such a heavy defeat, Salisbury resigned and handed over the Irish problem to Gladstone, then in his seventy-seventh year. The Liberal leader decided to introduce an Irish Home Rule Bill and by so doing he split the Liberal party. Chamberlain, leading the dissident Liberals, joined with the Conservatives to defeat the bill, and Gladstone then went to the country after only half a year in office.

During the short session, a Crofters Bill was introduced by the Government in response to the pressure exerted by the crofter M.P.s and their friends, mostly Radical, in the Commons. The bill pleased no one. The crofter M.P.s accepted it as better than nothing, but MacFarlane, M.P. for Argyll, described it as "a miserable, deluded, rubbishy measure". At the third reading, he and his friends voted against it as a protest at the Government's decision not to accept any of the amendments proposed by the crofter members; but on the last day of the session, just before Parliament was prorogued, the bill received the Royal Assent. The Crofters' Holdings (Scotland) Act, which gave the crofters security of tenure and provided for the setting-up of a permanent Crofters Commission to fix fair rents proved much more beneficial than the crofter candidates had anticipated and heralded a new era in the Highlands and Islands. The split over Irish Home Rule was to prove permanent in Britain. Those Liberals who opposed Home Rule (40 per cent of the Scottish Liberals) became known as Unionists, a name that came to be applied to Conservatives. At the time of the dissolution of Parliament, Col. Malcolm of Poltalloch, who had come forward as prospective candidate for Argyll, was referred to by the *Scotsman* in one paragraph as a Conservative and in another as a Unionist.

The elections of July, 1886, brought little change in the Highlands and Islands. The crofter party in all issues affecting the crofters received support from a few dozen, mainly Scottish and Radical, M.P.s as well as the Irish Nationalists and maintained its voting strength. Angus Sutherland in the county of Sutherland replaced the independent Liberal Marquis of Stafford, who resigned; but in Argyll, MacFarlane was defeated by the Conservative and Unionist Col. Malcolm of Poltalloch. There was little doubt that MacFarlane's defeat was due to his being a Roman Catholic, the Protestants of Argyll, like those in mid-Scotland, interpreting "Home Rule" as "Rome Rule". Fraser Mackintosh was the only Unionist among the crofter M.P.s. He was returned unopposed at the 1886 election but met with defeat in 1892, when Unionism was regarded in the Highlands as disloyalty to Gladstone, revered there as elsewhere in Scotland. At no election afterwards was there anything approaching the agitation, the excitement, the bitterness of these two years. Looking back from the viewpoint of almost a century later, we can see that the elections of 1884-86 formed a watershed in the political history of the Highlands and Islands.

Notes

1. Matthew Russell, chief magistrate of Stornoway in the 1880s, was grand-uncle of Sir Russell Johnston, Liberal M.P. for Inverness-shire.

2. The story of Dr MacDonald's electioneering in 1884 was published in the *Ross-shire Journal* in a series of articles in November, 1929, by "Senex".

3. The progress of the Disestablishment dispute may be studied in A. Stewart and J. Kennedy Cameron, *The Free Church of Scotland*, 1843-1910 (1911) on the one side and P.C. Simpson, *Life of Principal Rainy* (1910) on the other, and an impartial account is given in J.G. Kellas, "The Liberal Party and the Scottish Church Disestablishment Crisis" in the *English Historical Review*, lxxix (1964).

4. It was in August, 1884, that William Lever and his wife, on a steamboat cruise, spent a few hours in Stornoway and were so "enchanted by the natural beauty of the scenery" and "the charm and attraction of the people" of Lewis that more than thirty years later he purchased the island (Nigel Nicolson, *Lord of the Isles* (1960), 2).

5. The difficulties of travelling in the Highlands a century before the era of the motor car are well illustrated by the following extract from Duncan Cameron's diary:—

   Tuesday, 13th January, 1885 — Left Oban 4 p.m.; Stirling, 8.10; left by express for Perth at 10.29; arrived Perth 11.36; left for Inverness at 12.40 a.m.; arrived 8 o'clock. Fare 38/-. Breakfast 2/- and 1/- at Perth. Left for Strome at 9 o'clock; arrived 1 o'clock (17/1 fare to Portree). Left 3.45; arrived 7.15 p.m. Left 5 a.m. for Dunvegan; arrived 9.30 a.m.

6. For a discussion of the pros and cons of a separate constituency for the Western Isles, see the letter of the Duke of Argyll to Gladstone on December 4, 1884, published in the Appendix.

7. Cameron of Lochiel, canvassing on Reginald MacLeod's behalf in Lochaber before the 1885 election, met a Catholic priest, who, although a Conservative, refused to give MacLeod his vote as his ancestor had not come out for Prince Charles in 1745. (I.F. Grant, *The MacLeods* (1959), 590).

8. On the occasion of the Marquis's marriage to the daughter of the Earl of Rosslyn later in October, 1884, a general holiday was observed in Sutherland with bonfires, decorations, children's treats, Volunteer processions, balls and banquets. (*Northern Chronicle*, Oct. 22, 1884). His mother, the Duchess of Sutherland, Countess of Cromartie in her own

right, was proprietrix of Coigach, where, according to MacKenzie in his *Highland Clearances*, the tenants were among the most comfortable in the north of Scotland.

9. Reginald MacLeod, at a meeting of the Scottish Primrose League in Edinburgh after the election, ascribed the Liberal success to "new masses of ignorance sweeping the constituencies" and the electors being easily "misled by wretched falsehoods of the Liberal Party" (*Scottish Highlander*, Jan. 1, 1886).

10. It was in the Wick newspaper, the *Northern Ensign*, owned by Provost William Rae and later by his son, Sir Alexander Rae, that Angus MacKay, president of the Strathnaver Crofter Association, wrote trenchant articles on franchise extension and land law reform under the pen-name, "Free Lance". (Joseph MacLeod, *Highland Heroes of the Land Reform Movement* (1917), 68).

CHAPTER 8

THE CROFTERS ACT

The First Crofters Bills

During the year 1884, Sir William Harcourt, the Home Secretary, and the House of Commons were very much involved with the controversial London Local Government Bill, which Harcourt had to abandon after ceaseless opposition, and the Franchise and Redistribution Bills, which were to make the working class a dominant factor in politics from then onwards. The Prime Minister, Gladstone, who claimed to be "a full-blooded Scot" and who went to great lengths to redress Irish grievances, was sympathetic to the Scottish crofters but was too engrossed in the problems of Ireland and the Sudan to have time for the crofters' grievances. When in January, 1885, Sir William Harcourt, assisted by J.B. Balfour, the Lord Advocate, prepared a measure dealing with crofters' affairs, involving "the substantial application of the Irish Land Act to Highland parishes", Gladstone sent Harcourt a detailed analysis of the draft bill. Referring to the rights of proprietors, the Prime Minister wrote:

> "In point of moral title to live on the land . . . I scarcely know how to distinguish between the Chief and his followers. It was might, not right, which was on his side when after the '45 . . . he took to the rearing of rents, backed by the law, which took no cognisance of any rights but his."

Harcourt, in his speech in the House of Commons on November 14, 1884, announcing the dispatch of a military expedition to the Isle of Skye, had appealed to the proprietors in the crofting areas to put forward proposals making some concessions and invited them to get together to consider what should be done. At a conference of proprietors held at Inverness on January 14, 1885, more than half of those who attended were factors or chamberlains and only moderate concessions received consideration. The enlargement of holdings and the grant of loans to crofters were conceded but with the proviso that there should be no compulsion on landowners. A useful part as intermediary was played by Donald Cameron of Lochiel, a member of the Conservative opposition. By February 13, Harcourt, in consultation with the Lord Advocate, J.B. Balfour, and Lord Rosebery, at that time Under-Secretary in the Home Office, was able to inform Gladstone that the bill was ready for submission to the Cabinet; but it was not until May 18 that the Crofters' Holdings (Scotland) Bill was introduced by the Lord Advocate. The bill bore a certain resemblance to the Royal Commission Report but did not accept the Commission's recommendations for crofters' communes or for the compulsory purchase of land for enlargement of holdings (except with considerable restrictions). The bill received a fairly cool welcome, some people comparing it unfavourably with the Irish Land Act of 1881, on which it was based. But with the change of Government following the sudden defeat of the Liberals on June 24, the Crofters Bill was dropped.

Salisbury's "Caretaker" ministry gave way, after the election defeat in December, 1885, to Gladstone and the Liberals. By this time the office of Secretary for Scotland was in existence, the first holder, the Duke of Richmond and Gordon, having been appointed in the previous August by the Marquis of Salisbury. It was a period of resurgent nationalism (the Scottish Home Rule Association was formed in 1886) and Gladstone's choice for the post, Sir George Otto Trevelyan, was not popular in Scotland, where he was regarded as an Englishman, although through his mother he was descended from the MacAulays of Lewis.[1] It fell to Trevelyan to introduce the second Crofters' Holdings (Scotland) Bill, which he did on February 25, 1886. Already, the Radical Marquis of Stafford, M.P. for Sutherland, had attempted to introduce his own Crofters Bill, similar in its provisions to the Liberal bill of the previous year but with extra clauses dealing with compulsory acquisition of deer forests, made possible by government loans to help crofters stock any land granted to them. The Marquis's proposal that disputes between landlord and tenant should be settled by the local sheriff created some derision in Inverness-shire, where the sheriff, William Ivory, was regarded with little respect. Stafford's bill was introduced just before Salisbury's Government gave place to Gladstone's and was automatically dropped. Trevelyan did not last long as Scottish Secretary as he resigned on March 29 along with Joseph Chamberlain in protest against Gladstone's Home Rule policy for Ireland. As Trevelyan's successor, the Earl of Dalhousie, sat in the House of Lords, it was once again the Lord Advocate, J.B. Balfour, who was in charge of the bill's passage through the House of Commons.

Crofters' Holdings (Scotland) Act, 1886

There was widespread criticism of the bill when first published and H.L.L.R.A. branches all over the country passed resolutions condemning it as a landlord's bill; but the opinion of the crofter M.P.s generally was that it could be improved on its passage through

170

Parliament. Despite some criticism, mainly from crofters' friends, the bill survived its second reading. At the committee stage, several amendments were moved without success. Before the House went into Committee, Sir George Campbell, M.P. for Kirkcaldy Burghs, moved that no bill dealing with the crofting tenure would be acceptable which did not provide pecuniary assistance.[2] Sir William Harcourt, by this time Chancellor of the Exchequer, was against such expenditure as it would provide a precedent for identical requests from other parts of the country. The Marquis of Stafford cited the provision in the Irish Land Act for loans amounting to £5 million, and Campbell referred to other cases of Government loans, e.g. £100,000 to prevent the eviction of 30,000 residents of Bechuanaland by the Boers, but the amendment was defeated. In the committee stage, D.H. MacFarlane, M.P. for Argyll, was likewise unsuccessful in his effort to include the cottars (25 per cent of the people in the Highlands and Islands) in the provisions for crofters. Dr Clark, M.P. for Caithness, proposed to give the crofter power to assign his croft as in Ireland, where the tenant had free sale of improvements, but was defeated. The amendment moved by Dr MacDonald, M.P. for Ross and Cromarty, that all members of the Crofters Commission to be set up in terms of the Act should be Gaelic speakers was unsuccessful, but another amendment was carried stipulating that at least one member of the commission should have the Gaelic. The Lord Advocate's opposition to all amendments was supported by the Conservatives but created such frustration among the crofters' friends that on April 15 Dr Clark tried to stop further debate on the bill, declaring that in its present form it was just "a delusion and a sham". On May 6, at the Report stage Charles Fraser Mackintosh, M.P. for Inverness-shire, had his amendment to include Cromarty in the list of crofter counties reluctantly accepted by the Lord Advocate, and Sir George Campbell's amendment to add to the clause defining a crofter, "one who resides on his holding", the words "or near" was carried by 70 votes to 59 in a very late, sparsely-attended session, only to be defeated in the House of Lords and again when it returned to the House of Commons. On the motion that it should be read a third time, MacFarlane moved its rejection. It was on this occasion that he summed it up as "a miserable, deluded, rubbishy measure". The bill finally became law by receiving the Royal Assent on June 25, 1886, the day Parliament was prorogued.

Criticism of the Crofters Act

The Crofters Act of 1886, which M.P.s friendly to the crofters had denounced, at first pleased no one. To understand the reasons for the widespread opposition, it is worth while considering the main features of the Act:—

(1) Security of tenure for crofters, provided rent was paid, the croft not to be let without the landlord's permission, and the croft not allowed to deteriorate.

(2) Fair rents to be fixed by a crofters commission on application by either landlord or tenant.

(3) Compensation for improvements for a crofter who gives up his croft or is removed from it.

(4) Crofts not to be sold but may be bequeathed to a relative.

(5) Compulsory enlargement of holdings, with certain restrictions, applications to be considered by a crofters commission.

(6) A permanent commission to be set up to administer the Act.

(7) Compensation for a cottar who pays a rent for his holding which he leaves voluntarily.

The first three clauses, as detailed above, were based on the 3F's of the Irish Land Act of 1881 — fixed tenure, fair rents to be decided by a land court, and free sale of improvements. There was some advantage to the Irish tenant in regard to the sale of improvements being free from restriction; but in practice the Scottish crofter, living in a closely-knit community, would have little difficulty in finding a relative willing to accept and pay for the bequest of a croft. Security of tenure, reduced rents and cancellation of arrears changed the crofter's attitude, although some thought that all arrears should be cancelled as in Ireland. Later, with hindsight, historians, economists and writers on agricultural subjects have pointed out that the size of crofts was generally too small to make them viable and that not enough scope or incentive was given for the introduction of modern methods of cultivation. The new set-up in the crofting area, however, did create confidence to carry out improvements and a number of observers commented on the changes after 1886. Duncan Campbell, former editor of the Conservative *Northern Chronicle*, in his reminiscences wrote of Skye and the north-west mainland that "the advance has been most gratifying and in particular disticts almost marvellous". The Medical Officer of Health for Inverness-shire, Dr Grant, wrote in his report for 1890 and 1891 —

"Since the Crofters Act of 1886 much has been done by the people themselves to improve their dwellings and in Barra a skilled mason has been constantly employed in building houses of an improved type."

Enlargement of holdings was considered by Sir George Trevelyan, former Secretary for Scotland, "the very essence of the bill", which he had himself introduced. Certainly, compulsory enlargement of holdings was provided for but with so many conditions that it was difficult for any enlargement to take place. There had to be at least five crofters whose crofts were contiguous before the application would be considered and the land applied for must not be farmland and not under lease. Another objection to enlargement was the possibility of damaging the letting value of a farm or deer forest. Finally, the applicants must satisfy the Commission that they would be able to pay the rent and stock the land. It is little wonder that the familiar cry of "the land for the people" continued to be raised at political meetings, particularly by cottars, who were justified in their complaint that they had been completely neglected. Cottars received only one concession: they were given compensation if they had been paying a rent and voluntarily left their holdings. The appointment of a Crofters Commission was a necessary step towards fulfilment of the fairly limited aims detailed above and the Crofters Act may be said to have brought a new hope to the crofters and marked a watershed in the history of the Highlands and Islands. The Commission's work in drastically reducing rents and cancelling arrears was proof to the crofters that right had been on their side and strengthened their belief in the crofters' cause.

Crofters Commission

The Crofters' War did not come to an end with the passing of the Crofters' Holdings (Scotland) Act. Political agitation, grazing disputes, dyke-breaking, "No Rent" campaigns, military expeditions — all continued and on a greater scale than before. Implementation of the Act — the granting of security of tenure, the fixing of fair rents, the question of arrears, compensation for improvements — was entrusted to a small standing commission, appointed in accordance with the provisions of the Act. It was to comprise three members, one of whom should be an advocate of at least ten years' standing and one a Gaelic speaker. The three appointed by the Scottish Secretary, the Earl of Dalhousie, on June 7, 1886 (over a fortnight before the Crofters Bill actually received the Royal Assent) were David Brand, Advocate Depute and Sheriff of Ayr, William Hossack of Oban, Peter Macintyre of Mains of Findon in the Black Isle, a Gaelic speaker. They were to play an important part in the pacification of the crofting areas.

Sheriff David Brand, appointed chairman with a salary of £1200 a year (compared with his salary of £700 a year as Sheriff of Ayr) was the son of a Glasgow merchant, had no connection with the Highlands or Islands but was to spend most of the rest of his active life engaged in crofting affairs. In addition to his post as chairman of the Crofters Commission, he acted as chairman of a Royal Commission on the Highlands and Islands of Scotland from 1892 to 1895 (known also as the Deer Forest Commission) and he was also a member of the Congested Districts Board, set up in 1897. The Annual Reports of the Crofters Commission reveal a mind sympathetic to the crofters but realistic and objective. His *Report on the Social Condition of the people of Lewis in 1902 compared with twenty years ago* (called the Brand Report) is invaluable for the study of crofting life in the Hebrides. Brand was held in high regard by the islesmen: he was invited to act as chairman at the Annual Gathering of the Lewis and Harris Association in Glasgow in March, 1891, and also at a similar function of the Uist and Barra Association in Glagow in December, 1892. In his address to the Lewis and Harris Association, he praised the people of the Western Isles:

> "If I was placed in circumstances where I required the aid of men possessed of great powers of endurance, of self-denial, of absolute fearlessness, then I would choose a Lewisman in preference to the pale-faced artisan."

Appointed by a Liberal government in 1886, he served most of his time in office under Conservative-Unionist ministries, but was given the honour of knighthood in 1906, the year of the Liberal landslide victory and the year before his death.

The first task of the Crofters Commission was to collect information about the lands and rents of the applicants from factors, proprietors, old residents, clergymen, inspectors of poor in the various parishes with crofters' holdings. A crofting parish was defined as a parish in which there were at the time of the passing of the Crofters Act, or had been within 80 years before, holdings consisting of arable land, held with a right of free pasturage in common and in which there still were resident tenants of holdings, the annual rent of which did not exceed £35. Of the total of 163 parishes in the crofting counties — Inverness-shire, Ross and Cromarty, Argyll, Sutherland, Caithness, Orkney, Shetland — only 12 were omitted from the list of crofting parishes — 8 in Argyll, 2 in Ross and Cromarty, 2 in Inverness-shire. The Commission held hearings throughout the crofting areas (in some places more or less a repetition of the Napier Commission hearings), engaged surveyors to measure the ground, and in due course issued their findings, dealing with rents and arrears. In August, 1887, in order to expedite matters, a change was made in the procedure, whereby two of the members would hear evidence while the third would inspect the crofts along with a valuer; and in November, 1889, an Amending Act was introduced, enabling each of the three members to act individually along with valuers.

The Commission was from its inception designated the Land Court in certain newspapers in imitation of the Land Courts set up by the Irish Land Act of 1881, and the Commission exercised judicial functions throughout its existence until its disbandment in 1912 when the Scottish Land Court was set up. The first main survey of the Commission ended in May, 1891, with the decisions on the South Harris estate of the Earl of Dunmore. The reductions there were the greatest in the Hebrides: the average rent reduction was 48½ per cent and the amount of arrears cancelled 87 per cent. During the 26 years of its existence, 1886-1912, the Commission received 22,111 applications to have fair rents fixed, reduced rents on average by 24.5 per cent and cancelled 67 per cent of all arrears. In some areas the long period of waiting led to frustration so that the years 1886-1887 saw more agitation and violence than ever before, with the Government sending gunboats north to restore law and order.

In late September, 1886, there was held at Bonar Bridge in Sutherland the three-day annual conference of the Highland Land Law Reform Associations when preliminary steps were taken towards the formation of a united Highland Land League, comprising the London and Edinburgh Associations and the Sutherlandshire Association.[3] The general mood of the conference was one of confidence inspired by the passing of the Crofters Act and the successful showing by crofter candidates in the election in July. It was in the aftermath of this conference that the first hearing of the Crofters Commission was held in Sutherland, starting on October 13 at Dornoch and, after six weeks at Lairg and Bonar Bridge, returning to Dornoch from where on December 30 Sheriff Brand issued the Commission's findings. It had been a difficult start but Brand was praised for having done well. The crofters were fortunate in being represented by Kenneth MacDonald, Town Clerk of Inverness, and, in his absence, by Alexander MacKenzie, the "Clach".[4] One of the proprietors, Evan Sutherland Walker of Skibo near Dornoch, opposed the applications from his tenants (about 80 in number) to be heard. Most of the tenants had occupied their holdings on leases which expired at Whitsun, 1885 or 1886. After the latter date, Sutherland issued notices of removal to those who would not accept his conditions. On September 28 the estate manager with two sheriff officers arrived to evict Donald Fraser of Sleastery, driving off his cattle and pulling down some of his outhouses. But when they attempted to repeat the procedure at the house of a neighbour, John Logan, they were attacked by a large crowd of women and boys and driven back to Bonar Bridge, according to one reporter, "covered from head to foot with filth". Sutherland Walker refused to recognise the findings of the Commission but a small committee under Dr Gustavus Aird undertook the collection of the rents, which, after Walker had refused to accept them, were lodged in a bank and were ultimately handed over to the new owner when Walker sold Skibo.

The findings produced one surprise result, the rents being reduced and considerable amounts of arrears cancelled on all estates except those of the Duke of Sutherland, whose tenants' rents were increased by an average of 18.5 per cent, while tenants on the other estates (Skibo, Balblair, Rosehall, Gruids, Ospisdale) had rent reductions ranging from 17 to 51.5 per cent. There were two reasons for this surprise decision: the Duke's son, the Marquis of Stafford, had granted generous rent reductions in 1885 when elected M.P. for the county, and an addition of 1800 acres of hill grazing had been made to the Lairg tenants.

A.J. Balfour, Secretary for Scotland

After the Conservative election victory in July, 1886, the new Prime Minister, the Marquis of Salisbury, appointed his nephew, Arthur James Balfour, Secretary for Scotland: he was to hold many posts after that and become in time Prime Minister. Balfour was widely regarded as an aesthete, a dilettante, "the darling of perfumed drawing-rooms". He was himself going through a period of depression and doubt about his fitness for high office but he was to prove a resolute Secretary for Scotland and later Chief Secretary for Ireland, where he gained the nickname of "Bloody Balfour". He was not unacquainted with Highland problems; the large shooting estate of Strathconon had been purchased by his grandfather, and his father was responsible for the clearance of the strath. The future Prime Minister succeeded to the estate in 1869 but in 1885 he leased it as the income from the rents of his lowland estate in Whittinghame had slumped because of the depression in agriculture. He never again revisited his Highland estate and sold it in 1891 for £100,000.

He was succeeded as Scottish Secretary by the Marquis of Lothian in February, 1887, when he was appointed Chief Secretary of Ireland and during his brief tenure of office (16 months in all) Balfour was almost constantly engaged in planning and controlling military ex-peditions to the west and north of Scotland. His uncle, the Marquis of Salisbury, promoted him to the Cabinet on November 17, 1886, partly because Scottish affairs loomed large at the time, partly to improve the party's standing in Scotland (the Conservatives held only 12 of the 72 Scottish seats in Parliament), and partly because he wished to help his nephew in his political career. Much of the daily administration was carried on by the Permanent Under-Secretary, Sir Francis Sandford (later Lord Sandford), and the Assistant Under-Secretary, William C. Dunbar. As the Scottish Office was at Dover House in London, one of the administrative team (normally Dunbar) was stationed in the Edinburgh office, and communication was often by telegram. Balfour insisted on being sent copies of all letters and telegrams, and, in particular, the weekly police reports sent to the Sheriff of Inverness-shire. He wrote to his cousin, Lord Robert Cecil:—

> "The telegraph clerks in the Highlands are supposed to be in the interest of the crofters so I got the Foreign Office to provide us with one of their disused cyphers. We have all spent weary hours in trying to decipher telegrams so inaccurate they keep their secret from us as well."

At the end of August, 1886, Balfour met Malcolm MacNeill, who had been secretary of the Napier Commission in 1883, and entrusted him with a confidential mission of enquiry, in "the disturbed districts" of the Western Highlands and Islands. Balfour was being pressed by proprietors in the crofting areas for the dispatch of a military force to aid the police in maintaining order during the forthcoming months when it was anticipated that attempts would be made to interfere with the ordinary processes of the law over the question of non-payment of rent and rates. MacNeill was instructed to report on the attitude of the people to the Land League; to report on social and economic conditions generally; and to preserve complete confidentiality and not reveal the purpose of his mission to anyone. MacNeill left Gourock on a chartered yacht, the *Vindex*, on August 26, 1886, and in the next three months visited most of the towns and some of the villages in the crofting districts. As he avoided meeting anyone supporting the Highland Land League with one or two exceptions (among them Dugald MacLachlan, bank agent and lawyer in Portree, whom he described as "a sensible, reasonable person"), his report could hardly be impartial but it contained some matters of interest. For example, the opinion of another Portree lawyer, Alexander MacDonald, about the origin in Ireland of the crofters' agitation through the young Skye fishermen who began to make trouble on their return from Kinsale and through an Irish "emissary", MacHugh, soon afterwards in Skye, was confirmed by MacNeill himself and others. He also reported that it seemed

> "the settled conviction of all with whom I conversed that of the means by which discontent has been fostered none has produced such baneful results as the Royal Commission over which Lord Napier and Ettrick presided".

The wearisome hours MacNeill spent listening to the evidence submitted to the Commission, to which he had been appointed secretary, probably influenced him in supporting that opinion. Mr Roupell, a German connected with Harris through his marriage to the daughter of a Free Church minister, described the greatest fault of the people as "incurable laziness":

"They also spend too much time on church matters . . . Every death imposes idleness for several days, every marriage for about a week and all seem glad of the excuse".

This criticism could be considered in the light of Sheriff Brand's praise of the "Lewisman's great powers of endurance, self-denial and absolute fearlessness". The life of a crofter-fisherman was a seasonal one, arduous and dangerous at times and quiet at others.

Skye Hearings

The 1887 hearings in Skye started at the beginning of February and went on until the end of April, a period of changeable weather. On a sunny, fresh day, February 28, the Commissioners went from Portree to Glenmore and Unakill, two hamlets 5 miles away, to settle a dispute about boundaries which had been going on for years and which Lord MacDonald had asked the Commission to settle. On March 16, the Kilmuir delegates walked through two feet of snow 14 miles to Portree only to find the sitting cancelled. When Donald Beaton of Glenhinnisdal complained about the rent increase of £3.15/- on a £7.15/- rent, Sheriff Brand asked him, "Did Colonel Fraser do nothing for you when he raised the rent by £3.15/-?" Beaton replied, "Not in the least." Beaton was asked by MacDonald, the Portree lawyer, when the first rise of 10/- was made, he replied, "Under your father." MacDonald asked him further, "What was it for?" Beaton's reply was greeted with great laughter — "What do I know?" Sheriff Brand commented, "That is quite a fair answer: the tenants do not seem to know what this rise was for". MacDonald then asked Beaton, "When the rent was raised, was the price of stock high?" Brand again intervened, "That is a useful question but it cuts two ways sharply". Dugald MacLachlan, the Portree banker, who represented the crofters, was examining a witness when MacDonald objected but was told by the Sheriff, "Mr MacLachlan is quite entitled to put these questions". When Macdonald said, "Certainly, I don't mind", the Sheriff answered, "You are in quite a fever about it". MacDonald had a reputation for being hot-tempered: long before the crofting troubles he quarrelled with Sheriff Ivory at a meeting of the Skye Roads Committee when, as he said later, "We all lost our tempers". When Norman Stewart (Parnell) of Valtos was being examined by MacDonald, both factor and tenant lost their tempers. Stewart twice clenched his fist in a threatening manner, which induced Sheriff Brand to remark, "I think you two are standing too close to one another".

The disputes which set off the agitation in Skye — the Valtos and the Braes disputes — inevitably came under scrutiny again. The question of the Valtos souming was raised by Sheriff Brand, who asked MacDonald about the souming mistake. The factor replied, "The estate management as well as the British Parliament is subject to make mistakes and we found that we had been misled". Sheriff Brand remarked, "In fact, the tenants got the better of you", to which MacDonald replied, "Yes". In a printed version of the statement he made to the Commission, MacDonald gave his account of the souming dispute:

> "The tenants (of Valtos) averred at one time that their souming was only 6 and not 8 cows, but on oath some of them admitted the contrary; and in the belief that the souming was only 6 cows each, the proprietor reduced the rent some years gone by to £2.5s per lot (a reduction which no other tenants on the estate got) but he now adheres to the original souming and valuation."

William Malcolm, the valuator of Kilmuir estate in 1876, under rigorous cross-examination by Sheriff Brand, admitted that 25 per cent reduction on Kilmuir rents would be about right. The actual reductions for the whole estate were from £2,761 to £1,716, a reduction of 37 per cent. For Valtos township alone the reduction was from £80.10/- (which was the figure after the souming rebate on the rental of £95) to £51.7/-, a reduction of 37 per cent. A settlement of the dispute over the grazing on Ben Lee was made in favour of the Braes tenants, a lease of 1872 having been produced for the first time by MacDonald, the factor. The lease gave proof of the crofters' claim that they had no reduction of rent when the farmer, Angus MacDonald, took over the grazing in that year.

It was some time before the Crofters Commission visited Lewis, and agitation was simmering throughout 1886 and 1887 and led to violence in the winter of 1887-88. A conference of crofter delegates was held in Stornoway on December 2, 1886 in preparation for the Commission's hearings with the specific purpose of appointing an agent for all the Lewis crofters. A telegram had been sent to the veteran campaigner for the crofters' cause, John Murdoch, inviting him to represent them before the Commissioners, and he had accepted the invitation. The meeting was held in the Liberal party rooms and the chairman, Donald MacIver, used the occasion to attack the Conservatives' reduction of the mail service between Lewis and the mainland from six steamers to three, causing considerable loss to the fishing industry. A fortnight later, another meeting of crofters in Stornoway unanimously resolved to adopt a "Plan of Campaign" in imitation of the Irish and to carry on the agitation unless the deer forests and sheep farms were returned to the people and "until justice was triumphant and tyranny banished from the land". In Skye, the

179

following day, in freezing weather, several hundred Kilmuir crofters and cottars gathered at Loch Mealt, two miles south from Staffin on the east side of Kilmuir near Ellishader. Murdo MacLean, Lealt, presided and critical speeches were the order of the day, the delays of the Crofters Commission and the conduct of Sheriff Ivory coming under severe attack.

Chamberlain's Campaign

In the political wilderness after splitting the Liberal party over Gladstone's Irish Home Rule Bill, Chamberlain revived his old Radical Programme and announced his intention of introducing a bill to amend the Crofters Act. At a meeting of crofter and cottar delegates in Stornoway on January 5, 1887, with Donald MacKenzie of Bayble near Stornoway in the chair, a resolution was moved by Angus MacPhail from Arnol on the west side, praising "the recent powerful utterances" of Chamberlain about amending the Crofters Act. Two days earlier, Chamberlain informed Cameron of Lochiel, former Conservative M.P. for Inverness-shire, that he intended drawing up "the heads of a bill" for submission to proprietors' and crofters' representatives for their comments before introducing a bill in Parliament. It was not until May that this was done but in the meantime Chamberlain made a propaganda tour of the crofting area with his friend and fellow Radical, Jesse Collings, a Birmingham businessman and an advocate of breaking up large estates into small holdings (the "3 acres and a cow" of Chamberlain's Radical Programme at the election of 1885). They arrived in Lewis on April 20 and had a splendid reception in Stornoway, where the visit of a politician of such standing was sufficient excuse for celebration regardless of his politics. He had time for consideration of serious problems with the Chief Magistrate of Stornoway, Murdo MacLeod — the extension of the telegraph service to rural areas, the building and maintenance of piers and harbours. Although MacLeod's proposals were put forward primarily in the interests of fish-curers, the improvement of the infrastructure assumed greater significance in the next few years and formed the basis of the programme presented in 1889 by a supporter of Chamberlain, James Caldwell, M.P., on his tour of the crofting area. Chamberlain's representations to Government ministers were not very successful, but he was able to inform MacLeod that he had managed to persuade the Admiralty of the need for a coastguard station in Lewis. His tour of the island was marred by stormy weather and the absence of newspaper correspondents to report his speeches, the only horse and trap available in Stornoway having been commandeered for Chamberlain's party.

180

The whole tour of the crofting area was beset by criticism from those who blamed him for bringing about the downfall of Gladstone's government, thereby allowing the Conservatives to gain power, and also from Dr MacDonald, M.P. for Ross and Cromarty, who criticised him for interference in his constituency. Crofter M.P.s pointed out that he had not supported any of their amendments to the Crofters Bill on its passage through the House of Commons. In a letter, dated May 8, to Cameron of Lochiel, Chamberlain himself saw the situation as potentially dangerous unless appropriate measures were taken. He feared that at any moment there could be a rent strike and a repetition of what happened in Ireland. He argued that if a rent strike took place in Lewis and an army was sent, there were 2,000 Royal Naval Reservists (actually only about 1,000) trained to arms and splendid fellows, so that it would go hard with a small detachment of marines, and public opinion would not sanction a large expedition where people were unable to live in present conditions. Chamberlain's draft Crofters and Cottars Relief Bill, details of which were published in early July, had a chilly reception from crofters and proprietors. "The land for the people" had become the chief slogan for crofters and cottars (particularly the latter) at public meetings and demonstrations, and the cottars were yet again disappointed. Among the proposals included in this abortive measure was one empowering the Crofters Commission to designate a township a "congested district", wherein any crofter or cottar might apply for a new holding. The provisions for making crofters and cottars proprietors on the Irish model by paying increased rents over a period of 49 years, involving increased rates, did not appeal to people who were complaining about their inability to pay rents and rates, nor was the procedure for a crofter or cottar applying for a new holding much less complicated than that of the Crofters Act. The proprietors were even more critical. They objected particularly to the proposal, based on the Irish model, to cancel all or most of the rent arrears. Lord Lovat condemned the draft bill as bound to have disastrous effects, and MacLeod of MacLeod requested the Marquis of Lothian, the Secretary for Scotland, to defeat "a measure which could have the most prejudicial effects". These views were typical of Conservative opinion, and Chamberlain, seeing no assistance forthcoming, dropped the draft bill.[5]

In September and October, 1887, the *Scottish Highlander* published unsigned letters from a Lewis correspondent, almost certainly Alex. Morison of Stornoway, the first chairman of the Lewis branch of the H.L.L.R.A., who had been responsible for inviting Chamberlain to Lewis. He had been sent a dozen copies of the draft bill for distribution in order to obtain crofters' views and was naturally disappointed when Chamberlain decided not to proceed with the bill. Morison complained about "a nightmare of indifference", the crofters leaving it to Stornoway gentlemen to pay hall rents, lawyers' accounts, telegrams, subscriptions to the Land League — "hundreds of pounds spent by Stornoway H.L.L.R.A., but no longer". The townsmen seem to have been out of touch with the grass roots as the winter months brought more disturbances and agitation in several districts, a contributory factor being the return from the summer east-coast fishing of the young men.

Bankrupt Crofters

The Marquis of Lothian had succeeded A.J. Balfour in the spring of 1887 on the latter's appointment as Chief Secretary of Ireland. Lothian was to remain as Scottish Secretary until 1892, his period of office exceeding the total of those of his predecessors altogether. Educated at Eton and Oxford, he had entered the diplomatic service, and held posts in Frankfurt, Madrid and Vienna. He was one of the leading personalities in the movement for the appointment of a Secretary for Scotland and in January, 1884, he presided over a mass demonstration of all parties, classes and religious denominations in Edinburgh, at which a strongly-worded resolution was adopted unanimously, demanding unconditionally the appointment of a Scottish Secretary. When such an appointment came to be made in the summer of 1886, Lothian was considered by the Marquis of Salisbury for the post but was passed over on that occasion because of doubts about his health, and the Duke of Richmond and Gordon was appointed instead. One of Lothian's first steps was the introduction of a Crofters Act Amendment Bill prepared by Balfour and intended to close a loophole in the Crofters Act. Some landlords and factors had been suing tenants in court for arrears of rent and having them declared notour bankrupt because they failed to discharge their debts within the days of grace permitted them, thereby disqualifying them from making application to the Crofters Commission for fixing fair rents.

North Uist was one of the few places where the Napier Commission heard praise for the factor in 1883. According to Angus MacDonald, a crofter on the island of Boreray, "the factor is very kind to us". John MacDonald had been factor since North Uist had been purchased in 1855 from the trustees of Lord MacDonald by Sir John Orde of Kilmory in Argyll, and he could claim that there were no evictions in his time (but there had been large-scale clearances previously), no diminution of hill grazings, no increase of rents for small tenants, while Angus MacAulay of Middle Quarter stated in his evidence that generally tacksmen and crofters were on good terms. But the same could not be said of the crofters' relations with the proprietor, at any rate after the passing of the Crofters Act. The Crofters Commission began their North Uist hearings at Lochmaddy in September, 1887, and issued their decisions on December 8 of that year. Sir John had objected to nearly half of the 157 applications by tenants for fair rents and he had lost every case. Some of the tenants who had their rents reduced and their arrears cancelled thereafter paid only the reduced rent and no arrears. Orde then decided to make use of the loophole in the Crofters Act which allowed a landlord to evict a notour bankrupt, although this loophole had been stopped by the Marquis of Lothian's Amending Act of July 1887. Donald MacLellan, Tigharry, was one of those who paid only the rent fixed by the Commission and was made the victim of Orde's anger because at the Commission's hearing he had proved false an affidavit by the landlord. A decree for the sale of the crofter's effects was obtained in the Sheriff Court but was countered by the Commission sisting proceedings begun by the landlord. For a long time after the hearing of the case, Sir John pursued a vendetta against Thomas Wilson, solicitor, who had represented MacLellan, by forbidding his tenants to give him lodging on the island.

Commission Problems

The Crofters Commission widened the scope of its activities as time went on. Arising out of its statutory duty of fixing fair rents, the settlement of boundary disputes as between crofters and neighbouring farmers was undertaken at an early stage. In Skye, the much-vexed dispute over the grazing on Ben Lee was settled in favour of the Braes crofters. In Lewis, the estate management acted at the time of renewal of leases in anticipation of the Commission hearing. Three townships on the west side had restored to them in 1886-87 former grazings lost during the clearances in the 1850s — Borriston regaining Laimshader, Upper Carloway part of Dalmore, and South Shawbost part of Dalbeg. Similarly, on the east side of the island, the townships of Marvig and Calbost were given the tenancy of the grazing on Eilean Thoraidh. In Skye, a long-standing boundary dispute between Glenmore and Unakill, villages near Portree, was submitted to the Commission by Lord MacDonald in February, 1887. The Commissioners visited the area, interviewed about 20 men in each village, and in June gave their decision in favour of Glenmore, a decision repudiated by Unakill. Two townships near Broadford, Upper and Lower Breakish, in order to settle the difficult problem of access to Lower Breakish grazings, which were situated beyond those of Upper Breakish, made applications for lease of the same piece of a neighbouring farm. The Commissioners found themselves restricted by the provisions of the Act of 1886 and rejected the applications on the ground that the amount of rent arrears showed that the tenants were not able to stock the grazings desired. Applications for enlargement of holdings were hamstrung by the conditions laid down in the Crofters Act. Nearly 5,000 applications were granted during the period of the Commission's existence, 1886-1912, but the enlarged holdings tended to be unsuccessful because of mismanagement and, particularly, under-stocking.

In order to control and improve crofters' agricultural methods, the Marquis of Lothian was persuaded by Sheriff Brand in 1890 to introduce the Crofters Common Grazings Regulations Bill, which passed unopposed through Parliament. The intentions were good and the regulations should have been easy to observe as they were based on the traditional practices of the crofting communities. The soumings formed the basis of the regulations and varied from township to township —

Poolewe, Wester Ross — 3 cows and 1 stirk, 16 sheep for each croft
Gravir, Lewis — 1 cow, 1 stirk, 5 sheep per £1.10/- of rent
Carinish, South Uist — 2 horses, 4½ cows, 16 sheep for each full croft
Barvas and South Bragar, Lewis — 1 cow, 1 follower till a year old, 10 sheep for £1 of rent.

Other regulations provided for the control of heather-burning, peat-cutting, repair of dykes, employment of a herd, fixing of the date when sheep and cattle should be removed from the crofts and inbye land to the summer grazings.[6] There were, however, many townships where these regulations were not observed. Formerly, the village constable was able to exercise control in this sphere of crofting but the Crofters Act did not carry out the recommendations of the Napier Commission for the appointment of a village constable and the grazings committee was no effective substitute.

Notes

1. Sir George Otto Trevelyan's mother was a sister of Lord MacAulay, the historian and administrator, whose grandfather, the Rev. John MacAulay, Presbyterian minister of South Uist, did his best, along with his father, also a minister, to effect the capture of the fugitive Prince Charles Edward Stewart in 1746. Both Sir George Trevelyan and his son, George MacAulay Trevelyan, also earned fame as historians.

2. Sir George Campbell, M.P. for Kirkcaldy Burghs, had a distinguished career in India, where he was at one time Lieutenant-Governor of Bengal.

Although not active in the H.L.L.R.A., he was a consistent supporter of the crofters' claims. Detailed accounts of the Commons debates on the Crofters Bill by Joni Buchanan appeared in the *West Highland Free Press* in the summer of 1986, the centenary year. A proposal for a commemorative stamp to mark the anniversary of the Act was rejected by the Conservative Government.

3. For details of the amalgamation, see the last two paragraphs in Chapter 4.

4. Kenneth MacDonald, Town Clerk of Inverness for forty years, defended many crofters successfully during this period since his appearance at the Braes trial in 1882. Nicknamed *An Diabhol* (the Devil), he was small and slim in physique, in marked contrast to his colleague, Alexander Mac-Kenzie, the "Clach", who was described as of "Falstaffian proportions" by a fellow-journalist.

5. Despite Chamberlain's breach with his former Liberal colleagues, he still in 1887 impudently claimed a seat on the Opposition front bench; and it was at this time that Gladstone denounced him as "the greatest blackguard I have ever known".

6. For a list of grazing regulations laid down by the Commission, see Appendix.

CHAPTER 9

GUNBOATS TO THE HEBRIDES

Military Expeditions

A.J. Balfour's name has been associated with the military expeditions of 1886-87 rather than with the social and economic problems of the crofting area. On his first day in office he found himself in charge of an expedition to the Hebrides, to the Isle of Tiree. The decision to sanction the use of a military force had been taken by his predecessor in office, the Liberal Earl of Dalhousie. It was not the first military expedition in the Crofters' War and not all of them were effective in their aim of restoring law and order. Forces were sent to arrest men living in remote places — in February, 1883, the *Jackal* to Glendale to arrest John MacPherson and three others, and in December, 1884, the *Seahorse* to Loch Roag on the west side of Lewis to arrest eight men charged with deforcement of a messenger-at-arms. In each case things went quietly. The military expedition to Skye which arrived in November, 1884, was on a larger scale — a troopship (the *Assistance*), two gunboats (the *Forester* and *Banterer*), with 350 marines and 100 bluejackets. The expeditionary force, part of which remained in Skye until the following June, had little effect beyond hardening the resistance of the crofters to the existing system of land tenure but "nearly useless for the purpose of restoring law and order", as Balfour himself wrote in his memorandum to the Cabinet of September 13, 1886.

Duke of Argyll as Landlord

Tiree was an island different in many respects from Skye and Lewis, an island for years under the paternalist control of George John Douglas Campbell, 8th Duke of Argyll. He had succeeded his father in 1847, when he was 24, and he was faced with problems similar to those which confronted other landlords following the potato famine, problems made more difficult for them by the introduction of the new Poor Law in 1845, making poor relief payable from the rates. According to the Duke of Argyll, there would have been starvation were it not for the measures taken by his invalid father and himself. They used a Government loan of £10,000 (at 6½ per cent) to purchase Indian meal for distribution to the people in wages for work on systematic drainage of the land. Emigration was encouraged and subsidised so that over 2,000 persons (about 40 per cent of the population) left the island for the New World. Thereafter, by the annexation of the emigrants' "wretched little possessions" (to use the Duke's own words), and by a policy of consolidation of holdings and strict prohibition of sub-division, he laid the foundations, as he later claimed, for "a larger and more comfortable improved class of tenant". Of 194 tenants in Tiree in 1884, when the population was 2,733, 98 or just over half paid rents of more than £10 a year, in comparison with the average Skye crofter's rent of about £5, while it was estimated that there were about 300 cottars' families with little more than a patch of potato ground.[1] The Duke genuinely believed that so far as the people of Tiree were concerned, he had "redeemed them to a condition of comparative comfort and abundance", as he wrote in a letter replying to one from Henry Whyte ("Fionn", as he was better known). But, although rents had doubled and some tenants resembled farmers rather than crofters, others were obliged to give three or four days' labour to the Duke's factor, Hugh MacDiarmid, in the autumn and the winter, a practice which had died out in most other estates.[2] The Duke had taken an active interest in politics and had been a member of Gladstone's Cabinet until 1881, but as a Whig of the old school, he strongly disapproved of the Radical element in the Liberal party.

The Tiree men who appeared before the Napier Commission in 1883, like witnesses from other areas, described the evictions and mass emigration, the loss of the common grazings. For the landless cottars and squatters there might have been a livelihood in fishing but they lacked boats and there was no good harbour in the island. Those cottars who worked as kelp-gatherers for the North British Chemical Company complained that the company was in breach of the Truck Act in their method of paying wages. The Napier Commission had in Tiree, as elsewhere, the effect of producing a demand for a change of the existing conditions, which was kept alive by the formation of a branch of the Highland Land Law Reform Association. Meetings were held regularly: they were opened and closed with prayer, a practice which the Duke of Argyll characterised as "hideous aggravation". Proposals for open defiance of the law made by some of the seven hundred members of the League were deplored by the island ministers. A meeting of crofters and cottars at Balevoulin in November, 1884, was addressed by a Free Church minister, the Rev. Alexander Shaw, from Salen in Mull, who urged on his audience "the need for guidance from the Almighty as well as great caution, tact and wisdom", and apart from some of the crofters and cottars copying the "No Rent" campaigns in Skye and Lewis, things were to remain quiet in Tiree for some time. In May, 1885, the Chief Constable of Argyll,

Captain MacKay, was able to tell the Sheriff of Argyll that "the land Agitation is about dying out." But in July of that year serious complaints were made about the conduct of large numbers of the islanders raiding a ship, the *Cairnsmuir* of Leith, which had run aground. The ship's cargo consisted chiefly of beer, spirits and wine in cases, most of which had been washed ashore but only ten of which had been salvaged. The Deputy Receiver of Wrecks, the principal Customs Officer of the district, and the ship's officers were threatened with violence by large crowds of hostile islanders, and the numerous empty cases led the officials to entertain suspicions about the islanders having purloined the contents, particularly as they paraded in bands of 60 to 80 night and day along the shore. The *Scotsman* reporter added that "in some quarters this wrecking incident is regarded as the natural outcome of the agrarian agitation". It was probably because of this version of "Whisky Galore" that a notice was posted up on the doors of the churches in Tiree, prohibiting tenants paying less than £30 a year from using "whisky or any other spirits at weddings, balls, funerals or any other gatherings", and threatening eviction of anyone who contravened the said order.

Greenhill Farm Lease

The following year, 1886, trouble started over the expiry of a farm lease. The farm, called Greenhill or Grianal, many hoped would be divided up among neighbouring crofters and cottars. The Duke and his factor, Hugh MacDiarmid, however, advertised the farm for letting, which was bad enough — one prospective tenant, Angus MacLean of Tobermory, being forcibly prevented from viewing the farm — but consternation prevailed in the island when it was learned that the lease had been given to a well-doing crofter of Vaul, Lachlan MacNeill, a member of the H.L.L.R.A. and brother of the president of the Tiree branch, Neil MacNeill. On May 22, at a meeting of the branch the two brothers were expelled from the H.L.L.R.A. and a new president, Donald Sinclair, elected. When MacNeill came on May 28 to take possession of the Greenhill farm, he was met by a body of men, who compelled him to remove his stock; and a herd was appointed by Donald Sinclair on behalf of the rest of the crofters and cottars to attend to the 55 cattle and 17 horses they brought to graze there. The Duke of Argyll, nearly apoplectic with rage, reported to the Sheriff of Argyll about "the gross act of illegal violence" at Greenhill perpetrated, he wrote, by men acting under the direction of "some organised society whose means of action are the intimidation and coercion of the peaceful subjects of the realm". The Procurator Fiscal, after a visit to the island, informed the Sheriff that the Land

League were supreme there and that if arrests were to be made a considerable force would be necessary. He added that John Murdoch had also visited the island and had advised the people not to use violence against the police, should they come, and not to co-operate with them.

Police Expedition

To assist the messenger-at-arms, George Nicolson, and his concurrent in serving notices of interdict, which the Duke had ordered against 51 individuals, a force of 20 policemen from the mainland and 17 commissionaires, all ex-servicemen, from Glasgow was dispatched to Tiree on July 21, 1886. Proceedings against the crofters had been delayed until after the parliamentary election in the first fortnight of July as Colonel Malcolm, the Conservative and Unionist candidate for Argyllshire, was chairman of the county police committee, and the Duke, who fervently hoped that Malcolm would defeat the sitting member, Donald M. MacFarlane, a prominent member of the H.L.L.R.A., did not wish to spoil the colonel's chances by what would be unpopular action by the police.[3] (In a letter to Gladstone, Argyll had referred to MacFarlane at the time of his winning the seat in 1885 as "a thorough blackguard".) The police, headed by the Chief Constable, Captain MacKay, sailed from Oban in a specially-chartered steamer, the *Elfin*, but as there were no piers on Tiree they had to be ferried ashore at Scarinish in small boats. No help came from the watching islanders and getting the police on dry land took from 9 a.m. to 2 p.m. They then proceeded to Balemartin and Balephuil, where their progress was stopped by a crowd, some of whom took the heads of the horses drawing the machines or gigs carrying the messenger-at-arms and the police officers and told the poor Tiree men who had driven the gigs to take them back to Scarinish. The notices of interdict remained unserved.

Representatives of various newspapers covered the mission of the police. One difficulty which confronted them was the lack of telegraphic communication with the island, the nearest telegraph office being at Tobermory. The *Scotsman* reporter, who got no further than Oban and depended on hearsay, gave a lurid account of the deforcement of the messenger-at-arms, describing the impaling of the horses on barbed wire, the natives skulking behind hedges and blacksmiths forging pikes night and day. The sensational reports in the press induced the Secretary for Scotland to send a military expedition to Tiree. The decision to sanction the expedition was taken on July 24 (three days after the repulse of the police) by the Earl of Dalhousie, the Liberal Secretary for Scotland, but before a week was out he was replaced by the Conservative A.J. Balfour. In a letter which was sent to Balfour by the Duke of Argyll, who had received it from "an unnamed friend" in Tiree, the island was described as "under the rule of savagery, at the mercy of the rabble and the young people".

Military Expedition

The expeditionary force was composed of the turret ship H.M.S. *Ajax*, one of the largest warships in the navy, a troopship, H.M.S. *Assistance*, carrying 250 marines and 120 bluejackets between them, and a chartered steamer, the *Nigel*, with 40 policemen as on the previous unsuccessful mission. They sailed into Scarinish on Friday evening and on the Saturday morning disembarked on the shore. It was a very hot day and many of the marines in their heavy uniforms and carrying 20 rounds of ammunition found the 12-hour march round the island very heavy going indeed. Parts of the march were along the *machair*. At one place along their route, at Baugh, there lived a man with second sight who had twenty years before seen soldiers marching along the *machair* and there were many in 1886 who were able to recall his prediction. Although the Tiree people refused to co-operate with the police in identifying persons named in the notices of interdict, they kindly offered milk to the soldiers when they came to the doors of their cottages asking for a drink. The newspaper correspondents accompany the expedition were faced with a serious problem in getting their stories to their newspaper offices not merely because of the lack of telegraph communication in the island but also because the march round the island took place on a Saturday. The *Scotsman* reporter suggested to his fellow newspapermen that they should all delay sending their reports until the Monday so as not to offend local feelings about the sanctity of the Sabbath. On the following day, which was the Sabbath, it was discovered that he had sent off a carrier pigeon to the mainland with a full account of the events of Saturday's march. The pigeon was mobbed by seagulls and returned to the hotel at Scarinish, the pages of the *Scotsman* dispatch being scattered through the island and giving cause for great amusement. Two other reporters, with great difficulty because of the local feeling about Sabbath-breaking, managed to hire a boat to take them to Tobermory where they commandeered the services of the telegraphists, who sat up till 7 a.m. relaying their lengthy dispatches. On Tuesday, August 3, a meeting of the Tiree branch of the H.L.L.R.A. was held in Moss Public School near Greenhill farm, and the president, Donald Sinclair, proposed the expulsion of the *Scotsman* reporter on the grounds of his inaccurate statements and his breach of the fourth commandment. The Tiree leader's criticism of the Edinburgh correspondent was duly reported in the rival newspaper, the *Glasgow Herald*.

The marines made a second march round the island a week later on August 7 and arrested six men, who were charged later with the deforcement of the messenger-at-arms on July 21 and trespassing on Greenhill farm. They were Donald Sinclair, the president of the Tiree branch of the H.L.L.R.A., a cottar from Gortandonald, Colin Henderson, Hector MacDonald, Alexander MacLean from Balemartin, Donald MacKinnon and Lachlan Brown from Balephuil, the charges against Sinclair and the last two being later dropped. Sinclair claimed at a meeting in Oban, following the release of the prisoners on bail, that he had personally insisted that all meetings of the Tiree branch should be opened and closed with prayer, which he said was a sign of the righteousness of their cause. It was perhaps hypocritical for him or the other members of the branch to think that such prayers could justify whatever actions they undertook; but according to Dr G.B. Clark, the M.P. for Caithness and a prominent Radical, hypocrisy was not absent from the actions of the landlords. In a meeting in Glasgow only a few days after the arrest of the Tiree prisoners, he castigated the Duke as

"this elder of the Kirk, this sanctimonious prig, this pedantic priest of a played-out political gospel, who gloried in the policy of grab".

At the beginning of September, five more men were arrested for their part in the deforcement of Balephuil on July 21 and for the seizure of Greenhill farm — John Sinclair, John MacFadyen and Gilbert MacDonald from Balemartin, George Campbell and Alex. MacArthur from Ballinoe, the last-named being later liberated. The trial was held in Edinburgh, commencing on Monday, October 18, 1886, before Lord Mure, with the Lord Advocate prosecuting. The jury's verdict was reached by a majority of one but despite expectations of lenient sentences, the Tiree men were sent to prison for six months and four months — sentences which were regarded by the establishment as condign and salutary punishment for breaches of the law of the land and by sympathisers with the crofters as unnecessarily savage. It was pointed out by one critic of Lord Mure that some of the directors of the City of Glasgow Bank after its failure — over £6 millions were involved — had received sentences of only eight months a few years before. Petitions poured in to the Scottish Office from all over the country for the remission of the sentences but Balfour, advised by Sir Francis Sandford, the Permanent Secretary, who welcomed the sentences as likely to have a "wholesome effect" in Skye, refused to relent until January when three were liberated and the rest a few weeks later.

The displaced tenant of Greenhill was reinstated and the activities of the H.L.L.R.A. henceforth remained within the law. The reduction of rents carried out by the Crofters Commission, which visited the island in the summer of 1887, more than justified the crofters' claims that they had been rack-rented. On average, rents were reduced by 25 per cent and almost half of the island arrears of rent were cancelled. One man, Donald Kennedy, known as the King of the Moss, who had been paying £4 in rent for a croft on an exhausted peat moss, had his rent reduced to £1 and his arrears completely cancelled. As elsewhere in the Highlands and Islands the permanent Crofters Commission brought about an acceptance of the new set-up and the beginning of a period of security and improvement in living conditions.[4]

Rates Trouble in Skye

Before the Tiree prisoners came to trial, Balfour's attention was concentrated on another island, that of Skye, which was to experience its second military expedition within two years, the first having left the island only in June, 1885, after just over six months' stay. In the early part of 1886, the crofters and cottars had been waiting for Gladstone's Government to implement the recommendations of the Napier Commission Report of 1884, and, like crofters and cottars elsewhere, they expressed their disappointment with the Crofters Bill, which became law at the end of June, 1886, just before the dissolution of Parliament. But trouble was brewing in Skye over the non-payment of rent and rates. A "No Rent" campaign, started in 1884, had proved so effective that on Major Fraser's estate of Kilmuir, where the crofters and cottars were due to pay annually a total of £2,897, the arrears of rent amounted to over £6,000. The crofters, as time went on, were more and more reluctant to pay as they hoped for a reduction of rents when the newly-appointed Crofters Commission would come to Skye and a cancellation of much, if not all, of arrears, as happened in Ireland after the passing of the Irish Land Act of 1881. Tenants' rates were then of two kinds, the poor rates and school rates, and were invariably in Skye and elsewhere in the crofting area collected along with rents by the same persons — a practice deplored by the Inspector of the Board of Supervision in charge of poor relief, a Mr Peterkin, who visited Skye in April, 1886. Nor was it just crofters and cottars who were in arrears of rates: the landlords in most cases depended on their rents to pay their rates and were unwilling or unable to do so.

The need for a settlement of the rates problem became increasingly pressing in the summer of 1886. Alex. MacDonald, lawyer and bank agent in Portree, was not only factor for almost all the estates in Skye but was also a member or chairman of all the Parochial and School Boards in the island. In April, 1886, he was embarrassingly compelled to admit at the Portree Parochial Board meeting (at which he was chairman) that the largest arrears of rates were due by Lord MacDonald, for whom he was factor. A parliamentary return, which had been requested by Fraser Mackintosh, M.P. for Inverness-shire, and was issued in June, 1886, just before the dissolution of Parliament, gave full details of the arrears of school and poor rates for the year ending Whitsunday, 1886, and showed that in the Isle of Skye landlords' rates were £3,605 in arrears out of a total of £5,632 due; that tacksmen (mainly farmers) due to pay £2,556, were £1,004 in arrears; and that crofters and other small tenants, due to pay £1,123, were £591 in arrears. The difficulties for the Parochial and School Boards were obvious. The Parochial Boards began to obtain loans from the banks; but there was a limit to what bank agents were willing to advance in such uncertain conditions and in 1886 the banks refused further loans. Teachers in Snizort were informed by the Parish School Board in July of that year that they would have to depend on school fees as the Board had no money to pay salaries. Alexander MacDonald, seeing a complete breakdown in what are now called the social services, wrote urgently to the Sheriff of Inverness and to the Secretary for Scotland for assistance in ending the deadlock, arguing that another military expedition would be necessary to enforce the payment of rates as sheriff officers in Skye declined to serve summonses; John Lamont, a Portree sheriff officer, when he declined the duty, had said that he did not wish to have a hand in shortening his days "voluntarily".

Balfour's Skye Policy

Balfour did not take long to make up his mind after the conclusion of the Tiree expedition. At a private meeting with Sheriff Ivory of Inverness at the beginning of September, he indicated that the Admiralty would be prepared to send a gunboat with 50 marines to co-operate with the police in serving summonses for payment of rents and rates. Balfour regarded the police in Skye as "absolutely useless" for the protection of sheriff officers. They had (he said) been "demoralised by the ill usage" they had been subjected to by the people of Skye, who regarded them as "the emissaries of the landlords", mainly because the police rates were levied solely on the owners of lands. As for a military force to aid in the enforcement of the law, he was of the opinion that the large force sent in 1884 had been really useless through the dispersal of the marines over the island, which had led to fraternisation with the crofters, who stood in no fear of them; and he proposed that the marines should be quartered mainly in Portree and taken by sea to a landing-place nearest to the scene of action.[4]

The main purpose of the military presence was to provide support in the service of summonses, which would be applied for in the Sheriff Court before an expedition would arrive. When it became known, just as the expedition was ready for sailing from Portsmouth, that George MacDonald, acting for and on behalf of his brother, Alex. MacDonald, the Portree factor, had intended recovery action for payment of rates only against the crofters, (371 in all), Balfour was furious and threatened to withdraw the expedition unless proceedings against the landlords for recovery of rates were commenced immediately. There was a swift response from the Skye landlords, for a couple of days later all the proprietors in Skye (with one exception) actually paid their rates so that the way was clear for action against the crofters and cottars. The previous evening, Monday, October 4, Sheriff Ivory, Chief Constable MacHardy and a body of mainland police arrived at Portree in the *Glencoe*. Sheriff Ivory (almost certainly the most unpopular man in the Highlands and Islands) was met with a "perfect tempest of booing and groaning" all the way from the pier to the Royal Hotel. The arrival on the following day of H.M.S. *Humber* (1640 tons) with 75 marines and 85 of a crew was signalled throughout the nearby townships by the blowing of horns from the hilltops. The men of Kilmuir, who held a meeting at Garrafad, decided at the close of the meeting to march over the hill to Uig and there they discussed future tactics with the men of Uig until the small hours of the morning.

Skye Expedition — First Phase

The first phase of the expedition opened on Thursday, October 7, on the west side of Skye, the *Humber* conveying the marines and police from Portree. Messengers-at-arms, D.J. Grant and Alexander Mac-Donald, had been brought from Inverness and Edinburgh to enforce summary warrants for arrears of rates. Tenants then either paid up or had their goods poinded. At Glasphein, on the estate of Dr Nicol Martin of Husaboat, a number of tenants had their ricks of corn and stacks of peats poinded. No poindings took place for arrears of rent, the tenants merely being warned to appear in court. Some of the Kilmuir crofters had considerable arrears of rent to pay, a situation reflecting the protracted disputes between Major William Fraser and his tenants. Norman Stewart of Valtos (better known as "Parnell") was actually £41 in arrears on a rent of £6.12.6. Before the first phase ended, the *Humber* was recalled to Sheerness and replaced by two gunboats, the *Jackal* and the *Seahorse*, already used in previous

NOTICE

Whereas Riotous and Disorderly Persons have recently assembled at several places in Skye for the purpose of obstructing Officers of the Law in the execution of their duty, and whereby the said Officers and their Assistants have been obstructed and alarmed, **NOTICE IS HEREBY GIVEN** that such Assemblages are Illegal and Criminal, and that all persons taking part in them, even although they individually commit no Act of Violence, are Guilty of the crime of Mobbing and Rioting, and liable to be Punished therefor.   And **NOTICE** is further **GIVEN** that such Assemblages are hereby forbidden; that on the assembly of any such Riotous and Disorderly Persons in future, a Proclamation, in terms of the Riot Act, and to the following effect, will be made—

" Our Sovereign Lady, the Queen, chargeth and commandeth
" all Persons being assembled, immediately to disperse them-
" selves, and peaceably to depart to their habitations or to their
" lawful business, upon the pains contained in the Act made in
" the first year of King George, for preventing Tumults and
" Riotous Assemblies.

" GOD SAVE THE QUEEN."

And that if such Assemblage shall not disperse within one hour after such Proclamation, each person composing it will be Guilty of the said crime, and will be liable to Penal Servitude for Life, or for not less than Fifteen Years, or to Imprisonment for not less than Three Years.

By Order of the Sheriff.

H. C. MACANDREW,
Sheriff-Clerk of Inverness-shire.

Portree, 5th November 1886.

[Printed at the Courier Office, Inverness.]

THIS NOTICE CONTAINS A MISTAKE —
IMPRISONMENT FOR "NOT LESS THAN
THREE YEARS" INSTEAD OF
"NOT EXCEEDING THREE YEARS".

expeditions in the Hebrides. As these were too small for the number of marines engaged, they were given accommodation in the Skye Gathering Hall in Portree.

During the first phase, matters between the Sheriff and the Chief Constable reached a climax. For some time, Ivory had attempted to obtain police reports directly without going through the Chief Constable's office, and when Chief Constable MacHardy had justifiably refused permission, he was supported by Captain Munro, the Inspector of Constabulary in Scotland. When the policemen did not turn up for divine service on board the *Humber* on Sunday, October 10, the Sheriff expostulated angrily with the Chief Constable, who replied that it was the custom throughout Scotland for policemen to have freedom of choice in respect of religious services. The Sheriff insisted, however, that he would order the men to appear the next Sunday for divine service in uniform, to which MacHardy replied, "I beg your pardon but I cannot really carry out that order". On this polite but firm refusal, Ivory burst forth, "Be damned if I shall submit to such gross insubordination and disobedience from you. By God, I'll compel you to obey me". He then accused MacHardy of having grossly insulted Captain Errington and officers of the *Humber*. When MacHardy replied that he would apologise to Captain Errington, Ivory forbade him and when MacHardy insisted, Ivory said he would accompany him. Errington assured the Chief Constable that there had been no discourtesy, much to the chagrin of the Sheriff. Another row developed two days later, when the Chief Constable decided to give Superintendent Aitchison a rest and take his place on the *Humber*, while Ivory wanted Aitchison to accompany him, but Aitchison declared that he must take his orders from the Chief Constable. All this time, marines and policemen were sitting in open boats in drenching rain, waiting for the two officials to settle their argument. Finally, the Chief Constable went and Aitchison stayed behind. MacHardy's refusal to allow his policemen to wear the "Ivory medals" awarded by the Sheriff for the capture of "Parnell" in 1885 only added fuel to the fire. In a most violent outburst, Ivory criticised the Chief Constable in front of his own men; and MacHardy, who throughout had behaved with dignity, betook himself to Inverness to prevent a scandal.

Skye Expedition — Second Phase

The second phase of the expedition started on October 22 and as it involved poinding goods on the decrees for rates, it was expected that things would not go as smoothly as in the first phase. By November 7, when the second tour of the island was completed, Ivory could claim that the rates collected amounted to £3,030.15s., leaving only £69.10s. still outstanding. Trouble arose, however, at two separate townships on the Kilmuir estate on Monday, October 25, At Bornaskitaig, where the people gathered at the sounding of a horn when the marines and police were sighted, the messenger-at-arms, Grant, was faced by a line of women, arm in arm, blocking the doorway of a house, while the menfolk stood by. The Portree sheriff, Hamilton, who was accompanied by 12 policemen and 12 marines, ordered the police to arrest some of the men who had been obstructing the messenger-at-arms, and a mêlée developed. The police, trying to break through the line of women, were attacked in turn, the women throwing filth from a heap of manure at the door. The sheriff was pelted with clods and filth time and again and indeed never recovered from his injuries, resigning office some months later. The summonses were served, however, and six men who were arrested with the help of the marines were taken to Kilmaluag, where the *Seahorse* was waiting. At Herbusta, the messenger-at-arms, MacDonald, seeing a hostile crowd ahead of him, declined to proceed and after some talk with the crofters was assaulted with clods. No attempt at arrest was made but the messenger-at-arms declared himself deforced and along with the police, who waited in vain for the marines to arrive (they had been taking shelter from the weather in the lee of Kilmuir parish church), retired from the village. The arrest of the deforcers at Herbusta was to take weeks, the police making raids on the houses at all hours of the day and night. In the end, most of them, on the advice of the Free Church minister of Kilmuir, the Rev. John MacPhail, surrendered. The day after the two Kilmuir deforcements, another took place at Garalapin, not far from Portree, a crowd of men and women from the neighbouring townships of Uigshader and Peiness combining with those of Garalapin with sticks and graips to greet the messenger-at-arms, MacDonald, who was again deforced.[6] In an attempt to arrest the deforcers a few days later, plain-clothes policemen were sent out from Portree before daybreak to occupy the hills above Garalapin. After they had gone only half-a-mile, the ground officers, Charles MacLeod from Carbost and Norman Beaton from Portree, declined to accompany the police farther for the purpose of identifying the wanted men and Ivory had MacDonald, the factor, dismiss them right away. The raid was successful, nine men and one woman, Mrs Christina MacRae of Uigshader, being arrested.

Skye Expedition — Third Phase

The third phase of the expedition was expected to begin on November 8 with the removal of the stock and goods which had been poinded but no carters in Portree were willing to undertake the disagreeable task and Sheriff Ivory was forced to send to Inverness for two horses and carts, which duly arrived on November 9. The previous day, when a poinding sale of furniture belonging to John Nicolson, boatbuilder in Portree, was to take place, the local bellman could not be found to advertise the sale. One of the concurrents at the serving of summonses was induced to act as bellman for a fee of 25s, the sheriff himself fetching a bell from the Royal Hotel. It was on November 18 when MacDonald, the messenger-at-arms, officiated at the poindings at Peiness, Garalapin, Uigshader and Glengrasgo, that the famous poinding of Mrs MacRae's baby occurred. MacDonald, escorted by half a dozen marines and police, had entered the house of Mrs MacRae of Peiness to value the goods and chattels for poinding, and when he saw her two-month-old baby he said (as she thought, jokingly) — "I'll poind the baby too". His inventory however read as follows:— Dresser and crockery, 1s. 6d.; wooden seats, 2s.; spinning wheel, 1s.; 2 beds and blankets, £1; chair, 1s.; graip, 2s.; churn and top, 1s.; bed, 2s.; quantity of corn, £1; puppy dog, 1s.; cradle and child, 6d". The scandalous bad taste was given wide publicity and led to the suspension of MacDonald. (The poinded baby grew up a strong lad and in 1910 was employed as the "boots" in Portree Hotel.) The landlords and factors would have liked the expedition to continue for the sake of recovering arrears of rent; but proceedings for removal of tenants were abandoned after the Crofters Commission, then sitting at Lairg, declared on November 18 that all proceedings should be sisted in the cases of tenants who had applied to the Commission for the review of their rents.

Sheriff Ivory's Critics

Ivory's conduct of the expedition had by this time produced a storm of criticism. Following a public meeting of protest in Portree on November 1, John Gunn MacKay, a Portree merchant and a champion of the crofters, sent a letter to the Home Secretary (and a copy to the *Inverness Courier*) containing scathing comments on Sheriff Ivory's conduct and describing him as a "judicial monster". After the publication of the letter, MacKay was arrested and charged with "slandering, defaming and insulting" Sheriff Ivory and "holding him up to public ridicule, shame, execration and reprobation as being unjust, corrupt and oppressive in the execution of his functions". MacKay was liberated on bail of £100 but his case never came to trial. Nor was this the only case at the time which never came to trial. Two days after MacKay's arrest, the "Glendale Martyr", John MacPherson, was arrested in bed by marines and police and taken down to the waiting gunboat, the *Seahorse*, where he was charged with inciting the people to resistance, at a meeting at Colbost in October. He was kept in jail for a week, during which time several witnesses were precognosced without obtaining sufficient evidence and at the end he was liberated without a trial. On the evening of the same day, Saturday, November 13, the Rev. Donald MacCallum, parish minister at Hallin-in-Waternish, was sitting in the parlour of the schoolhouse at Valtos with William MacKenzie, the schoolmaster, when three policemen appeared and arrested him on a charge of inciting "the lieges to violence and class hatred". He spent the weekend in Portree jail, a strange place for a minister of the gospel. Like MacKay, he was liberated on £100 bail, paid by two Portree merchants, John and Donald Kemp. On November 18, A.J. Balfour received at his house in Carlton Gardens, London, a deputation of M.P.s and representatives of various societies sympathetic to the crofters, such as the H.L.L.R.A., and the Gaelic Society of London. Fraser Macintosh, M.P. for Inverness-shire, described the treatment of MacPherson and MacCallum as "harsh and inhumane". Balfour replied to criticism of Ivory and the suggestion that he was a "monomaniac" on the subject of crofters by affirming that he had been animated by "a high sense of responsibility", a claim which had some justification.

The expedition ended with the departure of the *Seahorse* and the *Jackal* on December 1, despite a request from the Skye proprietors that a gunboat, with 15-20 marines, should be left in the neighbourhood for two months. Sheriff Ivory (and A.J. Balfour) could claim that the expedition had been successful in the collection of rates and the vindication of the law. The crofters, however, felt justified in withholding their rents as in the summer of 1887 the Crofters Commission after their visit to Skye reduced all rents by varying amounts; on Kilmuir estate, notorious for its high rents, the reduction was 37 per cent and of the total of arrears amounting to £6,941, the large sum of £4,554 was cancelled. The trials of the Bornaskitaig deforcers were held in December in the High Court, Inverness, before Lord Mure, who after a long harangue about similar but worse cases in Tiree, sentenced them on the charges of mobbing and rioting to 3 months' imprisonment. The Garalapin and Herbusta prisoners had to travel to Edinburgh to the High Court to stand trial before Lord Young, who acquitted all the Garalapin men on the charge of mobbing and rioting and treated the Herbusta men leniently, stating that the affair was a "small matter" and "trifling in the extreme".

Lewis Troubles

The Crofters' Holdings (Scotland) Act of 1886 contained only one brief clause relating to cottars and the problem of cottars' rights was not to be settled for a long time. Their numbers increased with the natural growth of the population. Younger sons built houses on their fathers' holdings, which were divided and sub-divided. Some cottars had patches of potato ground and perhaps a cow, and some of the younger men could go as hired men to the herring fishing at Stornoway or on the east coast and in a good year earn as much as £20 to £25. But there were bad seasons such as 1881, 1882, and 1885, the year when 100 Lewis fishermen were stranded in Fraserburgh without money or food as they had failed to obtain employment. Herring fishing in the Minch was thriving and a lucrative trade with Russia had developed.[7] The Russians were willing to pay twice as much for the fat, oily herring (superior to all others except the Loch Fyne herring) as they would pay for east coast fish. But trawlers, mainly English, made their appearance in northern waters in 1882 and their inshore trawling was later to spoil the fishing grounds of Loch Hourn and other sea lochs in Wester Ross. The profitable herring fishing from Stornoway and Castlebay was in the early 1880s controlled by the fish-curers, who in 1885 and 1886 abandoned their old system of paying a fixed wage to the fishermen in favour of a fraction of the profit resulting from public auction of the catch. For various reasons, including over-production, prices fluctuated and it was estimated by Sheriff Fraser and Malcolm MacNeill that in the years 1886 and 1887 the fishermen of Lewis lost over £80,000 — a loss which was felt mainly by the cottars and squatters. Although no outstanding leader of the crofter movement came from the ranks of the cottars and squatters, they often formed the bulk of the support for the orators at Land League meetings and would vigorously applaud demands for land for the people. According to Malcolm MacNeill, who prepared a memorandum for Balfour after his confidential mission of 1886, Lewis was "swarming with squatters" and the Land League supporters were mainly "cottars, squatters and young men, especially Royal Naval Reserve".

The Highland Land League (to give the official title from the date of the conference at Oban in 1887) was not well organised in Lewis. The Free Church ministers on the whole remained faithful and sympathetic to the crofters' movement,[8] and as mentioned earlier, Principal Rainy along with other Free Church leaders had formed a branch of the Edinburgh H.L.L.R.A. in Lewis in October 1884. One notable exception was the Rev. Hector Cameron, Back, near Stornoway. With a great reputation as a preacher, he invariably upheld authority and the establishment and strongly opposed the crofters' agitation from the start.[9]

Before Principal Rainy's visit to Lewis in October, 1884, an independent Highland Land Law Reform Assocation had been formed in Stornoway by Alexander Morison, a commission agent, who appeared as a witness before the Napier Commission in 1883. It was Morison who invited Chamberlain in April, 1887, to visit Lewis and who took the credit for the efforts by Chamberlain and Collings to amend the Crofters Act. Chamberlain, who had been chiefly responsible for splitting the Liberal party over Irish Home Rule, also managed to split the Highland Land League but raised hopes that something would emerge. Whether it was the dashing of these hopes, or the frustration arising from the protracted delay of the Crofters Commission in dealing with Lewis applications for rent revision, or the destitution following on the failure of the fishing industry to provide a livelihood for cottars and squatters, or the active leadership of an incomer to the island, Donald MacRae, or a combination of all these factors which influenced events is debatable. At any rate there were two major disturbances which rendered necessary the dispatch of yet another military expedition to the Hebrides.

"Swarms of Squatters"

On the east side of Lewis, Park, the old deer forest of the Seaforths had been let during the nineteenth century to sheep farmers for whom several townships had been cleared and the people crowded into other villages. Similarly, on the west side, the creation by Sir James Matheson of Scaliscro and Morsgail deer forests and Grimersta fishings involved the removal of the small tenants miles away to Shawbost and farther north. The receiving villages had suffered by losing some of their grazing (often the best part) to the neighbouring farmers and what was left had to be shared with the incomers from the cleared villages. Thus, in the parishes of Lochs in the east and Barvas in the west, the villages were crowded with cottars and squatters; and, near Stornoway, a similar pattern prevailed where the best land was held by farmers and the peninsula of Point had too little land for too many people. Applications by 32 fishermen, squatters in the townships of Gravir, Calbost and Maravig, were made in 1881 and 1882 to Lady Matheson (her husband had died in 1878) but were treated contemptuously. Similarly, in December, 1886, a number of young able-bodied men from Arnol on the west side, who implored her for land at Dalmore or Park deer forest when the leases ran out, were referred to her chamberlain, William MacKay, who told them there was no land for them in Lewis but plenty in America. Whether it was to counter Land League propaganda or not, Lady Matheson in September, 1886, formed a branch of the Primrose League, founded by some Conservatives in memory of Disraeli, but few of the crofting community attended the Primrose League tea-parties, those who did having to suffer ridicule and worse. It was about this time that Lady

Matheson exhibited in the window of the Stornoway Post Office a message she had been sent in the form of a drawing of a coffin with an inscription, "Prepare to meet thy God". This "Valentine", as she called it in a sarcastic reply, also exhibited in the Post Office, was in imitation of the practice in Ireland but was regarded as the work of an employee of Lady Matheson's with a wry sense of humour.

Donald MacRae, Balallan

The major disturbance in Lewis in 1887 was a deer raid in Park in the month of November. The headquarters of the mass invasion of the deer forest was at Balallan, about 15 miles south of Stornoway and there is little doubt that the impetus to this sensational move came from the Balallan schoolmaster. A native of Plockton, Donald Mac-Rae had been dismissed in October, 1886, from his post of headmaster of Bridgend Public School, Alness, in Easter Ross, mainly because he was the active secretary of the Alness branch of the H.L.L.R.A. There were other reasons given — a dispute with the school board over the question of the school grant and the schoolmaster's salary, and the granting of a school holiday on the day of the H.L.L.R.A. conference at Bonar Bridge. A girl, who was the daughter of a member of the school board and had been strapped "too much", had refused to write an essay on the Bonar Bridge conference. Soon after his appointment to Balallan School the local crofters and cottars began to renew their interest in the agitation for land reform. Meetings of the branch were opened with psalm-singing and prayer and anyone suspected of having attended one of Lady Matheson's Primrose League parties was ejected to accompanying shouts of *"Mach leis! Mach leis!* (Out with him! Out with him!)". When Donald MacLeod, Balallan, was ejected, he was rebuked by the chairman:

> "If any Highlander is so low as to eat the crumbs that fall from Jezebel's table or sell his country for a cup of tea, then this meeting is no place for him".

In the summer of 1887, articles either written or inspired by Donald MacRae and dealing with destitution in the parish of Lochs appeared in newspapers sympathetic to the crofters like the *Scottish Highlander* and the *North British Daily Mail*, setting the scene for the dramatic events of November, 1887, and January, 1888.

Deer Raid

It was nominally in search of food that hundreds of men, mainly cottars, armed with rifles, guns and sticks, made their way into the deer forest of Park on Tuesday, November 22, 1887. Word of the planned invasion had reached the south but there was no organised resistance. On their way into the deer forest the raiders were met by Mrs Platt, the wife of the lessee of the farm and deer forest of Park, and Murdo MacRae, *Murchadh Mór* (Big Murdo), head gamekeeper. When Mrs Platt remonstrated with the raiders, one of them replied, "No English, my lady". Murdo MacRae, the gamekeeper, could hardly contain himself. *"An ainm Dhé, an e an caothach a tha oirbh?* (In

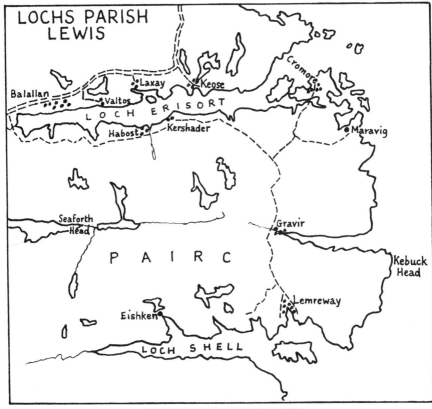

LOCHS PARISH, ISLE OF LEWIS.

God's name, are you out of your mind?)." For the rest of the day the raiders were dispersed and shots could be heard sporadically. Over three days of hunting the raiders killed possibly as many as 200 beasts, although a much lower figure, 15 to 20, was mentioned by the gamekeeper, Murdo MacRae, at the trial. The number of deer in the forest before the raid was estimated at 500-600. One group of raiders, led by Sandy MacFarlane from Maravig, met by accident near Loch

203

Brollum Douglas Thornycroft, Mrs Platt's brother, accompanied by gillies. After exchanging a few pleasantries, one of the gillies produced a picnic-basket and the food was shared with the raiders, the unexpected lunch topped off by a dram. This incident was referred to by defence counsel, Thomas Shaw, Q.C., in order to disprove the charge of forming part of a riotous mob. That night over a hundred raiders camped out near Loch Seaforth at Airigh Dhomhnaill Chaim, the site of a shieling called after Donald Cam MacAulay, seventeenth century chief of the clan MacAulay of Uig in the west of Lewis. Large canvas sails and masts had been put together to form a tent to give the raiders some shelter as they dined on venison (probably not so edible but still enjoyed by the raiders). A grace was delivered by one of the older men, who offered thanks for the bounteous provision the Lord made for them.

The following day, Wednesday, November 23, when more deer were killed, Sheriff Fraser and Superintendent Gordon made their way from Stornoway to the deer forest. Sheriff Fraser, in marked contrast to Sheriff Ivory in Skye, took a sympathetic interest in the conditions of the cottars. Later, at a meeting in Stornoway called to consider relief measures for destitution, Fraser referred to "the pinched and poverty-stricken-looking children" he had seen in Balallan. With the raiders, his first policy was one of persuasion. At Ruadh Cleit, in the middle of the deer forest, the Sheriff and the Superintendent came upon a group of raiders carrying guns. The Sheriff asked them to disperse and, when they refused, he read the Riot Act in English and Gaelic; but the raiders, who doffed their caps in deference to the Sheriff, maintained that they had taken part in the raid only because their families were facing starvation.

Surrender of Ringleaders

The Sheriff spent the night in Park Lodge but the Sheriff's party was accosted on their return journey by a young man carrying a gun and a stag's head, which he was taking home as a trophy of the chase. He was Donald MacKinnon of Balallan, a keen member of the Highland Land League. MacKinnon foolishly challenged the strangers, whom he failed to recognise in the dark, and threatened to shoot if they moved. When the Superintendent declared his identity, MacKinnon realised the enormity of his offence and fled, reaching Balallan in a distressed condition. There he met with Donald MacRae, the schoolmaster, who advised him to disappear for a while; but MacKinnon, still distraught, did not take the advice and on Saturday set off for Stornoway, where he surrendered to the police. He was interviewed by William Ross, the Procurator Fiscal, who seems to have persuaded

MacKinnon to give evidence for the Crown and regain his freedom. With the help of MacKinnon, the Procurator Fiscal drew up a list of men to be arrested. The task of arresting the raiders and the organisers was given to Police Sergeant Smith, a native of the parish of Lochs. Smith, "a shrewd man, with the approval of Sheriff Fraser, a pacific man" (in the words of the Glasgow *Daily Mail*) first went out to Balallan, where he informed MacRae of the dispatch of a military expedition to Lewis, already on its way, and suggested that it would be better for everybody if the raiders surrendered quietly. MacRae, who was quite prepared to answer for the part he played (he was later charged with instigating a riotous mob), believed that the others, accused of having "formed part of a riotous mob", were equally innocent of the charge. A trial, he felt, would give him an opportunity to present a case for the Lewis people. He told Sergeant Smith he would go quietly and he would answer for the others doing the same.

In all, 14 surrendered but only 6 were brought to trial, which was held in the High Court of Edinburgh on January 16 and 17, 1888. The accused, Donald MacRae, Roderick MacKenzie, merchant, chairman of the Balallan branch of the Highland Land League, and John Matheson, faced a charge of instigating the raid, and the last-named, along with Murdo MacDonald, Malcolm MacKenzie, and Donald MacMillan, all of Balallan, was accused of having formed part of a riotous mob in the deer forest of Park and intimidating Murdo MacRae, gamekeeper, and others. Thomas Shaw (later Lord Shaw) acted as defence counsel for Donald MacRae and Roderick MacKenzie, and, in a masterly cross-examination of the witnesses for the prosecution, destroyed the case for the Crown. In his address to the jury, he attacked the chief witnesses for the Crown, Donald MacKinnon, Murdo Martin and Malcolm Kennedy, three of the ringleaders in the raid and now witnesses against their fellow raiders. "If Donald MacKinnon had not been here, there would have been no case." Despite the summing-up of the judge, Lord Moncrieff, against the accused, the jury took less than half an hour to return to the court with a verdict of "Not guilty" on all charges, The verdict was greeted with cheers from the public gallery and outside a crowd followed MacRae, borne shoulder-high down the High Street to the Waterloo Rooms, where the hero of the day made a stirring speech.[10] He attacked the *Scotsman*, which a month before had denied there was any destitution in Lewis but was now publishing reports of the most harrowing conditions in the island. The problem of destitution was to remain before the public for a long time: Sheriff Fraser and Malcolm MacNeill of the Board of Supervision (for Poor Relief) produced in 1888 a report on the cottar population of Lewis, and Sheriff Brand, chairman of the Crofters Commission, produced, in 1902, another report with the title, *Report of the Crofters Commission on the social condition of the People of Lewis in 1901 as compared with twenty years ago.* Lewis and other parts of the Highlands and Islands were to be the subject of many more reports in the years to come.

Arrival of Gunboats

Three days after the raid began, a detachment of 82 men and 5 officers of the Royal Scots was sent from Maryhill Barracks, Glasgow, by the early morning train, arriving at Stornoway by steamer at 11 p.m. They were greeted in a friendly way by the people as they marched, headed by two pipers, from the quay to their billets at Manor Farm. It had originally been intended to send a detachment of the Seaforth Highlanders but the Commanding Officer objected as the regiment included so many men from the Highlands and Islands. On the same morning as the Royal Scots left Glasgow, H.M.S. *Ajax* (which had been engaged in the Tiree expedition) sailed from the Tail of the Bank with 400 men on board. Off the Mull of Kintyre, the *Ajax* ran into a "perfect hurricane" and damaged its rudder so badly that it had to be towed ·back for repairs. A fortnight later the gunboat, *Seahorse*, arrived in Stornoway with 40 marines to relieve the Royal Scots and in the New Year still another gunboat, H.M.S. *Forester*, arrived with marines transferred from the damaged *Ajax*.

While the Lochs raiders were awaiting their trial, the rest of the people in Lewis were agog with excitement over incidents much nearer Stornoway and also on the west side in the parish of Barvas. The land hunger had not abated but had rather increased by Lady Matheson's continued refusal to meet the wishes of the cottars. Malcolm MacNeill, whose confidential mission of inquiry at the end of 1886 had led him to report, after his visit to Lewis, that "squatters abound everywhere", had made a fair assessment. Some crofts at 25 shillings rent contained as many as four separate dwellings, the holdings having been divided and sub-divided by the people "with utterly reckless improvidence". On June 19, in the midst of the Golden Jubilee celebrations, a lengthy telegram had been sent to Queen Victoria on behalf of "27,000 souls of the crofter population of Lewis", imploring her to

"request Lady Matheson, the proprietrix, to restore unto us our land, formerly tilled by our ancestors, at a fair rent ere the Jubilee year closes".

News of the Deer Raid stimulated a revival of agitation among the more militant cottars and led to a disturbance of an unprecedented nature. On Wednesday, December 21, 300 landless men from Borve and Shader on the west side, headed by two pipers and in military formation, marched on to the large farm of Galson and gave warning to the farmer, Mr Helm, to leave Galson when his lease was up. Three days later, a procession of several hundreds from the Point district marched to the farm of Aignish near Stornoway and informed the farmer, Albany Newall, that they required his farm for starving cottars and their families. From Aignish, they carried on to Melbost farm, where, in the absence of the farmer, Thomas Newall, they passed resolutions in favour of re-allotment of the lands of Lewis. At a meeting in Eye churchyard on Thursday, December 29, Newall was accused of desecrating the churchyard by letting his cattle graze there; and after speeches by prominent Land Leaguers, it was decided to march on Aignish farm and remove Newall's stock on Monday, January 9. There was no attempt to maintain secrecy about the intended raid, which seemed bound to produce a confrontation. The authorities reacted swiftly to the threat of a disturbance with the arrival of the *Forester*. In the meantime, deputations of crofters from the west side and from Tong arrived in Stornoway on January 5 to present petitions to Lady Matheson. Her ladyship relented sufficiently to receive Roderick MacLeod, Shader, Donald MacDonald, Borve, and a delegate from Tong, but remained as stubborn as ever. "These lands are my property and you have nothing to do with them".

Battle of Aignish

By 10 o'clock on the morning of Janary 9, 1888, 400 to 500 men from various townships in the Point district had gathered on the hill in front of Aignish farm. Long before daybreak a detachment of Royal Scots

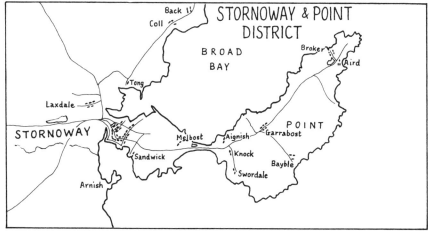

STORNOWAY AND POINT DISTRICT, ISLE OF LEWIS.

207

had marched to Melbost farm nearby, and a company of marines, fully armed and accompanied by police, had taken up their stations at Aignish farmhouse, there to wait in silence for the crofters and cottars to make a move. As day was breaking, Sheriff Fraser arrived from Stornoway with the Deputy Fiscal, John Ross. After some time had elapsed, a body of 40 to 50 men dashed down from the hill towards the farm steading to be faced by the Sheriff and a dozen policemen. Sheriff Fraser, who earned praise for his good sense and tactful conduct on this day, warned the men in Gaelic of the consequences of their actions. When the raiders, shouting and brandishing their sticks, started to drive off Newall's cattle, they were stopped by police and marines, and after a stiff struggle 12 of them were arrested. The most serious incident of the day occurred when the prisoners were being led off to Stornoway. The crowd became incensed when the Deputy Fiscal, with a revolver in his hand, went to the assistance of two policemen struggling with a prisoner. The Fiscal was quickly

TROOPS IN ACTION AT AIGNISH, ISLE OF LEWIS, 1888.

overpowered and at once a dozen marines with fixed bayonets advanced to ward off his assailants. A South Bayble man, Donald MacDonald (nicknamed the "Captain") bared his chest and challenged the soldier, "*Sath an sud do bhiodag* (Stick your dagger in there)". For a few moments, crofters and marines stood in confrontation, and then suddenly the tension was relaxed when the "Captain" shouted to the soldiers, "*Falbhaidh agus mharbhaidh na cearcan: cha neil an corr a dh'fheum annaibh* (Go home and kill the hens: you're fit for nothing else)". By this time a messenger had reached Captain Farquharson in charge of the Royal Scots at Melbost farm, but even with the help of the soldiers it was with great difficulty that the prisoners were brought to Stornoway and from there to the gunboat, *Jackal*. They were to face trial in the High Court in Edinburgh at the end of January before Lord Craighill, described in the *Scottish Highlander* as a "brow-beating judge".

Trial of the Aignish Rioters

All the accused were cottars or sons of cottars, fishermen or sailors by occupation except William Crichton, a mason from Aird, and all resident in Point, eight of them from Aird and Broker, townships at the extreme eastern end of the Eye Peninsula. Crichton had been released on bail and when he made his appearance in court, the charge against him was dropped. All the accused pleaded not guilty except Murdo MacDonald, who appeared on a separate charge of having attempted to break down the fence at Aignish farm on the night of Friday, January 30, and received a sentence of only 6 months. The other accused had been arrested at the first onset against Newall's cattle and, as often happens in cases of mobbing and rioting, were not necessarily the most active and aggressive of the rioters. But Donald MacKenzie (51), Aird, was unable to deny having delivered an intemperate and inflammatory speech at the meeting in Eye churchyard on December 24 when, according to police evidence, he declared that he was prepared to shed the last drop of blood to carry out the resolution of the meeting to drive Newall's cattle off the farm of Aignish. William MacLeod (63), Aird, was said to have told the crowd, after his arrest, to go home but, nevertheless, received the same sentence as most of the others. Colin Nicolson (31), Bayble, claimed to have been opposed to the raid and had become involved in the crowd by accident on his way to Stornoway to collect some wood. Another accused, John MacKay (26), Aird, also pleaded accidental involvement in the riot. He had left home in order to gather edible sea-weed on the machair and had crossed over to Aignish out of curiosity. According to police evidence, however, he was in the forefront of the rush to drive off the cattle and was carrying a heavy stick. Donald MacLeod (21), Sheshader, returning from Stornoway with medicine for his invalid mother, was similarly the victim of what seems to have been indiscriminate arrests. The defence lawyers had a difficult task, as, unlike cases of deforcements in Skye and Lewis, the accused were not engaged in an effort to protect their property but were acting in a premeditated campaign against other people's property. The defence offered by the accused and by their lawyers was unconvincing. The object of their demonstration, they claimed, was primarly to visit the graves of their ancestors; but considerable publicity had been accorded to the churchyard meeting and particularly to threats of expelling the farmer's cattle. The accused were tried in successive batches and the juries lost no time in bringing verdicts of guilty, all receiving sentences of 12 months' imprisonment except Donald MacKenzie and Alexander MacLeod, who were sentenced to 15 months, and Malcolm MacKenzie and John MacLeod, Broker, who were given only 9 months.[11]

On the other side of the island, persistent attempts had been made for months to break the dykes between farms and the grazings of neighbouring townships. Policemen had been drafted in to keep watch on the dykes and on the night of January 16, 1888, a clash occurred at Borve between a group of young men and the police watchers, three of the police being injured. When news reached Stornoway of the incident, the Sheriff set off on the gunboat, *Seahorse*, for Port of Ness, with police and marines, and a force of Royal Scots marched across the island to Borve. Five men were arrested, taken to Ness and thence by sea to Stornoway. In the High Court, Edinburgh, they were acquitted mainly because of the uncertainty of identification of the culprits in the darkness. One of the accused pleaded an alibi, maintaining that he had been with his sweetheart from midnight until 4 o'clock in the morning. Dr Ross of Borve, in his evidence for the defence, confirmed that this was a common practice in the district, adding that in the three years he had been in Borve there had been no illegitimate birth.

In the two years since the passing of the Crofters Act there had been much talk about violence in Skye and Lewis but, all things considered, the crofting community had gained little by their confrontation with the authorities, and there was a conspicuous absence of violence following the heavy penalties imposed in 1888. All the time of the clashes between the crofters (or their supporters) and the armed forces, the Crofters Commissioners were carrying out their duties in a plodding but painstaking manner, bringing about a better atmosphere in the crofting area. The security of tenure granted by the Act made it possible for the crofters to look forward in confidence to the future: for the cottars and the squatters their problems remained.

Notes

1. In 1951 the population of Tiree numbered 1200, more than a quarter of whom were squatters and their families. By that date, Tiree was almost entirely a crofting island, practically all the large farms having been broken up. (F. Fraser Darling, *West Highland Survey* (1955), 54).

210

2. MacDiarmid was known as *Baillidh Dubh* (Black Factor), the word *Dubh* being used in a pejorative sense. Similarly, Principal Rainy of the Free Church College was known in the Highlands and Islands as *Rainy Dubh* (Black Rainy) because of his views on church union.

3. The Duke of Argyll, writing to Gladstone on December 6, 1885, denounced MacFarlane's "Bribery of Promises, one being to Fishermen that they should get all the Salmon as well as all the Herring" (Gladstone Papers).

4. A Gaelic version of the Tiree expedition in 1886 ("Aimhreit an Fhearainn ann an Tiriodh" by D.E. Meek) is included in *Oighreachd agus Gabhaltas*, edited by D. MacAulay (1980). The author, who incorporates local tradition in his account, is highly critical of the account in *The Old and the New Highlands and Hebrides* (1917) by James Cameron, who relied mainly on contemporary newspaper reports.

5. For Balfour's exposition of his Skye policy, see his Memorandum for the Cabinet in the Appendix.

6. The messenger-at-arms, Alexander MacDonald, later averred that two of the accused (one of them a woman) had threatened to take his life "by putting the graips they held through his guts".

7. For details of fishing based on the Western Isles, 1873-82, see tables in Appendix.

8. See "The Ministers and the Crofters' Agitation" in Chapter 4.

9. In a recent biography of the Rev. Hector Cameron by the Rev. Murdo MacAulay there is no mention of Cameron's denunciation of the Highland Land League.

10. Robert Bontine Cunninghame Graham, M.P. for North-West Lanarkshire, who was sent to prison for his part in the Trafalgar Square demonstration on "Bloody Sunday", November 13, 1887, sent a letter from prison to the press, praising the Lewis raiders, adding that deer-killing was not a criminal offence in Scotland. Two Gaelic versions of the Park Deer Raid have appeared in recent years — John M. MacLeod's "Reud na Pairc" in *Oighreachd agus Gabhaltas* (1910), and *Creach Mhór nam Fiadh* (n.d.) by Norman MacDonald.

11. A Gaelic version of the "Battle of Aignish", Aimhreit Aignis by John MacArthur, is also to be found in *Oighreachd agus Gabhaltas* (1980).

CHAPTER 10

AFTERMATH

Destitution in Lewis

The subject of destitution received wide publicity in the national press both before and after the Deer Raid in Lewis in November, 1887. It was not the first time that the standards of housing and diet in the crofting community had been commented on, mainly by people sympathetic to crofters. An older generation could recall tales of near-starvation at the time of the potato blight in the late 1840s, when, although there was nothing resembling the scale of the disastrous potato famine in Ireland, many families in the Hebrides were reduced to living on shellfish. Were it not for the efforts in the large cities to organize relief funds, the death roll would have been several times greater. In the early 1880s there was widespread destitution in Skye and Lewis as a result of storm damage. Sir William Collins, the former Lord Provost of Glasgow, who played an active part in raising relief funds, stated in his evidence to the Napier Commission in 1883, that as the result of a storm of unusual severity on November 22, 1881, about 1,200 boats had been destroyed or damaged, corn crops had been scattered, and on the island of Iona all the peats had been blown into the sea. The winter of 1882-83 was even more disastrous. The potato crop had been a complete failure in Skye and Lewis, and a gale on October 1 swept away corn crops and hay, destroying 250 boats in Skye and 136 in Lewis and partially destroying 132 and 56 respectively. One effect of the loss of boats was to restrict still further the meagre diet of the people by their being deprived of the opportunity to fish. Relief funds in Glasgow, Edinburgh, Greenock and other towns made possible the distribution of meal and seed potatoes, payment for which was expected but in many cases not exacted.

The articles which appeared in the *Scottish Highlander* in the summer of 1887 on destitution in the parish of Lochs in Lewis were unsigned but were almost certainly written by Donald MacRae, who was appointed schoolmaster at Balallan in January, 1887. The first article criticised the Rev. John MacDougall, Free Church minister in Lochs, who had written to the *Spectator* about the destitution in Lochs, as a result of which he had received a cheque for £20 from Joseph Chamberlain and other gifts totalling over £100. He was criticised for restricting the distribution of the gifts to his own part of the parish of Lochs and at the same time he was accused along with other Free Church ministers of failing to support the movement for land law reform. The *Scottish Highlander* correspondent claimed that:

> "God never willed, nature never meant, townships to exist such as Gravir, Cromore, Kershader, Arivruaich, Ranish, Grimshader and Keose, while Park and Aline should be consecrated to deer . . . Until the restoration of Park and Aline to the people of Lochs there will be chronic famine in Lochs."

Donald MacRae, if, as was likely, he was the anonymous correspondent to the *Scottish Highlander*, contributed several articles on destitution in Lewis in the same vein. He may have been genuine enough in his views, having come from the more affluent district of Easter Ross, but the *Scotsman* regarded the articles very cynically as mere political propaganda. Writing in July, 1887, MacRae described landlordism in Lewis as an "uninterrupted torrent of robbery and plunder", and the tenantry in a more miserable plight than anywhere else in Christendom except, perhaps, the Irish of Clare and Connaught. The Deer Raid in November organised by MacRae was ostensibly in order to provide food for starving people. After the Deer Raid, national newspapers such as the Glasgow *Daily Mail* and the *Scotsman* portrayed the cottars' plight with lurid pictures of the worst of the hovels in Lochs, much to the annoyance of crofters in the district.

Sheriff Fraser was one who took the charges seriously and in January 1888, along with Malcolm MacNeill of the Board of Supervision, undertook an inquiry into the extent and character of a measles epidemic raging at that time and of destitution in general in the island, enlisting the assistance of medical officers and parochial boards. Part of the trouble in Lewis was the vast number of cottars and squatters. Sub-division of crofts had been permitted short-sightedly by the notorious chamberlain, Donald Munro, who used only to impose a fine of £5 on anyone, often a younger son, building a house on his father's croft or on the verge of the common grazing. The number of cottars in the parish of Barvas had formerly been artificially small, but the chamberlain in 1883, William MacKay, entered in the new rent ledger several persons hitherto paying rent to crofters. Nearly all who were asked by Sheriff Fraser for their views commented on the unusually good corn and hay harvests and potato crop in 1887. Dr John Dewar, Medical Officer for the parish of Lochs, stated that he had read about destitution in the press but had heard nothing of it in the parish. The Rev. Hector Cameron, Free Church minister at Back, near Stornoway, was emphatic about the absence of destitution, adding that the harvest had been the best for years, but pointed out that because of the unprecedented failure of the fishing industry and the exceptionally low prices for stock there was very little money about and that could lead to destitution among cottars and squatters in the spring. The Rev. Angus MacIver, Uig, was equally emphatic about the absence of destitution in his parish, characterising the newspaper reports as "calumnious". Dr Charles MacRae, Medical Officer for Stornoway parish (which included several crofting townships), pointed out that the good harvest and "the well-known Lewis generosity of those having food in supporting neighbours", had helped to relieve the distress of poorer families. William MacKay, the Lewis chamberlain, mentioned the various advantages that Lewis paupers possessed in comparison with people in other districts — with the fuel (peat) good and accessible, they also could grow potatoes on some spot given by a relative, and they could obtain fish at times of plenty as gifts from the successful fishermen.

In a house-to-house visitation arranged by Sheriff Fraser, details of 108 houses were collected in the parish of Lochs on the east side of Lewis and Barvas on the west side, two areas with large numbers of cottars and with much division of crofts. Many crofters were not much better off than the cottars. Most of them possessed potatoes but little meal. In some cases the livestock was minimal — only one old cow, one stirk, and one sheep. This was in January, when the inquiry was carried out, with a prospect of worse to come in spring or early summer, when the stirk or sheep might have to be killed off. The report did not mention the hens which scratched a living at the door or even inside every house; but they helped a family to supplement their meagre diet. If there were any doubt about the extent of destitution in Lewis, there could be little argument about the defects of many of the houses, in which cattle and human beings lived under the same roof, sometimes without any partition between them. The slow improvement in housing standards in Lewis in comparison with Skye, Tiree, Barra and the western mainland after the passing of the Crofters Act was attributed to the very high proportion of cottars and squatters in Lewis. In 1899, the Medical Officer of the parish of Barvas described a typical crofter's house, adding that to one unaccustomed to such houses they appeared "cheerless, wretched and comfortless", while the inmates as a rule compared favourably in physique, general well-being and immunity from disease, with those in better houses. Lord Napier, in his evidence to the Royal Commission on the housing of the working classes in 1884, stated that although the worst black houses in Lewis were "confined, dark, miserable and unhealthy", the people, especially the men, were "unusually healthy, long-lived and among the most moral in the United Kingdom". The difference between the sexes was probably due to the greater amount of time spent by the men outdoors. But, according to Dr Roper of H.M.S. *Jackal*, who carried out a survey of Lewis people, the women and girls

214

over 17 years were "extremely healthy and strong", performing many arduous tasks such as carrying heavily laden creels of peats and potatoes, while some of them were engaged as gutters during the herring season.[1]

Harbours and Railways

In 1888, after the trial of the Lewismen captured at Aignish, the period of the crofters' defiance of the law and violent confrontation between threatened tenants and the emissaries of the law was at an end. The heavy sentences imposed in Edinburgh acted as a deterrent, and the crofters' attention turned to the progress of the Crofters Commission through the crofting communities and the generally favourable decisions, while in Lewis the question of destitution was a main topic of concern to the people and their Lowland friends. In the spring of 1889 the western and northern Highlands and Islands, however, were agog over the prospect of new harbours and railways, a subject which had tended to be forgotten during the previous years, when the emphasis in the crofters' agitation was on land tenure, rents and grazing rights. The Napier Commission had given serious consideration to ways and means of improving the fisheries of north-west Scotland. In the Commission's report in 1884, Lord Napier wrote:

> "By far the greatest number of crofters and cottars in the Highlands and Islands are wholly or largely dependent for their subsistence on their earnings as fishermen."

The Commission's recommendations on fisheries included the following:—

(1) Harbours, piers and landing-places to be built and paid for out of public funds;
(2) Assistance to fishermen with purchase of boats and tackle, in loans at 3½ per cent, the loans to be repaid within 7 years;
(3) Improvement of postal and telegraphic communications;
(4) Extension of existing railways, e.g. Garve to Ullapool;
(5) Construction of new lines to reach the west coast and of light, narrow-gauge railways in Skye and Lewis, to be financed by the Government.

In April, 1889, James Caldwell, M.P. for the St Rollox ward in Glasgow and a supporter of Joseph Chamberlain, toured the north-west and the north of Scotland, the districts where the people's livelihood depended on the fishing industry, addressing meetings and holding out prospects of prosperity. He advocated the measures recommended by the Napier Commission; and in a letter to Caldwell after he had published his programme, Chamberlain congratulated him on his achievement, which confirmed the opinions formed in

1887 on his own tour of the north-west of Scotland. In his letter, which was published in the press, Chamberlain went on to sneer at Gladstone and the Liberal party, of which he had been a member, for their failure to effect the necessary improvements in the fishing industry; and there was little doubt that the chief incentive, so far as fishery improvements were concerned, was, for Caldwell and Chamberlain, the opportunity of winning support for the Liberal-Unionists. Meetings were held in villages in the islands and also on the western seaboard, and petitions were sent to the Scottish Secretary, the Marquis of Lothian. The first reaction of the Scottish Office was cautious. To a letter from one of the Stornoway magistrates, J.N. Anderson, enclosing a petition from a public meeting, Lothian replied by asking to what extent the district would be likely to support the cost of the proposed harbours in Lewis.

At the end of May, Lothian decided to visit the north-west himself. His tour in the Admiralty yacht *Enchantress* started at Oban on June 7, 1889, and his first call was at Roshven, a small place at the mouth of Loch Ailort, which had been mooted as the possible terminus of a railway from Fort William. In Skye, he attended a meeting in Portree, presided over by Alex. MacDonald, solicitor and banker, who stressed the inability of landlords to undertake such projects as those proposed, the Government having reduced their rents. At Broadford, Lord MacDonald presided and would not permit questions about the land; and at Dunvegan, where the subject of a light railway was foremost in people's minds, John MacPherson of Glendale protested about being rebuffed when he raised the question of land for the people. In Lewis, Lothian visited many places both on the Minch and the Atlantic sides, suitable for harbours and piers. Reference has already been made to the destruction of boats in the storms of 1881 and 1882, mainly for lack of shelter. There was a terrible price to pay for the fishing in the Atlantic Ocean, one of the stormiest zones in the world. In the thirty-five years before the Napier Commission, 293 fishermen from Lewis lost their lives at sea. During the gale of March 18, 1889, 12 fishermen from Ness near the Butt of Lewis were drowned. There were many reasons for a disaster on such a scale — the type of boat, the dependence on sails only, the lack of lighthouses on an exposed, rugged coast; but the teeming wealth of fish was an irresistible attraction and a necessity for the native inhabitants as well as the incomers from other parts. The Scottish Fishery Board, set up in 1882, had made grants towards improvement but without much effect, the sums allotted being inadequate, as in the case of Ness harbour, and the project suffering from the multiplicity of authorities. The only immediate result of Lothian's tour was a grant of £30,000 to West Highland parishes in relief of local taxation, which had been drastically reduced through non-payment of rates with adverse effects on education and poor relief.

A later result was the appointment of yet another Commission, the announcement of which came just before the end of 1889. The terms of reference were wide. Because of much destitution and consequent disturbances, the warrant of appointment read, it would be the duty of the Commission to consider what measures, if any, could be taken by Her Majesty's Government to remedy those evils by developing the natural resources of the region and to report on various schemes and proposals already made. The warrant continued:—

> "It is proper to point out that Her Majesty's Government does not contemplate any expenditure of a purely charitable character or such as merely aims at the relief of temporary distress or the temporary employment of labour; nor do they wish to establish at public expense any competition with existing private enterprise."

The Commission, which was appointed by the Marquis of Lothian, was officially known as the West Highlands and Islands Commission but was generally designated the Walpole Commission, so called after the chairman, Spencer H. Walpole, Lieutenant-Governor of the Isle of Man. He had a reputation as a historian (he had produced a biography of his grandfather, Spencer Percival, the British prime minister who was assassinated in the House of Commons), and he had been an Inspector of Fisheries from 1867. Once again, the inhabitants of the crofting region were visited by an official body of strangers, and the same witnesses appeared at the Commission's hearings to give evidence. Complaints were made about the Commission's hurried and cursory inspection of sites. Fraser Mackintosh, M.P. for Inverness-shire, raised the subject in the House of Commons, criticising "the flippant manner and hostile cross-examination of witnesses". The Commission's first report, which appeared in August, 1890, contained a comprehensive survey of the many proposals put forward, prefaced by some derogatory comments on the people of the region as having "a disinclination to work at a regular job", and "little evidence of any systematic method" of fishing. The Commission expressed support for extension of the proposed West Highland Railway from Banavie to Mallaig and of the Highland Railway from Strome to Kyle of Lochalsh as worthy of financial assistance but would not recommend any grant for the proposed Garve to Ullapool line.[2] The suggested light railways in Lewis (Stornoway to Carloway, Barvas, Ness and Gress), and in Skye (Portree to Uig, Dunvegan, Glendale), were considered as unlikely to be profitable and were therefore dismissed as impracticable, but subsidies were approved for steamers on certain routes. Grants for improvement of some harbours, all in the

Isle of Lewis (Ness, Carloway, Portnaguran) were recommended, as well as lighthouses and beacons at a number of places on the west and north-west of Scotland and also an extension of telegraphic communications, work on these to start at once. The rejection of the proposal for light railways on Skye and Lewis was criticised by Liberal M.P.s as unjustifiable, especially as the Government had so recently allocated £300,000 for light railways in part of Ireland. The difficulty in implementing plans to facilitate speedy arrival of fresh fish at more accessible ports was that of funding; and the Scottish case seemed less urgent to the Conservatives, who were prepared to accept Gladstone's mission to pacify Ireland, short of conceding Home Rule. The Marquis of Lothian was reported as having serious differences with the Chancellor of the Exchequer, W.H. Smith (the founder of the wholesale newspaper business), who, like many chancellors before and after him, was unwilling to approve any novel plan involving increased expenditure and subsequent higher taxation. A grant of £15,000 was, however, made for the construction of a new road from Carloway to Stornoway, seven miles shorter than the existing road by Callanish, but the sum proved inadequate, and the road was left unfinished until 1912, when the Secretary for Scotland, Lord Pentland, managed to carry the project to completion. The Pentland road fell into desuetude after the First World War and survives as a relic of a policy that was one of "too little, too late". The proposals of the Walpole Commission were embodied, with modifications, in the Western Highlands and Islands Works Act of 1891, which helped to lay the foundation of a period of comparative prosperity for the crofter-fishermen in the early twentieth century.

Disunity in the Movement

The Bonar Bridge Conference of the H.L.L.R.A. in 1886, the first after the passing of the Crofters Act, marked, as already stated, the culmination of the process of amalgamation of the three constituent bodies, the London, Edinburgh and the Sutherland associations, into the Highland Land League. Paradoxically, the conference also marked the beginning of the break-up of the Highland reform movement. The Sutherland Association, with its 3,000 paid-up members, was even reluctant about merging with the other less financially sound associations, with which their relations had not been over-friendly in previous years. The official name from the time of the 1887 conference at Oban was changed to the Highland Land League, but instead of greater unity, stresses and strains developed. At first, the chief complaint was of the inactivity of the leadership. A Central Executive Committee had been appointed at Bonar Bridge with

Angus Sutherland, M.P., as convener, but had never been convened; and another committee elected to draw up a draft bill for land law reform, with Dr MacDonald, M.P., as one of the conveners, had likewise not met. The 1888 conference of the Highland Land League was held at Inverness without Angus Sutherland, who, his critics pointed out, had not attended a meeting of the League outside Sutherland for two years. At the 1889 conference in Stornoway, the London members, who had previously been castigated by Alick Morison for their support of the Irish Home Rule movement, actually proposed that executive members should be chosen from the Highlands or Islands, a move intended to close the gap developing in the League. The conference ended in harmony with the appointment of Donald MacRae (Balallan) as travelling and organising secretary of the League. His salary was not guaranteed but depended on subscriptions, which included 20 guineas from Dr MacDonald and amounted to £120 altogether at the conference. MacRae set about his duties immediately after the conference, addressing 30 meetings in Lewis in the next six weeks. His political ambitions became obvious as time went by and as a result he attracted jealous criticism.

The crofter party in Parliament appeared to lose momentum after 1886. It was divided over Irish Home Rule, as was indeed the Liberal party in the United Kingdom generally. At the second reading of Gladstone's Irish Home Rule Bill in June, 1886, which brought about the overthrow of Gladstone's government, 38 Scottish Liberals had voted for the bill and 23 against. Among the 38 Home Rulers were two senior members of the crofter party — Charles Fraser Mackintosh and Dr Charles Cameron. The former changed his views and became a Unionist, while the latter, with his Irish background, remained loyal to his nationalist convictions and also upset most Scottish Liberals by his sponsorship of a Disestablishment Bill during the Liberal ministry of 1892-95. The incursion of Chamberlain into Highland politics caused bitter feelings in the Liberal party with two warring factions — the Liberal Unionists, who claimed to have forced the Conservatives to initiate a programme of public works in the crofting area, and the Gladstonian Liberals, who blamed the Liberal Unionists for having ousted a Liberal ministry and made possible a Conservative ministry. The Walpole Commission and its recommendations deepened the schism but the crofting community remained on the whole loyal to Gladstone at election times. The members of the Sutherland Association in Glasgow blamed Angus Sutherland's inactivity in Land League affairs as responsible for the lack of any proposals for harbours or railways in Sutherland in the Walpole Commission's recommendations. As a member of the Deer Forest Commission, he seemed to side with the landlord representatives rather than with those sympathetic to the crofters; and in 1894 the Glendale branch of the Highland Land League gave vent to their wrath over what one of them called the actions of "Judas" Sutherland. When later in the same year he resigned his seat in Parliament on his appointment as chairman of the Scottish Fishery Board (with a salary of £800 a year) his reputation sank to a low ebb. As early as 1890 Dr MacDonald had intimated his intention to resign his seat on health grounds but changed his mind after a London business man, James Galloway Weir, had been invited to represent the Ross and Cromarty constituency. MacDonald's popularity slumped drastically but his resignation ultimately came about in time for Weir to canvass the electors and gain a victory for the Gladstonian Liberals in 1892. Another elder statesman of the crofter movement, Charles Fraser Mackintosh, retired from the political scene after his defeat by Dr Donald MacGregor, a supporter of Gladstone, who in his eighty-fifth year formed his fourth ministry and made a second attempt to persuade Parliament to agree to Irish Home Rule. His bill was passed by the Commons but was thrown out by the Lords, and Gladstone, troubled with failing eyesight, resigned office in favour of Lord Rosebery. Two other crofter M.P.s, Dr Charles Cameron and Donald MacFarlane, who held their seats, were rewarded for past services in Gladstone's honours list, Cameron receiving a baronetcy and MacFarlane a knighthood, but both were defeated in the general election of 1895.

"The Land for the People"

All through the eighties and nineties and even up to the First World War, the Liberals in the Highlands and Islands fought elections with the slogan, "The Land for the People", but whether under a Liberal or a Conservative government, crofters and cottars waited in vain for legislation which would enable cottars to obtain holdings. The setting-up of county councils by the Local Government Act of 1889 raised the hopes of the crofting community, especially when the first elections resulted in majorities for Land Leaguers in most of the crofting counties. At the first meeting of the Ross and Cromarty County Council, the convener, Sir Kenneth MacKenzie, managed, however, to prevent discussion of questions of a political and controversial nature. The Inverness-shire County Council, which chose another proprietor, Donald Cameron of Lochiel, as convener but with a larger representation of members favourable to the crofters, rejected the convener's proposal to exclude from their discussions topics of a political nature but without achieving any benefit for the cottars. At later triennial elections Land Leaguers had less success, some members deciding not to seek re-election, partly because of frustration arising from tedious debates and the difficulties involved in travelling to and from the county town, such as Inverness or Dingwall. One measure of the Liberal government which was appreciated by Inverness-shire County Council was a grant of £3,000 for construction of roads, although members from the Hebrides complained about the allocation of funds, as their successors were also to complain in the twentieth century. Other county councils received similar grants, and although inadequate for the needs of the inhabitants of many areas, they helped to improve the quality of life in scattered townships.

Another Royal Commission appointed by Gladstone to consider crofters' and cottars' grievances at first raised hopes but proved disappointing. The terms of reference unfortunately restricted the commissioners to an inquiry as to whether —

"any, if any, land" (in the crofting counties), "now occupied for the purpose of a deer forest or for grazing, not in the occupation of crofters or small tenants, is capable of being cultivated to profit or otherwise advantageously occupied by crofters or small tenants".

Sheriff Brand, the chairman of this Deer Forest Commission (as it was called), had shown himself sympathetic to the crofters in the Crofters Commission hearings, and three of the members had been active supporters of the crofters for many years — Angus Sutherland, M.P., John MacLeod, secretary of the Sutherland Land League and editor of the *Highland News*, and the Rev. Malcolm MacCallum, president of the Argyllshire Land League and brother of the Rev. Donald MacCallum; but they were in a minority, with the chairman giving his casting vote in favour of the landlords when necessary, and Sutherland, as time went on, tending to agree with the landlords. The Commission's report, which appeared in April, 1895, contained a list of lands on sporting estates suitable for grazing but not suitable for arable cultivation. The report disappointed crofters and cottars. To most small tenants, whose livelihood was fishing and grazing of cattle and sheep, the reservations of the Commission were irrelevant. A new bill, introduced by Sir George Trevelyan, amending the 1886 Act in minor details, omitted mention of the cottars, as in previous amending bills, but discussion of its provisions was short-lived, as the Liberal ministry was replaced by the Conservative ministry of the Marquis of Salisbury and the bill was dropped.

Another attempt to implement the recommendations of the Deer Forest Commission was made by the Conservatives in 1897 by a decision to set up a Congested Districts Board. The decision was based on the success in Ireland of a body of the same name, formed as part of the Conservative policy of enabling the Irish small tenant to become owner of his holding. The success of the Irish policy was made possible by the grant of a large sum, ultimately £20 million, for the provision of loans to purchase lands, the loans being repayable over a period of 49 years. The Scottish Congested Districts Board was given a wide range of powers, for example, the right to purchase land for the creation of crofters' holdings, the construction of roads, piers, harbours, and the improvement of crofters' livestock; but from the start the Board was hampered by lack of funds and the absence of a properly organized administration. As happened in 1887 with Chamberlain's draft bill, crofters looked askance at proposals to transform them into owners of their lands. Their objections were based mainly on the fact that as owners they would have to pay double the tenant's rate, added to the annuities necessary for the repayment of the loans; and the crofters felt that the total cash outlay would be more than they could afford. Another factor influencing their attitude was their reluctance to lose the protection of the Crofters Commission as a court of justice in the event of a dispute. Some estates were purchased and considerable sums of money spent in the process, but in nearly all cases the crofters preferred to retain their tenant status, a notable exception being the Glendale crofters.[3]

A Decade of Peace

The 1890s proved to be a decade of peace, marked by a general improvement in the standard of living in the crofting districts, particularly for the crofters, no longer forced to "thole a factor's snash", with their security of tenure, low, fixed rents, better houses, and grazings restored. Life also was better for the cottars and their families. For the latter (and for younger sons of crofters), the opportunities to seek a new environment multiplied with the passing years; and for those who stayed at home, there was a reasonable chance of an acceptable livelihood because of the general prosperity of the fishing industry despite the trawler. The advance in communications of all kinds brought about more frequent contact with the outside world; and a young man, desirous of learning a trade and with relatives in one of the large cities to provide board and lodging, would opt to serve his apprenticeship away from home in, say, Glasgow, which city in time accumulated a considerable Gaelic-speaking population. Similarly, in the 1890s, domestic service, a low-paid but honourable occupation at that time, attracted young women who sought a livelihood away from home. In many cases, elderly parents, unable to call on the assistance available in the modern welfare state, benefited from regular remittances from their sons and daughters in the south. The improvement in educational facilities was general. In Lewis following a financial crisis in 1889, when, because of non-payment of rates and maladministration, three school boards became bankrupt, a successful salvage operation was performed by a young Inspector of Schools, John L. Robertson, a Lewisman, who was accorded great praise in the Brand Report of 1902 for his energy, tact and sympathy. The abolition of school fees and the improvement of township roads led to better attendance and a consequent higher standard of pupils' attainments. More and more pupils were able to proceed to higher education and the crofting districts produced a steady stream of entrants to the medical profession, the ministry, teaching and the police forces, who, however, tended to earn a living in the south. Not all the developments of the nineties could be attributed to the crofters' agitation of the eighties but 1886 marked the turn of the tide, and the publicity given to the crofters' campaign resulted in a favourable reception for the young people from the Highlands and Islands in their new environments.

The political aspect of public life in the nineties has already been discussed. The changes brought about by the extension of the franchise and the reforms in local government such as school boards and county councils created opportunities for public service unprecedented in the crofting communities apart from the duties and obligations laid upon elders and deacons in the presbyterian churches. Religious disputes began to weaken the loyalty and solidarity of the Free Church. The passing of the Declaratory Act by the General Assembly in 1892, modifying the rigid standards of the Kirk, led to a small secession and the formation of the Free Presbyterian Church, still loyal to the principles of 1843 and, in particular, to the strict observance of the Sabbath. Another more serious schism came about in 1900, when the majority of the Free Church, led by Principal Rainy, joined with the United Presbyterian Church to form the United Free Church. The remnant, known as the "Wee Frees", was well represented in the Gaelic-speaking areas but there also the split led to mutual recrimination; and John MacPherson of Glendale was only one of a number of crofters' leaders who suffered in consequence.[4]

In the cities on the mainland the Highland societies became non-political again. Another Gaelic Society was formed in 1887, this time in Glasgow, by Magnus MacLean, professor of electric engineering in the Technical College there, Malcolm MacFarlane, Archibald Sinclair and John MacMaster Campbell, sheriff of Argyllshire. Sheriff Campbell was one of those who founded a few years later An Comunn Gaidhealach (The Gaelic Association) for the encouragement of teaching of Gaelic, the study of Gaelic literature, history, music, and the wearing of Highland dress. The following year, 1892, the first Mod was held in Oban, with only ten competitors. Those organisations had little impact on the crofting way of life but they provided a bond of friendship between the resident population in the Highlands and Islands and the expatriates. The soirées and Annual Gatherings of the societies helped also to preserve the songs and memories of the period of the clearances but, until the centenary of the Act of 1886, little knowledge of the Crofters' War.

Notes

1. Few commentators on the low standards of living in Lewis and other crofting areas were aware of the conditions prevailing in the large cities. Lord Napier, giving evidence to the Royal Commission of Inquiry into the Housing of the Working Classes in 1884, stated that in Glasgow 25 per cent of the population lived in single-roomed houses, lacking the simplest amenities. An inquiry in Edinburgh in 1861 revealed that there were in the capital city 1,530 single-roomed houses, each occupied by 6 to 15 persons, 125 of them mere cellars without windows. The public conscience was stirred in the late 1880s by the revelations in the 12 volumes of *Life and Labour of the People of London* by Charles Booth, a wealthy shipowner, who estimated that over 60 per cent of the population of East London were below the subsistence level, and by the founder of the Salvation Army, William Booth, in his *In Darkest England — The Way Out*, with its portrayal of the "submerged tenth" of English society.

2. Speculation had been rife since Caldwell's tour of the north-west in the spring of 1889. The most publicised proposal, involving a terminus on the coast to link up with Lewis, was to construct a branch line from Garve to Ullapool; but an influential pressure group, that of Stornoway fish-curers, preferred a line from Achnasheen to Aultbea, which was reckoned to be fractionally shorter. Other suggestions were — Lairg to Loch Laxford and Invershin to Lochinver.

3. When Lord Leverhulme offered every crofter in Lewis a free gift of his holding in 1923, the offer was refused. The crofters' reasons were not quite the same as in the period of the Congested Districts Board, when the amount of the owner's rates combined with the annuities was the main stumbling block. In 1923 most of the crofters paid no rates at all and they feared (wrongly) that they would lose the right to compensation from a landlord if they wished to renounce the holding.

4. The Scottish law courts' decision to uphold the claim of the new United Free Church to all the property of the Free Church was much resented by the "Wee Frees" and in Lewis tempers ran high when the church at Ness built by local people was taken over by a small minority of United Free Church adherents. The Government reverted to its policy of the eighties and sent a gunboat to keep the peace. The Free Church remnant took their case to the House of Lords in 1904 and won, the Government finally stepping in to arrange a fair distribution of the property.

APPENDICES

APPENDIX A

A Factor's Letters

To tenants of Digg, Isle of Skye.

12 January 1882

Dear Sirs,

I am in receipt of your letter which I have forwarded to Captain Fraser. I have no doubt Captain Fraser will be willing to do what he can for your accommodation and comfort but you address him as if you were proprietor of the land and not he and you address him as if you had a right to fix your own Rents, which you must know perfectly well you have no power to do.

There must always be poor people in the world who are not so well off as others, and if a Tenant happens to be so poor that he cannot pay his Rents his first remedy is to give up his holding. There is no use in any Tenant thinking that he can fix his Rent and pay up what he thinks proper himself. I am very much surprised that any sensible man should think anything of the kind and far more that they should put it in writing.

Captain Fraser has given you a most liberal deduction for the present year and you should gladly avail yourself of it and pay your Rent honestly and cheerfully as you can. I shall expect to see you all at the Rent Collection at Uig on the 31st curt with your Rents. There is not the slightest doubt that Captain Fraser or any other proprietor would view with much more favour anything you had to say provided you just came honestly forward like men and then stated your complaint. In writing as you did you must certainly have done so without due consideration.

Yours faithfully,
Alex. MacDonald

To A. Robertson, Calligary, Armadale.

30 January 1882

Dear Sir,

I am in receipt of your letter claiming payment for seven days' work for putting up a small piece of handrail at the Quay at Armadale. I cannot understand this. I know perfectly well that any tradesman could put up that rail and take it down several times in the time you mention. I am perfectly willing to leave the matter to the judgement of Mr. Barron or any other respectable person in case I may be mistaken but I cannot pay Lord MacDonald's money away in such a way or for such an account as you render without being satisfied that it is correct, which I certainly am not at present. I return the accounts.

Yours truly,
Alex. MacDonald

To J. Lamont, Ground Officer, Uig.

4 February 1882

Sir,

I am extremely surprised that you have not yet settled your Rent although I have repeatedly written to you for payment. I find you most difficult to deal with in every way. I have told you more than once that if you alleged that you should get credit for anything for which you did not get credit, you had simply to produce a Receipt for it as I always do with such receipts and cheques so that there can be no mistake.

I was very much surprised the other day to hear that you pulled down a house belonging to a sister of yours who is unable to support herself and would not give her any quarters. I hope this is not true and shall thank you to let me know as to this and also as to payment of your Rent.

Yours truly,
Alex. MacDonald

To J.D. Brodie, W.S., Edinburgh

17 April 1882

. . . About the threat to drive Mr. MacKay's sheep off Ben Lee at Whitsunday, my ground for that is that the tenants have been publicly boasting it in Portree. I cannot at present give the names of those making the threat but it is perfectly true that the threat has been frequently given utterance to. In the meantime we cannot, I think, take action. There is watch and ward kept night and day against all comers. On Saturday I got a threatening letter which I handed to the Procurator Fiscal, threatening me with a visit of Captain Moonlight if I demanded any rents from the tenants. Until the Sheriff and Fiscal have those engaged in the deforcement apprehended and punished we can do nothing.

All Skye is watching this case. If we yield, the small tenants will try to take possession of every farm in the country and goodbye to Rents peaceably paid! I hope the authorities will make no mistake and not under-estimate what they have to cope with. They have found everything I forewarned (although I pretend to no special wisdom) coming to pass, and unless a severe example is made of the deforcers, there will be worse to come.

(MacDonald and Fraser Papers)

APPENDIX B

State of Lord MacDonald's Rental and Deductions, 1881

Rental

Land Rental	£10,800
Rent of Shootings	1,525
Revenue from Portree Harbour, say	400
	£12,725

Deductions

Public and Parochial Burdens, say	£2,600. 0.0
Interest on Debt affecting Estate	4,000.15.6
Rent Charge on Improvements outlay	496. 2.0
Rent Charge for recent Improvement outlay	194.13.8
Dowager Lady MacDonald's Jointure	1,000. 0.0
Fire Insurance Premiums	58. 0.0
Interest of £1,267.3/- due to Somerled Lord MacDonald's Executry	50.13.6
Gamekeeper's wages and game outlay, say	150. 0.0
Wages of Ground Officers, etc.	100. 0.0
Repairs to Buildings and Fences, say	500. 0.0
Miscellaneous outlays by Factor, say	100. 0.0
Factor's and Clerk's Salary £360 and law business £150	510. 0.0
Lady MacDonald's pinmoney and allowances for children	400. 0.0
Yearly allowance to Mrs Langham	100. 0.0
	£10,260. 4.8
Net Revenue	£2,464.15.4

Factor £250
Clerk   80
———
      £330
———
Not   £360

(Lord MacDonald Papers)

APPENDIX C

Valtos Tenants — Stock and Rents, 1881

Lot	Tenants	Depand-ants	Cows	Stirks	Horses	Sheep	Rents £.s.d.
1 {	Widow Margt. Macdonald Donald Lamont	8	4	1	1	10	15.10.0
2 {	Lachlan Macqueen Norman Stewart	18	3 2	2 2	1 1	4 12	15. 0.0
3 {	John Stewart Malcolm Stewart	15	3 2	3 3	1 1	8 12	16. 0.0
4 {	Norman Macdonald Norman Macdonald, jun.	14	2 2	1 1	1 1	2 3	16. 0.0
5	Martin Martin	8	4	1	1	12	16. 0.0
6 {	Donald Matheson John Lamont	8	4 2	2 1	1 1	10 7	15.10.0
			33	17	9	80	94. 0.0
	Angus Nicolson, Herd, for herding	2	—	—	—	
			35	17	9	80	94. 0.0

N.B. — There were in addition 5 cottars — Angus Bethune, Ewen MacQueen, Angus Lamont, Angus Nicolson, Alexander Gordon — with 21 dependants.

(MacDonald and Fraser Papers)

APPENDIX D

Herring Fishing — Stornoway District, 1873-82

	STORNOWAY SECTION			BARRA SECTION		
	No. of Boats Fishing	Total No. of Crans of Herring	Estimated Value	No. of Boats Fishing	Total No. of Crans Caught	Estimated Value
1873	599	39,642	£99,105	435	35,258	£105,774
1874	656	36,383	90,958	670	27,900	83,700
1875	711	33,446	83,615	542	10,108	30,324
1876	803	7,434	18.585	268	7,911	23,733
1877	688	57,708	144,270	398	23,855	71,565
1878	581	53,743	134,358	290	11,860	34,080
1879	750	41,291	103,228	334	24,225	72,675
1880	852	65,088	162,720	549	36,758	110,274
1881	691	28,309	70,773	594	13,641	40,923
1882	691	42,996	107,490	609	2,984	8,952

Cod and Ling Fishing — Stornoway District, 1873-82

	No. of Cod, Ling, etc.	Estimated Value
1873	482,000	£24,536
1874	325,000	16,754
1875	472,000	25,145
1876	196,000	11,343
1877	485,000	25,476
1878	624,000	34,523
1879	830,000	35,611
1880	498,000	24,959
1881	304,000	16,223
1882	359,000	19,405

(Napier Commission Report, 1884)

APPENDIX E

Highland Land Law Reform Association of London Office-bearers, 1883-84

President — D.H. MacFarlane, M.P.

Vice-Presidents — Professor J. Stuart Blackie; Henry Broadhurst, M.P.; Thomas Burt, M.P.; G.B. Clark, M.D., F.H.C.S.E.; James Collings, M.P.; Rev. J. Thain Davidson, D.D.; C.R. Drysdale, M.D.; Howard Evans, Esq.; Daniel M. Forbes, Esq.; J. Chisholm Goode, Esq.; Daniel Grant, M.P.; J.S. Stuart Glennie, Barrister-at-law; R.C. Hedderwick, Barrister-at-law; John Houston, Barrister-at-law; W.A. Hunter, Barrister-at-law; Rev. John Kennedy, D.D. (late of Stepney); J. Seymour Keay, Esq.; J. Boyd, Kinnear, Esq.; Rev. A. MacAuslane, D.D.; John MacDonald, Barrister-at-law; John MacKay, C.E., Hereford; Malcolm Mac-Kenzie, Guernsey; C. Fraser Mackintosh, M.P.; Angus Mackintosh of Holme; C.S.B. MacLaren, M.P.; J. Nicol, Esq.; Rev. H. Sinclair Paterson, D.D.; J. Dick Peddie, M.P.; W. Peterson, Esq.; Professor E. Robertson, London; J. Forbes-Robertson, Esq.; John Slagg, M.P.; Samuel Storey, M.P.; P.A. Taylor, M.P.

Committee — G.B. Clark, Chairman; Bennett Burley, Duncan Cameron*, E. Cattanach*, J.C. Durant, H.C. Gillies, W. Graham, Donald Grant, J.L. Joynes, J. MacDonald, Kenneth MacLean*, Malcolm MacLeod*, H. MacNeill*, Dr A.L. MacPhail, James A. Manson, J. MacDonald Murray*, W. Reeves, T. Reid, A. Watt*.

Hon. Treasurer — Angus Mackintosh, Esq. of Holme.

Hon. Secretary — Donald Murray, Esq.

* Executive.

(Duncan Cameron Papers)

APPENDIX F

H.L.L.R.A. Branch Rules

Copy of Resolution of the Bernesdale Highland Association, November 6, 1884.

I. — That this meeting be called "The Bernesdale Branch of the Edinburgh Highland Association."

II. — That the following be the Office-bearers of said Association, viz.:—

> John Macmillan, President
> Neil Macleod, Secretary
> William Maclure, Treasurer

III. — Fee of Membership, One Shilling.

1st resolution — That this meeting, approving of the objects of the said Association, recognises its necessity, and pledges itself to give it a cordial support.

II. — That this meeting desires to express its sense of the urgent necessity of such legislative measures as will recognise the right of the occupier of the soil, and protect them from the hardships and oppression to which they have been so long subjected.

III. — That this Association is committed to report to the Centre Association any cases of alleged grievance which they may have to complain of, or may come under their notice in any part of the parish.

IV. — That this meeting, while resolved to vindicate their rights in every legal way, strongly disapprove of any counsels that resist the law, and recommend all parties to do their utmost to pay their rents.

V. — That this Association is committed to render all assistance in their power to secure a reform of the Land Laws, such as Fair Rents, Fixity of Tenure, and Compensation for Improvements.

(Lachlan MacDonald, *Position of Bernesdale Crofters from 1843 to 1886*)

APPENDIX G

A Western Isles Constituency

Duke of Argyll to W.E. Gladstone, December 4, 1884

— Today I had a conversation with young Munro Ferguson (elected M.P. for Ross and Cromarty in August, 1885). He advocated that the Hebridean Islands should be formed into a separate constituency as otherwise they will swamp the mainland constituencies to which they are attached and return Land Leaguers.

I fear there can be no doubt that a Land League on the model of the Irish and the leaders of which are working with Parnellites more or less, have got hold of all the Hebridean islands, which are now divided between the counties of Argyll, Inverness, Ross and Cromarty. Novar tells me that the mainland constituencies would return such members as himself with tolerable security but that the Islanders will only too probably go in for regular Leaguers.

The extraordinary ignorance of many of these poor people is incredible. Novar thinks that unless the Islands are separated and erected into a constituency by themselves about five seats will be lost to the Liberals . . . Novar is one of the most creditable young men whom Scotland has sent to Parliament. He tells me that he doubts whether he has a chance if he is to be swamped by the cottars and crofters of the Lewis, as he cannot support the wild notions they have conceived.

A Scotch Parnellite Party embracing some five county members and co-operating with a certain number from the Cities would be a formidable addition to the Party of Disorder. The displacement of such men as Novar by such men as Fraser Mackintosh would be damaging to the House of Commons.

(Gladstone Papers)

APPENDIX H

Grazing Regulations

The committee appointed by the crofters of Lower Shader, Lewis, having made application to the Crofters Commission in 1892 for approval of certain rules, the Crofters Commission disapproved of the Rules proposed and advised:—

(1) The Committee shall assign or apportion 1 cow, 1 stirk and 15 sheep to each share of the total number of 60 full shares into which the right of grazing was divided under the Fair Rents application disposed of in 1888. 1 cow equals 5 sheep, 1 horse equals 8 sheep.

(2) The Committe shall have full power to engage a herd if necessary to look after the stock and lay down regulations for stock management.

(3) The Committee shall see that all sheep are sent to the hill pasture not later than 15th May each year and all cattle removed to the shielings or summer grazings by 1st June.

(4) Heather burning and peat cutting to be regulated by Committee and ground officer.

(5) Each crofter to build or repair the dyke as of old and help keep in repair under the direction of the Committee.

(6) The Committee shall have power to levy assessment for a herd's wages, dipping, or smearing.

(7) The Committee shall have no power to authorise erection of any dwelling or house on the common pasture.

(8) The Committee shall have full power to stop interference in common pasture by cottars or others.

(Report of Crofters Commission (1893))

APPENDIX I

A.J. Balfour's Skye Policy

In Skye, at this moment, it may be said, that, broadly speaking, neither rates nor rents are paid by Crofters, excepting when it happens to suit them. No officer can serve a writ without protection; and for purposes of protection, the police are absolutely useless.

The uselessness of the police arises from more than one cause. The force, according to an English, or an Irish, standard, was probably not very efficient to begin with. They have been recently demoralized by the ill-usage they have received from the population of the island; ill-usage usually altogether unpunished, and never punished adequately. The people, on their side, having successfully defied the police for nearly five years, now hold them in the uttermost contempt and the contempt is largely supplemented by detestation, founded on the belief that the police are rather to be regarded as the emissaries of the landlords than as the vindicators of the Law. The circumstance that, according to the Law of Scotland, the local police rate is entirely levied upon the owners of land, gives countenance to this idea.

It is manifest that this condition of things cannot be allowed to continue, and the question therefore arises what practical steps ought to be taken by the Government to remedy it. Two possible courses seem to be open. The first is to increase and arm the police force in such a manner that they may be able to vindicate their authority by sheer force. The Chief Constable of Inverness informs me that if 150 or 200 men could be provided and armed with revolvers this might be done. But there are two objections to it. The first is, the difficulty of collecting 150 police at all (the total police force of the county is only eighty men), and the absolute impossibility of collecting them secretly. The second objection is that, though such an armed force might bear down all resistance, yet every authority whom I have consulted is agreed in saying that this could not be done without bloodshed, and probably loss of life. Nothing short of bitter experience will convince the people that the police, whom they have so long trampled on with impunity, are really to be feared.

The second course is to support the police with marines. It may be urged that this has been tried before, and with but very small success. There appear, however, to have been grave errors of management in the previous military expedition to Skye. The force employed was large, but it was scattered over the island in small groups, under no official supervision, with little to do but fraternize with the crofters, and without being put to any useful purpose. The friendly relations

234

between the marines and the crofting population in the disturbed districts, desirable enough in itself, reached under this system such a point that the latter, in some cases, actually seem to have believed that in case of emergency the marines would side with them against their officers. The whole expedition appears to have been extremely costly to the county of Inverness, but nearly useless for the purpose of restoring law and order.

After a consultation with the Sheriff and Chief Constable of Inverness, I am inclined to think that if the errors which experience has shown to have vitiated the policy of the last expedition were avoided, the Law might be enforced without very great expense, and without any bloodshed at all. All authorities whom I have consulted are of opinion that the people will never for an instant attempt to resist the forces of the Crown; partly through fear of the results, and partly because they recognize in them what they decline to recognize in the police, ie., that they are emissaries of the central authority. Macleod of Macleod, a resident landlord, and lately an eminent civil servant, has gone the length of telling me that he believes that ten marines would be quite sufficient to protect the police in the execution of their duty in any part of the island.

I am inclined to think, and the Law Officers for Scotland, with whom I have consulted on the whole question, agree with me in thinking, that the policy here sketched out is likely, if all goes well, to have a salutary effect. But its execution depends on the discretion of the chief executive authority on the spot, who is entirely independent of any central control, and whose management in the past has certainly not been above criticism.

Memorandum for Cabinet, September 15, 1886
(Scottish Office Files)

INDEX

241

242

250